THE PEOPLE
IN MY HOUSE

THE PEOPLE IN MY HOUSE

By
Libby Earle Henry
Mark Hubley

☽

triple h publishing
HHH

triple H publishing

Louisville KY

ISBN 978-1-7321461-2-9

As regards, *The People In My House*, certain facts are a matter of record, and can be found at the county clerk's office, in public databases, or in the files of publications. The events portrayed in the book are told to the best of my ability, which might be different from other people's. Most names have been changed to protect their identities, and others have not, particularly those who are a matter of public record.

Libby Henry

Acknowledgement:

To my many friends, Monroe Jett for his time and contribution to my book, Susan March, Tiffany Hendrick, and Tina Carroll, who have donated their time to read and give valuable feedback, you all have given the kind of unwavering support that gives friendship a new meaning. To Lisa Mayes Lawler who created the Facebook support group, The Secret Lives of White-Collar Wives, which has provided me with the courage to persevere with my story. Also, many thanks to Dr. Valerie Wise for editorial insight, to Will Rosenthal for proofreading skills, and to Emily Hubley for her design contribution to the book cover.

"There is no greater agony than bearing an untold story inside you."

~ Maya Angelou

"If I go down, I'm taking you with me!" Ted yelled out the window as he plowed through our side yard in his SUV. My car was parked behind his so rather than wait for me to move he was going cross-country. Peeling off down the road he yelled, "You're a co-conspirator, Libby!" Standing in the driveway my worst fears took on clarity. Ted was talking about mortgage fraud, and that somehow how I was implicated.

My hands trembled and sweat was running down my back. We lived in a fish bowl. No.1 Indian Hills Trail was the first house on the main artery of the neighborhood. Once you stepped outside you were on display. Under most circumstances I wouldn't have trailed Ted outside. Making a spectacle of myself in front of passersby was something I normally would never do. I cared what my neighbors thought.

Today was different. We were in the middle of an ugly divorce and Ted had come over unexpectedly. He frantically searched the house for something, though he didn't tell me what. I had just learned a day earlier that Ted had committed fraud and was in serious trouble with the FBI.

"Ted, what have you done? Answer me!" He looked anywhere but at me, going through the drawers of his desk. "STOP! I want to know the truth. You owe ME the truth!" He snatched some paperwork from his desk, looked at me and coldly said, "I don't owe you anything, bitch!"

CHAPTER 1

My name is Elizabeth Earle Henry ("Libby") and this is my story. My earliest memory is being scolded by my mother for wetting my bathing suit bottoms. It was a lavender two-piece. The top had thin horizontal lines and the bottoms had a heavily pleated skirt. Beal (my mother) was screaming, "Libby! Damn you, why didn't you go to the bathroom?" She yanked down my bottoms and spanked me. I was ashamed and I didn't know why. I was three years old.

I was a spirited little girl with a lot of energy. When I woke up, I was a thoroughbred running out of the gate. That wasn't welcomed in a household with a mother whose interests lay mostly outside the home. Beal didn't like to play with me, or my sister. If you did get a game of checkers out of her you had lobbied for days. "One game, Libby, then find something to do!" She resented every play and couldn't get the game over quickly enough.

Beal didn't like to be bothered and, oh boy, did I bother her. I wanted to play with Beal because my sister, "Virginia" and I never played with one another. Beal had seen to that. She scripted our young lives early on. When I was born, apparently the nurses remarked what a pretty baby I was. They asked Beal if she had penciled in my eyebrows. "Everyone

1

remarked about your eyebrows, Libby. Everyone in the hospital," she would say pointedly in front of Virginia, only to make Virginia jealous. Each time Beal recounted that story a piece of my sister faded.

Beal assigned all her attention-seeking needs on the new baby. She never had any of hers met as a child. Her sister, "Faye," was the favorite, so now it was Beal's turn to choose a favorite. I was the favorite and Virginia was not. The stage was set. "Libby, I had to take you all shopping separately as children. People remarked on your curly hair and green eyes and your sister was soooo jealous." Beal was all about divide and conquer. When Beal was growing up her younger brother and sister were thick as thieves, and she was the one left out. Beal wasn't going to be left out again, so she made sure her daughters were at odds, however unnatural that might be. It's not hard to imagine how Virginia felt. She was shy and introverted; my personality could not have been more opposite.

My family tree has some unusual branches. My father, "Earl," was twenty-one years older than my mother, two years older than her parents. He was born in 1918 and she in 1939. Earl left the family dairy in Mount Sterling and went to work for Dixie Dairy in Lexington, Kentucky. Beal was my Dad's secretary. I guess it's the old cliché, middle-aged man has mid-life crisis, which leads to an affair with his young attractive secretary. He was married and she was a young woman looking to the future. I don't know how long they carried on before my father left his wife, but I do know he later regretted it.

Soon after my father divorced, he married my mother. Later on, he sadly confessed to my sister, Virginia, "If only I were a younger man, Virginia, I would leave." Virginia was always afraid Earl was leaving. He unfairly burdened her with the woes and cares of his marriage, which only added to her insecurity.

Virginia was born in 1964 and I followed in 1968. My father was having his second family at the same time his two children from the previous marriage were having their first. Two of his grandchildren were older than Virginia and four were older than me. We came out of the womb instant aunts.

Beal was from Waynesburg, an insular farming community in Lincoln County. People there live by a strict moral code and her family had strong ties to the fundamentalist Baptist church. She grew up on "Fishing Creek" in a clapboard house without a bathroom or electricity, the eldest of three. She had big dreams and wanted an education. With the help of a kind uncle, she attended Cumberland College where she earned an Associate's Degree. She then transferred to the University of Kentucky. Her uncle died and without support or encouragement from her parents, she quit school and took a job as a secretary where she met my father. At that point she apparently left her strict moral code back in Waynesburg.

As a child my home life was confusing. Beal was always angry with Earl for reasons I didn't understand. After work Earl frequently patronized The Patio, a bar located in the St. Mathews Mall. This held up dinner as Beal made us wait until he came home. He was stalling; he didn't want to come home. My mother forbade drink in the house and that's what he needed most. I was usually playing in my room with my Lincoln Logs or singing loudly to "The Orange Bird Song." It was my favorite Walt Disney record. Riding my rocking horse, I played it over and over and over and over.

"Little Orange Bird,
Little Orange Bird,
In the sunshine tree,
In the sunshine tree.
Won't you sing something sunny
Just for meeeee.....
Think funny thoughts
Think funny thoughts
Or sunny words,
Or sunny words,
That will make me happy
Little Orange Bird."

It was the most happy song in the world. I loved that bit of sunshine in my gloomy home. My performance was regularly interrupted by Earl,

"Libbah, turn that racket down! Get this mess cleaned up!" Earl liked a clean house, an impossible demand for a young child with a singing career.

When I started sleepwalking, Beal screamed at me. Neither she nor Earl offered comfort. She mocked me the next day and days thereafter, "Libby, you were talking in your sleep again." She made fish lips and said, "The fish are going to bite me!" Maybe fish scared me in my dreams. Beal questioned me about my nightmares, "I just think it's funny that you're afraid of fish," and then she made her fish lips face again. I was scared of her, like the nightmare had come alive. When I wasn't scared, I felt ashamed and sad.

I continued having nightmares as I got older. I was also talking in my sleep. I don't know if that was a result of the chaos in my home but it was unacceptable to Beal. When I was a teenager, she pulled up a chair and took notes.

"So who is this James boy?" she asked.

"I don't know, Mom, who is this James boy?"

"You were talking about him in your sleep, Libby." I was talking about him in my sleep? Beal was suspicious.

"I bet you do know, Libby!" I had developed a sense of sarcasm.

"Ooooooohhh...that James boy!"

Being a child in their household was hard. My father had already raised a family and was not available. Earl completely re-invented himself after marrying Beal; he had to. Moving to Louisville he took a job with an insurance company. He was middle-aged, with a young wife and new family. He also made regular trips to Mount Sterling to look after his aging parents. No wonder he didn't have time for his energetic little daughter.

I started to show anxiety-driven behaviors. I wet the bed, washed my hands compulsively, had nightmares and then there was the sleep walking. One time I crawled into a bottom drawer to cry, and Beal took pictures of me. I still have those. In the picture I don't have pants on. I didn't want my picture taken and it made me cry harder.

By the time I was four I suffered severe urinary tract infections. Having to use the bathroom all the time, I was punished every time I got out of bed. "Libby, get back in that bed!" Beal shrieked. The infections got so bad that I was put through a battery of frightening tests at the hospital. They prescribed medication for me. I wish they had provided some for Beal too.

I craved attention when I was little, and it was my half-sister, Lottie, who gave it to me. I love my half-sister, Lottie, and her kids were a great comfort to me. Lottie's youngest, Patty, was two months younger than me and we were as close as any two sisters except I was her aunt. When they visited, the otherwise slow heartbeat of our home quickened. My house came alive. Patty and I ripped and roared. One of our favorite things was to jump from one twin bed to the other without falling on the floor. Our imaginations were big. On the floor lay treacherous territory filled with crocodiles and poisonous snakes hoping for a misstep. I became upset when it was time for my nieces to go. Once I hid in the yellow Karman Ghia that my sister Lottie drove. I believed no one would miss me. I wanted to escape. I made a second attempt at escape not long after, losing myself in an All Mart, a one-stop store with a variety of merchandise. Questioning me in the fishing and tackle department, security asked, "Is your name Libby?" I shook my head no. They weren't buying it, and I was returned to Beal. Damn.

One day melted into the next. A family outing consisted of visiting multiple grocery stores searching for the best prices, pulling weeds in our rented garden off Dorsey Lane or going to visit my grandmother in the hospital. She had broken her hip. I was left in the lobby for hours. Back in the early 1970's, you had to be a certain age to go to a patient's room, so I amused myself. It gets pretty boring for a young child in a hospital lobby. My choice of entertainment was a King James Bible on the coffee table or some tattered *National Geographics*. Naturally, I found my way to the gift shop. Buying the giant stuffed panda bear was out of the question. I wasn't left any money. I liked that bear. I would have settled for a dum-dum sucker.

Earl was doing what most sons of aging parents do, showing concern and looking after them. The problem was he had young children who needed him too. Earl was in his mid-fifties, his mother was in her seventies, and I was five.

Weekends I watched other families pack up and go to the swimming pool. I wanted to go with them. Watching through my window as station wagons packed with inflatable rafts, picnic baskets and excited neighborhood children drive off on incredible adventures, I ran and begged my mother to go to the pool too.

"Libby, we are not going and that's that!"

"But why can't we go?" I didn't quite grasp that Beal couldn't swim or that my father had no interest in taking our family to the pool, or anywhere else for that matter. Nothing was ever explained. They had no room for children in their lives. Virginia and I were like collapsible chairs they put in the car and set up wherever they needed or wanted to go. I wanted to set up a blanket at a picnic, or go someplace together. Earl was more interested in Marshal Matt Dillon preventing lawlessness on *Gunsmoke*. He was worn out and I had a lot of energy.

Beal, though, was involved in different activities outside of home. When I was very young, one of these was the Kentucky's Junior Miss, a pageant based on achievement and talent. She took Virginia and me with her to many of the practices and meetings that led up to the crowning. I loved watching the girls compete. I took a dance class so dancing was the talent that interested me. All of the girls were beautiful. They seemed like live versions of the Miss America Barbie Doll I carried around. I sat in the auditorium while the girls practiced, and looked through the pageant program. Studying each girl's picture, I picked my winner. My winner was solely based on how much they looked like my Barbie doll. I think Earl used the same system. One year a girl who won was unlike all the previous winners, she wasn't thin or as conventionally pretty. The pageant wasn't a beauty contest, but after her crowning I heard adults talking in hushed tones about how she didn't look like a "Kentucky's Junior Miss." As I grew older, I felt differently about the pageant. No longer something I looked forward to, it became another way for Beal to

6

make me feel inadequate. "Libby, if you had studied harder, you might have had the grades to be a Junior Miss." I can't remember ever wanting to be a Junior Miss. I wanted to have friends and get out of the house. Bringing home the crown was the farthest thing from my mind.

First grade was a disaster. I was emotionally ill-prepared for school. I wasn't socialized. I felt different from the other children. When it was time for lunch I was allowed to sit in the classroom while the other children went to the cafeteria. In trouble a lot that year, I was suffering at home and not wanting to cooperate with my teacher's instructions. I couldn't focus. It was probably a mix of ADD and the emotional abuse I endured. Mrs. Dayworthy had no tolerance for my lack of focus. Forcing me to sit under her cavernous desk, the other children laughed and snickered while I hid my face. I might as well have been in the circus freak show.

"Libby, why are you so embarrassing?" Beal wanted to know why I acted out at school. Beal was masterful at playing the model parent and presenting me as a willful child whose actions were a mystery to her. It's not as if I sprouted from the ground like that – I was reacting to my home-life. That was a long year for me; trouble at home, trouble at school. Beal served on the PTA and I was making her look bad. You didn't make Beal look bad without consequences. Yelled at and sent to my room – sometimes hit me with a switch, but the worst thing was the way she belittled me and compared me to the other children.

"All the mothers are talking about you, Libby!" Why can't you be good like the other children? None of those kids like you, Libby!" Cutting me with her tongue, that was her biggest weapon. I would rather have gone out and cut my own switch.

That summer we had company staying with us. Wanting to play dress up, I went to my mother's room and put on what looked like a princess dress. I proudly came out to show off my new look. Unfortunately, it was a negligee, and I terribly embarrassed Beal. "Libby!" she roared, "Take that off!" I didn't get a chance to take it off. Grabbing me, she stripped me naked and forced me to sit on the family room sofa with our company. No one did anything or said anything. A part of me died that day. I stopped trusting adults, accepting I was bad. That moment in time was a turning point.

By middle school, things hadn't changed in my house. Beal cooked, ironed, screamed, watched TV and went to church. My father hadn't changed either. He worked, paid the bills, and bucked Beal's system by having drinks after work. The Patio in St. Mathews had long since closed so Earl frequented Flaherty's. Beal was always yelling at Earl about drinking. "Earl, you smell like a distillery!" This became so commonplace I just closed my bedroom door and put on an album. "Games People Play" by The Alan Parson's Project was one of my favorites and I appreciated the irony. Music was my way of dealing with Beal's chronic ranting; I wanted to drown out the high-pitched shrieking. A pair of earphones from a garage sale was a savvy purchase.

Grovenut Baptist Church was paramount in Beal's life. It's a beautiful white church with stately columns framed by hundred-year-old oaks. Never missing Sunday school or church service I was always amazed by Beal's ability to morph into someone different once she was walking on holy ground. IT WAS SHOWTIME! She greeted each member with her "sweet voice" and plastic smile. "Why hello, Julia Lee. I saw your winning pie at the fair…Ginger makes the most wonderful pies and when Bobby Jack is in town he always stops by Ginger's for a slice and…." My mother is a one-upper. The conversation always comes back to her. She always knows someone who does it better or has it better. Losing interest, Mrs. Lee gently patted my mother on the shoulder. "I better go find Jim." This was something Beal had a habit of doing. Every conversation is a U-turn back to her and her experiences. Reading people's body language and sensing their desire to get away I felt bad for my mother. Beal has a fault. She doesn't recognize the body language and facial cues of others. She keeps talking until her audience escapes.

Earl never attended Sunday school. He arrived in a separate car for church service and left immediately after the last hymn was sung. It was an extension of their separateness as a married couple. Church made me uncomfortable. Not measuring up to the other families according to Beal, she made that abundantly clear at supper each Sunday; it was always about someone else's daughter who had gotten into the pageant or how proud someone must be of the accomplishments of their children. Virginia and I have never fulfilled her expectations. Forcing me to sing in the choir with my froggy voice, Beal was always disappointed when I didn't get the solo. I hated the choir. One time at a kid's party, Beal grabbed me out of the pool and trundled me off to choir practice. When she brought me back, all the other little girls wanted to know what happened. It was so unfair, but that was Beal. To this day I still hate church music.

We were not a functioning family, and we never had been. I guess every Sunday was a harsh reminder of the void in Beal's life. When I was young, it puzzled me to see families participating together in church activities. As I got older, I became envious. Seemingly happy and openly loving with one another – I wanted to feel that too.

Julie Ames and I grew up going to Grovenut Baptist Church. We also attended school together for a year. Julie was an old soul for an eighth grader. Julie says that year I tried to sell my mom off as "cool." I wanted to have the house where the kids came over. I guess that shows how badly I wanted to be accepted and how much was missing in my home life. I wanted us to be a normal family.

The summer of 1981 marked a turning point in my relationship with Beal. I had listened to her judge others my whole life, myself included. Self-righteous Beal the Baptist did no wrong, was always perfect, never at fault. It was ALWAYS someone else. Beal had mastered the art of blame shifting. Although not an angel, I wasn't always wrong. In my house I didn't have a voice, and my feelings were never validated. I had to swallow my feelings. If Beal was angry, Virginia better not be happy or the smile was slapped off her face. And if Beal was in a good mood, "Why are you looking so sullen Libby? Git off of it!" and off I go to my room.

It was early June and I was over at a neighbor girl's house. Laying out in the sun working on our tans, I was relaxed and enjoying the smell of fresh cut grass. My friend Rebecca and I were waiting what seemed an eternity for the song we requested to come on the radio, "The Best of Times" by Styx. I could never have enjoyed a moment like this at my house. Beal didn't believe in tans, at least not for me. She said the sun would ruin my skin. I had tried a couple of times on an old green blanket, but she periodically poked her head out the rear of the house. She reminded me of the bird in a cuckoo clock.

"Libby, you are ruining your skin! Libby, did you hear me?" Of course, I heard her, but I pretended not to. Not until her giant shadow blocked out the sun.

"I said you are ruining your skin!"

"Mom, I'm just getting a little color." It was futile, so I just packed up my blanket and went inside. From that point on I only damaged my skin at my friends' homes.

Rebecca and I were talking like middle school girls do when she told me another girl liked the same boy I did. Rebecca saw I was angry. Later she intentionally invited him and the girl to her pool to make me feel worse. When I saw him there I was so upset I rode my bike home immediately. I was crying. Beal spotted my tear-stained face when I came through the door.

"What's wrong with you, Libby? Are you pregnant?" WHAT?? I was 13. I was stunned. It felt disgusting and I didn't know why. I couldn't utter a word. Finally, I answered with a resounding, "NO!"

"Well you're crying, aren't you?" I don't know how she came to the conclusion that a crying teen girl equals pregnancy, but she had. I explained I was just upset at a friend. She responded with "What did YOU do?"

"Nothing, I didn't do anything and you should not have said 'THAT' to me." I experienced a myriad of emotions, rage, confusion and shame.

"Libby, I didn't do anything wrong! You're just so upset." Beal didn't apologize or offer something consoling. Beal never apologized for anything. Ever.

Later that summer I was hanging out with some of my relatives. We were in the back bedroom all piled up on cherry-wood twin beds, talking about who-knows-what when the conversation turned towards

Beal. "Your mother had an affair with our granddaddy." Time stood still. I knew my father had been married before, but what I didn't know was that my mother was his mistress. It wasn't something I had ever considered or thought about. Beal's personal life was her business, but I couldn't let it go. Beal!...Beal, The Baptist who condemned women as long as memory served, committed adultery and was a hypocrite? The same person who considered anything remotely sexual, vulgar, had an intimate relationship with a married man? Beal regularly invaded my privacy looking for material to blackmail me with. She scoured my diary looking for sinful thoughts or events (the little gold lock was no match for Beal). Reading about the boy who pecked me on the lips at the skating rink, she left me feeling dirty for writing about him. I was shocked learning about Beal and Earl, but after getting this information, I was empowered. Beal no longer the voice of righteousness, I might tell her, "You had an affair!" the next time she confronted me.

High school proved to be the start of an ongoing war between my mother and me. I joined Kappa Chi, a high school sorority. One of the new pledges and I hit it off right away. Nicole and I shared a common sense of humor, I'd always been drawn to funny people and her mother was fun to be around too. She was cool and more liberal than any mother I had ever met. That was fine by me because I was used to an oppressively strict mother. Nicole's mom was the first adult who respected and treated me like a person. Seeming like friends, as well as mother and daughter, they had a relationship the likes of which I had never seen before. I liked Nicole's mom a lot and began to feel maybe there were some adults I could confide in. We became close and Beal took notice.

There was another mother on the PTA with Beal who lived in Nicole's neighborhood who didn't approve of Nicole and her mom. She put the bug in Beal's ear, or so Beal said. I think Beal saw me gravitate towards another mother, and feeling threatened, Beal went after her. This was around the time I really began to push back and challenge her authority. I was bad. I talked back to her, broke the rules, and smoked cigarettes. Beal saw this as a sign of loose morals and promiscuity. My hormones were kicking in, and I felt like I couldn't do anything to please Beal, so I openly defied her. Beal called Nicole's mother and they got into it. Beal threatened Nicole's mother with a restraining order. Beal wanted to pick my friends. She wanted to pick my boyfriends. She wanted to be in charge.

My friendship with Nicole continued. I learned decades later from a boy I dated in high school that Beal had called him to use his influence to break up our friendship. He was sixteen years old. Beal was the master at trying to manipulate people to do her dirty work.

Beal harassed me constantly. The more she harassed me, the more I rebelled. One particular evening, following me around the house ranting on how Nicole was a bad influence, she said I would become a loose girl if our friendship continued. "Loose" was an unfamiliar term, but I knew she meant I would become a slut. "Everybody is talking about you two," Beal chided. "They saw you two at Mr. Gatti's." (our favorite pizza parlor), I never knew who "Everybody" and "They" were. This disapproving group of people governed my life, and was apparently stalking me as well. There was no basis for Beal's disparaging comments about Nicole.

I went into the bathroom. Beal stood outside and continued berating me. Feeling the anger bubble up inside, I was shocked by my reflection in the mirror. My cheeks were red and my face felt warm. I couldn't take it anymore. I opened the door, and words flew like speeding bullets.

"Who are you to judge anyone? You had an affair with Dad!"

Dashing to my room, I locked the door. Beal pounded and demanded to be let in. Watching the door quiver, I thought she might break through. She was in a rage, knowing I knew the truth and at whoever had divulged her secret. The door stopped quivering. It was quiet for a minute, but then I saw the doorknob start to loosen. Beal had gone to the utility room and retrieved a screwdriver to dismantle the doorknob. I braced for impact. Flinging the door open she started screaming. She got as close as she could and gritted her teeth.

CHAPTER 1

"Who told you that?" I didn't answer. "I'm calling your father."
I heard Beal on the phone, "Earl, you call Lottie right now! Libby is
saying we had an affair." If there was such a phone call, I wasn't privy.

My dad wasn't happy when he came home and, perhaps, rightfully
so. The grilling for information seemed to last forever. Sweat formed on
my brow as they questioned me under the investigation lamp. Both were
desperate to discover the messenger. Beal was frantic. Earl was furious.
I was frightened. Earl had had a drink or two. This had become the new
normal. I would get home from school and the fighting would start.
Maybe it wasn't every day, but that's how I remember it. The messenger
remains unknown.

By the time freshman year ended, I really just wanted to hang out
with friends and enjoy the social side of high school. I didn't have the
insight to realize I was so empty inside that I constantly was searching
for ways to fill the void. I hated being home so much that I would walk
on foot to my friends' homes even if they lived a car ride away. Naturally
Beal was angry. She was always angry. She began calling the police and
reporting me as a runaway. Of course, she failed to tell them how she
verbally abused me, spit in my face, or butted up against me attempting
to provoke me so I would hit her. One time I came out of the shower
and found two plain clothes policemen in my bedroom. I told Beal I was
going to a friend's house to get away from her and she called the police.
They were nice and asked me why I was running away? I told them, I
wasn't, just going to a friend's house like I had done before to watch
TV because I didn't want to fight anymore with my mother. I was told I
couldn't just leave without my parent's permission and that was the end
of the conversation. It was uneventful. They left my room and she never
called the police again, or if she did, I imagine they realized I wouldn't
be crossing state lines.

Beal was the PTA president so I never attempted to talk with my
counselor or teachers, and who was going to believe me anyway? I was
just a girl who couldn't get along with her mother, a girl who acted silly,
a girl who used humor to mask her pain. Beal settled into her role as a
mother who had a daughter she couldn't control quite nicely. It brought

13

her attention she craved. It brought her attention she never got from her parents. It brought her attention the world wasn't giving her previously.

Our battling escalated the older I became. During my sophomore year I came home with a progress report with a poor grade in geometry and Beal tried to slap me. I had had enough. I grabbed her wrist. "You're not going to slap me anymore." Beal was smart and calculating. I watched with amazement how her enraged face suddenly produced tears.

"Libby! Look what you have done!" She was acting as if I had taken a 2 x 4 to her head.

"I didn't do anything to you, I stopped YOU from slapping me."

Racing from the family room into the kitchen I heard her rustling around in the cabinets. I was confused. Beal didn't walk away from an argument. What was she doing? No phone call to my father? The cabinet door slammed shut, and she came back to the family room with a giant bottle of generic aspirin. "You're making me do this! She turned the bottle over into her mouth and ran down the hall. In disbelief, I was scared. Once it fully registered what she was doing, I ran down the hall. Opening her bedroom door, I saw her in the bathroom. The door was open a crack, and she was spitting out the aspirin. She used her index finger to scrape out the remaining pills. I slunk out of the room and waited in mine.

I was supposed to cook the broccoli for dinner. The saucepan was already sitting on the stove. Not knowing what to do, I knew she was not in any danger because she spit out the aspirin, but I didn't know what she would do next. My heart was pounding and my mind raced. My mother had just attempted suicide and it was my fault. Snapping back into the present I saw her walk by my room. It was a short walk to the kitchen and she could always be heard clanking around making dinner in there. Silence. Crickets. I heard nothing. I tiptoed on socked feet down the hall and peered around the corner just in time to see her position herself on the floor. She was pretending to be dead. Going back to her bedroom I called my father's office, but he had long since gone and was probably holding a stool down at Flaherty's before facing the music. I looked down at Beal telling her I knew she wasn't dead and that I had seen her spit out the aspirin. She didn't flinch. I could have drawn a chalk outline of her body as still as she stayed. Instead, I stepped over her pretend lifeless body and opened the freezer. I pulled out the Green Giant frozen block of broccoli, filled the saucepan with water and waited for it to boil, all the while looking back at my mother on the floor.

Feeling uncomfortable with my back turned, I hopped up on the Formica counter so I could keep an eye on her and the saucepan. It was almost dinnertime so I knew my father was moments away. Imaging his face when he walked through the door was not comforting. Earl had not been the type of father to challenge Beal, let alone resolve family issues, but this was different. He would have to act. The side of my hand was getting hot from the steam. I dropped the broccoli into the saucepan. Beal was still lying there, breathing, car lights shined in my face, and I waited to hear Earl slam the door of his Pontiac. He always entered the house through the utility room on the side. The outside door opened quietly, but the door to the inside always screamed when it opened. It announced everyone's arrival.

Earl arrived. Beal was on the floor and I sat wide-eyed on the counter, "Beal, what the hell are you doing?" I expected him to toss his overcoat in the air and rush to her side. He didn't. He turned and took notice of me. I blurted out, "Mom poured aspirin down her throat and is pretending to be dead on the floor." Beal then pushed herself up by the palms of her hands and was resting comfortably on her side. The miraculous resurrection spoke in what was more of a bark.

"Libby has a failing grade in math!"

"Libbah, are you not studying for your subjects?" Frozen as the broccoli, trapped in a block of ice, it was more of the same. Beal behaved in any manner she liked and Earl looked away. Beal got up and cooked dinner like nothing had happened. Earl shook his head and looked at us, "Why can't we just have peace?" Walking away to his nightly routine, he changed and neatly hung his clothes up before dinner. That night we sat under a poorly lit hanging fixture, around the small kitchen table and ate broccoli, except I didn't eat. It was rubber.

I don't remember the next day at school. I do know I didn't tell any adults about what happened. I didn't tell my sister who was away at college. It would have been completely out of character if I had called my sister. We had no relationship growing up. She was just another girl doing time on Broadbend Road.

Continuing with my persona as the girl who didn't take life too seriously, I just wanted to have fun. I was compartmentalizing my life without realizing what I was up to. I wandered aimlessly. I remembered having goals, but they weren't the right goals for Beal. Apparently, I told her I wanted to be a children's doctor when I was very young. I don't remember my career choice but I was married to it for years. I was no different than the little boy who wants to be a fireman or a policeman. The difference was MY job paid well and would bring Beal glory, so she took it literally.

By the time I was in high school I was doing the bare minimum. I wasn't always like that in school. In sixth grade, for some reason, everything clicked and I made straight A's for the whole year. Focusing at school had always been a struggle for me, but as my home life spun out of control it was virtually impossible. I guess there was less chaos at home that year. Needless to say, I was not meeting Beal's needs, and she and Earl were not meeting mine.

CHAPTER 2

My sister, Virginia, dated Tommy Pride for most of her high school years. Tommy was congenial. He played football for Eastern High School, and I liked him – he was almost an older brother. When I was in eighth grade he was a senior.

Tommy was someone you could confide in. When I had just gotten my permit, I drove Beal's car into a ditch. I was driving without permission, so walking home I was nervous. Tommy saved the day by rescuing the car. It was our secret. I liked having someone I could trust. Trust just didn't exist in our house. Earl liked Tommy too and so did Beal. A LOT.

Tommy came from a family with problems of its own. Earl had grown up through the Great Depression and he couldn't stand seeing Tommy cold or hungry. So, when Tommy's family turned him out and he was sleeping on a golf course, Earl immediately took him to buy a warm coat. I was only thirteen and didn't really understand what was going on.

Meeting Tommy had opened doors for Virginia. When Virginia was in eighth grade, she had gone to a party at Lonnie Buckley's house with all the cool kids. There was some pot smoking, so Virginia called Beal and told her she was uncomfortable. Beal came, picked her up, and Virginia thought everything was okay, but that's not how Beal was. Climbing up and down the phone tree in her role as PTA president she spoke to each girl's parents, so when Virginia went back to school, Virginia was the "Narc." Going out with Tommy, Virginia put some of that behind her.

Tommy and Virginia both went to the University of Kentucky after high school and continued to date. Three months before spring break, Tommy and Virginia broke up. The relationship had run its course according to Virginia. While on spring break Virginia met a guy unbeknownst to her that was not only in the same fraternity as Tommy but would become her future husband. She and Ryan hit it off right away.

When Virginia gave Beal the news, she didn't take it well. Beal chided, How could you? How horrible! Now you're dating a Catholic!" Beal went ballistic. She called Ryan, the "fish eater." Virginia expressed her feelings to Beal, but Beal was having none of it. Beal loved Tommy, and it was more Beal's relationship with Tommy than Virginia's.

I was fifteen years old and didn't know about the goings-on as concerned my sister and her new boyfriend. As far as I knew she and Tommy were still like two peas in a pod. Imagine me at my friend Krista's house. We're in the bathroom sampling some of her new Mary Kay makeup when Krista's mother calls up, "Libby, your moms on the phone."

"Libby, I need to talk to you about something." I thought I was in trouble because you never knew with Beal. "Tommy has come over...." Beal never gets right to the point, so all this time all kinds of things are going through my mind and I'm wondering what have I done now? Was Virginia okay? What did anything have to do with Tommy?

"Tommy has come over and talked to me and your father, and he would like you to go to his fraternity dance with him." I didn't understand.

"What dance are you talking about? Where?" I watched the condensation on the windows in Krista's bedroom.

"At UK," Beal said enthusiastically and I still wasn't getting it, "with Tommy!"

"He wants you to go as his date to the Old Bluegrass Ball, Libby! It is a grand event and you'll be wearing a dress just like Scarlet O'Hara!"

I got it. It felt dirty, and Beal was disgusting. Everything about Tommy changed. No longer the older brother – he was looking at me in a different way. This was my confidant who pulled my car out of the ditch, the guy who took my nieces and me to the amusement park when we were younger, and the guy I thought one day was going to marry my sister, so it was disturbing on so many levels. Beal was ready to serve me up on a platter, and I felt compromised; I don't believe Earl was in on this.

"No! I won't go. I won't do it!"

Beal was angry and I didn't want to go home. I knew there was going to be war.

"This is a great opportunity for you. It's on campus." She was trying to sell it. She wanted to keep Tommy in the circle. She wanted to hang onto him, and she was willing to sacrifice me for her own purposes. This became a pattern as I got older.

I put the whole Tommy incident behind me. I knew Virginia and I wouldn't have a conversation about it either. We never had sisterly conversation so I knew that wasn't going to start now. That was fine by me. I felt ashamed by Beal's attempt; I didn't know how to make sense of it. The truth is I was learning how to sweep disturbing events under the rug and act as if nothing happened. Beal was a good teacher.

That summer, I met Blake in a shopping center parking lot where teenagers gathered. Spinning around the lot in my friend, Kelly's, MG Roadster we selected a parking spot next to an open-air Jeep. The guys in the Jeep started talking and invited us to join them. My eyes fixated on the driver who introduced himself as "Blake." His friend quickly followed, "I'm Andy." I barely heard him. Blake was dark headed with eyes that almost looked black. He was impossibly good looking and quick-witted. I was attracted right away. Somewhere in the conversation they told us they played football for Trinity, an all-boys Catholic school. Trinity was a football powerhouse. I wasn't surprised; they had overdeveloped muscles to prove it. Flirtatious exchanges continued as long as curfews allowed. The night ended with swapped phone numbers and plans to meet again. Kelly and I were pleased. We had met two guys from a different school, and that seemed exciting. The next weekend we were invited to Andy's stepfather's boat. We had a great time. Blake made it clear he was interested and asked me out.

He arrived at my house the next Friday. Exactly as expected, he came to the door and was introduced to my parents. Earl was receptive, he played high school ball and also in college for Purdue. When the obligatory meet-the-parents conversation concluded they walked us to Blake's Jeep. We were just about to pull out of the driveway when I realized I had forgotten my purse. Quickly, I ran and grabbed it from a chair in the living room. I had one foot across the threshold when Beal stopped me and said, "He's sooo good looking," in a low throaty tone. It was so uncomfortable. The same feeling washed over me as when she tried to coerce my going to the fraternity dance with Virginia's boyfriend. I swiftly stuffed that in my back pocket.

Soon, Blake and I dated exclusively. Every waking moment I was consumed by thoughts of Blake. When is he going to call? When am going to see him? What am I going to wear? What's he going to think of my new outfit? I thought about him all the time. And then there was my mom. She didn't care what I did if I was with Blake. I could pretty much do what I wanted as long as I was with him.

Earl was on board as well. One of Trinity's practice fields was across from his office. He often watched team practice, but now that his daughter was dating the quarterback, he took special interest. Blake was talented and a star, and for the first time Earl took pride in me and participated in my life.

Later that year, Beal signed me up for "Teen Beauty Classes" sponsored by Bacon's, a local department store, claimed to be Louisville's oldest. The classes taught young teenage girls about proper make-up application, style, physical fitness, and how to model clothing. At the conclusion of the series, a hand-picked group were selected to be on their teen board and serve as style ambassadors for the store. My sister had taken the classes before me and I was excited to take them as well. I loved fashion.

One of our classes was about learning to walk a runway. A representative from the Cosmo Modeling Agency was there to teach us proper technique. She introduced herself as Linda Granger. I, like every other girl, stood in line until we were cued by Ms. Granger to walk across the floor as if we were modeling. At the end of class I was gathering up my belongings when Ms. Granger approached. "You have a very unique look and I wondered if you would like to come by the agency for an interview?" I don't remember if she had a business card or told me to have my parents call, I said okay, not really sure.

That night I told my mother about the lady from the agency. Beal shrieked in excitement. She couldn't get to the phone fast enough. "Libby has been chosen to have an interview at the Cosmo modeling agency." Not having stepped a foot inside the agency, Beal was talking magazine covers. Beal got her big break!

The agency was intimidating. Pictures of famous models adorned the walls. Sitting with Beal I felt awkward and out of place. It wasn't long before Ms. Granger appeared and we were ushered into an office. The owner of the agency sat behind an oversized desk. I noticed the office was chic and modern, with a style I had never seen before. My house was pre-historic. The conversation, as I remember, called for me to take their classes and make an appointment for headshots. There was also a contract. I'm not sure if WE signed right then and there or if WE took it home and signed. Beal was so happy, and I was glad that I had done something deserving of her approval though not sure modeling was for me.

I began taking the classes at Cosmo soon after WE signed the contract. The class was full of wannabe models. They were a friendly group of girls and I soon forged a friendship with a girl named Kate. I could tell she was serious about pursuing a modeling career. I was not, but I was going with it.

Classes at Cosmo were similar to the Teen Beauty classes except it was a smaller group of girls.

We were taught how to walk the runway, strike poses, and apply makeup naturally. There was great emphasis on our makeup application. The agency wanted to relieve us of our frosty blue eye shadow and fuchsia lipstick. It was a sacrifice.

The girls took the classes seriously, and I watched them. Whereas I was unsure, they were confident. Whereas I was detached, they were committed. Not sure how I felt – I was going through the motions. I felt less defined by imagining myself a model than by my relationship with Blake. I was happy in Blake's shadow. I preferred being in the background to a cover shot on a magazine. I didn't want to be focused on, and if asked, I might have realized I was confused. The other girls knew what they wanted. I studied them with a sense of curiosity. Being so in tune with oneself was foreign to me.

It didn't take long to realize that I wasn't comfortable in front of the camera. Each girl had a private photo shoot with Tom, Cosmo's photographer. I felt like the photographer saw straight through me. It was different from taking pictures with my friends. Tom, the photographer, was a stranger. Trying to fake it, of course, I couldn't wait for it to be over. This was in contrast to the self-appointed photographer I was with my friends. I could always be found with a camera.

Trinity beat St. Xavier, their biggest rival, and the headline on the front page of *The Courier-Journal* read, "Blake Warner Makes the Difference!" I felt important. That summer when I first met Blake, the modeling agency picked me and another girl to go to New York for "Go-Sees" which is when the girls go meet clients to see if there's interest.

I don't have memories of what transpired between meeting Blake and leaving for New York. I do remember, secretly, not wanting to go on the day I left. I was content walking in Blake's shadow. That was a safe place and I didn't have many. I don't remember who drove me to the airport. My only memory of that day is sitting on the plane next to Celia, the girl Cosmo sent to New York with me. She was a natural beauty with poker-straight hair and blunt-cut bangs. Celia had porcelain skin and a wide smile. She was a few years my senior and far more sophisticated, poised and confident. Modeling had already taken her out of the country. IT showed. I wasn't emotionally prepared to be a model, but I went along with it.

We sat next to one another. Celia pulled a cigarette from a golden case. I asked if her mother knew she smoked. "Oh God Yes!" she replied. I thought of all the times I had been caught by Beal. "Libby, nice girls don't smoke!" Searching for evidence my mother rifled through my purse on a regular basis. I would have never bought an attractive cigarette case it would be confiscated immediately.

Actually, Beal was right. I shouldn't have smoked. It was amusing, though, that she equated not being nice with smoking. By those standards, Beal smoked three packs a day. I was so used to hiding when I smoked, I hesitated when Celia offered me one. "What the hell," I thought, "It's not as if anyone knows me or cares." I lit up and began filling the cabin with smoke rings.

Upon arrival in New York, Celia caught us a cab. I was dropped at a chic looking high rise with a doorman. It surely signaled an upscale apartment upstairs, but reality proved otherwise. A river of dirty clothes flowed from room to room, and crawled up the walls as if met by a dam. Stunned, now I appreciated Earl's quest for orderliness in our home.

"Hi, I'm Jackie!"

"I'm Libby," I replied.

"Ah'm Libby," she parroted, "are you from Alabama?"

"No, I'm from Kentucky."

"Ah'm from Kentucky" We both started laughing.

"Where are you from Jackie?"

"Ah'm from Portland." Light red hair and freckles belied the impression that she was a model, however, her portfolio was incredible. She was like a house with good bones that isn't appreciated until it's been renovated. Make-up and hair transformed her into a beautiful creature. She had modeled in Japan and appeared regularly in Montgomery Ward print ads.

Jackie had been in New York for a week, so she showed me around. I waded through clothes that were begging to be washed, arriving at an empty bunk. The apartment had two bedrooms. One had three sets of bunk beds and the other had a queen bed. I assumed the chaperone stayed in the one with the queen bed.

"Where's the chaperone?" I asked.

"What chaperone? There's a twenty-one year old girl staying here named Kris." Jackie replied. Kris was definitely NOT the chaperone. There wasn't a chaperone. Kris was older and we asked her questions about modeling, but we were on our own. Kris went to the clubs and stumbled in with her boyfriend almost every night. How "NO chaperone" had been lost in translation between my local agency and Beal was a mystery to me.

Quickly getting myself settled I meandered into the kitchen. Flipping on the overhead light I interrupted a gathering of cockroaches on a forgotten piece of pizza. The kitchen and I would not be friends. My new menu was like eating at a poolside concession stand. I had no complaints. My meals were coming from the convenience store on the corner or restaurants within my budget. At home I was accustomed to the same weekly menu: Pot roast on Sundays, leftovers on Monday and the dreaded meals, Swiss Steak with overcooked brussels sprouts and liver with hardboiled eggs. I couldn't get enough of my poolside concession stand.

Three more girls moved in the next day. They were from all over the country. Two of them I liked, but not the third. I don't remember her name, but she was obnoxious and grated on my nerves. At 5'8", I thought I was tall, but "The Grate" as I came to call her, towered over me at 5'11". Every time Jackie and I were in conversation "The Grate" butted in with unsolicited opinions or blindsided us with unrelated useless facts. "The Grate" was like the annoying child no one wants to babysit. Jackie and I moved our conversations to the balcony where we could smoke and talk in peace. "The Grate" didn't like smoking, so I made sure cigarettes were always within reach.

Acclimating to New York City was not easy. All the girls had different daily schedules or "Go Sees" as the agency called them. We navigated our own way, which required zigzagging through the city.

My lean budget didn't allow for multiple cab rides, which took the guesswork out of finding my appointments, so I became a New Yorker overnight traveling by subway, buses and by foot. I relied on the kindness of strangers when maps failed me. My accent was especially helpful when lost. The quid pro quo for receiving directions was to answer questions about Mars, I mean the South. They just wanted to hear me talk. I was amused, not offended. The only time I took offense was from the Grocery Store Man at the convenience store on the corner. He was a short, stump of a man with wavy black hair and a thick mustache. "Grocery Store Man" wore the same clothes every day, a short sleeved, collared shirt with tan pants and a worn black leather belt. An assortment of ink pens weighed down his shirt pocket in reserve, in case he lost the one behind his ear.

It was an old store in need of a facelift. The doorway had peeling paint and the floor had swells. Entering, one immediately was greeted with an overwhelmingly pungent smell. I thought it odd that a store that sold food smelled so bad.

"Where youse from?"

"I'm from Kentucky," I replied. He leaned over the counter and looked at my feet.

"Just checkin' to see if ya have shoes."

I went to that corner store every day and every day he had something to say about my accent. Yes, he did and I didn't think he was funny and I don't think he meant to be. I should have written my order on a piece of paper and handed it over. "Grocery Store Man" never took a day off, maybe he slept on a cot in the back.

I got used to my "Go See" routine pretty fast, but I never got used to some of the photographers. It wasn't unusual to pose in a bra and underwear. If you didn't like it there were twenty girls behind you who didn't mind. "It's just like wearing a bikini," one of the photographers said. But no, it's not like wearing a bikini.

We were sent on "Go Sees" to gain experience and build our portfolios. Looking back, I see how exploitative some of the photographers really were. I wish I could say it was random, but it wasn't.

One night one of the male executives, "Dave," from the modeling agency took the girls I was staying with and me to a nightclub. It was electric inside. My body pulsated with the music. Revolving lights cast colored shadows all over the dance floor. I don't know about the others but I felt like a little girl. I didn't know what to focus on, so I found myself pivoting around like a tiny ballerina in a jewelry box. There were beautiful people everywhere. Dave ordered drinks for all of us, it didn't matter we were underage. No one questioned Dave. He seemed to know the staff very well. Once our drinks arrived, he left us to explore. Jackie and I broke off from the other girls; I told her, "Let's shake The Grate."

We wandered around with drinks in hand and tried to look like we belonged. I don't remember what I was drinking. It looked like a tall Shirley Temple but it didn't taste like one. I sipped on California Coolers back in Kentucky. Jackie and I were taking our second lap around the club when Prince and the Revolution's "Let's Go Crazy," began to play. Quickly we ran onto the dance floor and morphed into a couple of Mexican jumping beans. We danced ourselves silly until Dave summoned us to the limo at the curb outside. I felt giddy. Alcohol, of course, had nothing to do with the whirling sensation.

"Jackie, I'm hungry," I said.

"Me too," she replied. "Maybe we can stop at Taco Bell, Libby?"

"No way! I've already been told I needed to lose five pounds. No way is he going to stop. Jackie, we can order a pizza when we get back to the apartment." I felt like it was taking forever for Dave to get into the limo and where were the other girls? We hadn't seen them for hours. "The Grate" had probably trapped some unsuspecting guy and was boring him with her arsenal of useless facts. I peered out the window and watched Dave talk with two other men. He reminded me so much of Luke Spencer from *General Hospital,* my favorite soap opera. He had that whole long permed hair thing going on. His pastel coral shirt and baggy linen pants looked exactly like something "Luke" would wear in the tropics searching for Laura. Finally, Dave poked his head in and said, "It's just us."

Where's everyone else?" Jackie questioned.

"I got them a taxi an hour ago" Dave explained. "Kris had a headache and the other girls were ready to go. It's just you two dancing queens and me." Good, we were "Grateless."

The next couple of days were really busy. I had been booked to do a shoot at the Twin Towers, and one at a non-disclosed location. You never knew what to expect on a shoot, except the unexpected. I learned quickly. The day of the shoot at the Twin Towers I expected to be photographed in one of the towers or at least have them behind me. The photographer I shot with that day was a woman, a cool woman who took smoke breaks throughout our session. "My boyfriend hates smoking so I sneak them on the job." I thought it funny that a grown woman had to sneak cigarettes.

She searched around the grounds for a site until she decided on what looked to me like a bunch of large rocks, the kind you find around train tracks. She had me lie on them to create an earthy image. I rolled around as the shutter clicked. By the time we finished shooting a primer of rock dust had settled over my body.

The next day's shoot was daunting. I was dressed in an oversized pink and yellow striped shirt and bright yellow pants at a beer garden during happy hour. Models are forbidden to get tans so I was unusually pale for mid-summer. I hated being pale. I longed to slather on some iodine and baby oil and bake my body. The photographer had me stand on a giant liquor barrel in the middle of the garden. All around me were people in work clothes drinking and suddenly I was the entertainment. Comments were hurled from every direction. "Hey baby show us a little skin!…I'll take your picture!...Smile for the camera!" poured out from drunken mouths.

"Just ignore them Libby and focus on me," the photographer instructed.

"Oh sure," I thought. I was nothing but a piece of chum circled by sharks. I had no idea how to be natural in front of that particular audience. It was a long shoot.

"Libby, Libby, Libby on the Label, Label, Label," Jackie sang in my ear.

"Jackie, It's 7:30 in the morning. I don't have to be anywhere."

"You Will Like, It, Like It, Like It, On the Table, Table, Table," she continued.

"Jackie, if you are going to wake me up so early, I would appreciate a soft wake-up."

I don't have to be anywhere either, Libby! My shoot got cancelled. Let's go play in the city today!"

"Alright, let me go back to sleep!"

Ten-thirty rolled around before I woke up refreshed. Jackie had apparently run out of her early morning energy. She lay lifeless in her bunk. Immediately, I seized the opportunity to wake her up with the help of an archaic alarm clock that had been left in the apartment years ago.

We decided on UNO's pizza for lunch. I had never heard of UNO's, in Kentucky, Mr. Gatti's and Pizza Hut were the kings. Jackie explained it was deep dish Chicago style pizza like I had never heard of the concept.

"Jackie, I live in Louisville, not in the hills. I've had deep dish pizza before." Jackie was just as much a smart ass as I was.

"Good thing I get to eat with my hands, I haven't quite mastered the use of a knife and fork!" While waiting for the pizza, we mapped out our day. John Casablanca, founder of the Elite Modeling Agency, which represented us, was taking all the girls to a fancy restaurant for dinner so we both wanted to dress especially chic. John was a strikingly handsome man of Spanish descent.

"Where's the check?" I groaned. "It's been forever! Oh my God what's that Jackie?" The restaurant was shaking.

"Why are you laughing?"

"It's the subway. What did you think it was? An earthquake?" Jackie teased.

"Let's go, smart ass!"

Roaming in and out of boutiques we searched for perfect outfits, but I don't recall finding one. My recollection is that I found long shimmering geometric earrings and borrowed a white strapless dress from Kris. All the girls took special care to make sure hair and make-up was model perfect. I was no exception, we all clamored for mirror time. I found it ironic that an apartment for models lacked appropriate mirror space.

Our limo arrived at 7:00. We piled into the elevator and the door opened to a mirrored wall. The reflection that met me was not a group of girls with no make-up on their way to "Go Sees" all day. This group was a leggy bunch glammed up in brightly colored heels and short dresses. As soon as the doorman opened the door we were greeted by John Casablanca with open arms and he kissed each of us on both cheeks. I tried to enter the limo as elegantly as I could. We all were trying our best to be cool and collected. "Girls, girls, how are you this evening?" We responded with a collective "Great." John told us a reservation had been made at one of New York's finest French restaurants. I clenched my teeth at Jackie with excitement. John popped open a bottle of Champagne and removed flutes from another compartment. He poured and we passed them along until every girl had a glass. "Cheers girls!" "Cheers," we echoed. Sweet carbonated bubbles tickled my tongue. "The Grate" blathered non-stop about her day until John redirected the conversation. It was obvious she was trying to impress him. The Grate, however, *did* look beautiful. She had her sandy blonde hair in a French twist and her make-up was flawless, her sapphire eye shadow contrasted perfectly with her dark brown eyes. Her look could have graced any magazine cover. Modeling is the perfect career for "The Grate" I thought. No speaking.

The restaurant was everything I had imagined. Angled black leather chairs surrounded tables with white linen and grey walls were adorned with colorful paintings. Every table had a mirrored pyramid in the center. There was an abundance of plates resting on a silver charger. I was glad I had read Amy Vanderbilt's book of Etiquette that Beal insisted I read. Beal could fake suicide before dinner, but by the time she was resurrected, you had better use the right fork.

I had been to plenty of nice restaurants but none like this. John immediately had the waiter bring champagne. I noticed the bottle right away. It was beautiful, with flowers painted on the sides. Jackie whispered it would make a great souvenir. All the champagne bottles I'd ever seen had labels on them, but not this one. The waiter came round to each of us and filled our glasses even though we were underage.

John ordered everyone's meal in French, and I was fascinated. I only agreed to the duck because it came highly recommended and I wanted to feel Parisian. By the time dinner arrived I was floating. I have no memory of eating. I can only string together what I remember in a "montage sequence." I was drinking champagne, I was laughing, I was floating and the next thing I knew I was on the floor in the bathroom and Jackie was waking me up. I had passed out in a chic French restaurant. The black-and-white tiles of the floor were in 3D. I still don't know how I walked out. Maybe, divine intervention. The intervention abandoned me in the limo on the way back to the apartment. Riding backwards sent me over the edge and a tidal wave of nausea hit me, I leaned over and threw up on the floor. I was in bad shape. The second wave hit me in the elevator where I was sick again. The next time I opened my eyes it was day. Jackie filled in what I couldn't remember.

"Well, at least you didn't say anything stupid? One minute you were fine and the next you were on the bathroom floor." Jackie was kind enough not share that detail with the others. She also informed me "The Grate" got sick too…once she got home."

"Lucky Grate," Jackie burst into laughter.

"That does NOT make me feel better Jackie! Oh my God, what did John say?"

"Nothing, he wasn't in the limo."

"Really?"

"Yeah, he sent us home in one limo and another was waiting for him."

"Thank God!"

Arriving at the agency the next day I expected the worst. No one said anything, no one ever did. I left New York that weekend. I was ready and I said my good-byes. Jackie and I vowed to keep in touch, which we did for some time. Weekly letters became monthly and then our correspondence dwindled to nothing.

I was so thrilled to be coming home I couldn't contain my excitement. I knew everyone would want to hear stories about what it was like to be a model in New York, but all I cared about was seeing Blake. I remember sitting anxiously at La Guardia, in a good way, waiting to board. I had taken great care at the apartment to look perfect before I left New York behind. I wanted to make sure the mousse I used to sculpt my hair held my new style in place. Quickly, I fished out a compact in my purse for a glance.

"Excuse me, Miss. Are you a model?" My eyes focused on a yuppie couple and their young daughter.

"Yes," I replied, feeling like a complete phony.

"My husband and I both thought you must be a model." I smiled graciously. I assume my new style gave me away. Nobody had thought I was a model when I arrived in New York wearing a plain tank dress and old Keds.

Mentally I left modeling back in New York. When my plane touched down at Standiford Field, I couldn't have been happier. I was back in my safe pocket of the world. I wanted to tell Beal that my welcome to New York consisted of liquor and a sleepover offer from a man two decades older than me. Beal only was interested in being regaled with stories of high fashion photographers and the photo shoots she assumed were launching my career. She had visions dancing in her head, visions of my picture splashed across magazine covers.

Settling back into high school life was like slipping on a pair of comfortable old shoes. Of course, I spent as much time with Blake as was allowed, which was a lot. Beal had lots to brag about now. I was dating Trinity's quarterback, and I was an aspiring model on the cusp of hitting it big. I did print ads for local department stores and runway shows, but in no way was I about to make an effort at becoming a household name.

Appearing in local print ads proved another way Beal lived vicariously through me. When ads ran for Shillito's, the department store I modeled for, Beal called everyone she knew. It wasn't about me it was about her. Beal wanted the glory and she used me to get it. One afternoon, she asked if I wanted to go shopping at Shillito's. Wandering through the racks of clothes I found a dress I loved. Beal came back to the dressing room and gave her approval as I turned around in the three-way-mirror. She happily agreed to buy it. When I met her at the counter, I found her spreading the newspaper ad across the counter. Walking towards her, she pointed her finger at the ad and then at me, declaring to the sales girl, "It's Libby, its Libby!" I was so embarrassed. The sales girl wasn't much older than me, and her eyes were glazing over as Beal force-fed her every detail of my life. When the sales girl's eyes met mine, I quickly looked down from humiliation. Beal never took a breath throughout the whole transaction. On the way to the car I was quiet. Beal never liked quiet.

"What's wrong with you? I just bought you a dress, damnit!"

"Mom, that was so embarrassing. I can't believe you carry that ad around with you. That sales girl couldn't have cared less." Beal's face turned blood red.

"Oh, you're embarrassed, are you? I embarrass you? You're the embarrassment! In first grade no one liked you and no one wanted to sit next to you!"

That was Beal's way. She never acknowledged or validated my feelings. For some reason, she always reached back into the past and told me horrible things about myself to switch focus.

"Mom, you aren't listening to me."

"Libby, I have had enough out of you! I'm going to take that dress back!" I gave up appealing to Beal. She had an arsenal of put downs and it wasn't worth being belittled anymore. Beal kept her word and snatched the bag from the back seat of the car and scurried inside. Later that night she came to my room and told me I could have the dress if I said I was sorry.

"I haven't done anything to be sorry for!"

"Well then, Libby, the dress goes back!" I assumed she took the dress back, but a month later she asked me to pull a handbag down from her closet that was out of reach. In the back of the closet I saw the crumpled bag with the dress inside. I guess taking the dress back to the sales girl would have been too embarrassing for Beal. The dress remained in her closet for years and possibly is there today.

I was grateful when the modeling buzz died down. I gladly embraced my high school routine. I wouldn't let modeling take all that away. The attention that came from being Blake's girlfriend was exhilarating and that was enough excitement for me. For the first time in my life I felt like somebody. For the first time, Earl seemed interested in my life. It wasn't my life he was interested in though it was Blake's. Earl was struck with Blake. I was struck with Blake. Beal was struck with Blake. My family's preoccupation with Blake was filled to capacity.

When I was with Blake, Beal's rulebook was thrown to the wayside. I could go over to his house and stay for hours without interruption as long as she believed I was really at his house. Beal hardly ever took me at my word. I was relentlessly questioned. I'm surprised she didn't set up a metal table and chair, blinding overhead light, and a lie detector for my interrogations. Her real concern was that I might not be dating Blake anymore, but rather sneaking over to Alex's house. Imagine that, a single sixteen-year-old girl? How tragic?

Beal, always highly suspect of my actions, started tracking me. I noticed my dad's car in the church parking lot across from Blake's house one night. There was a clear view. A young oak barely camouflaged her in the driver seat. Horrified, I pretended not to see the car on the way home. I went to my room, shut the door and never said a word to Beal. I didn't sleep well that night. I knew the stalking would not end.

One evening after Blake and I were leaving mass, he revealed he knew my mother was sitting out in the parking lot. By the time he discussed it with me, he had already discussed it with his parents. Beal had been staking out his house for weeks, but I hoped it had gone unnoticed. Unfortunately, a kiss goodbye in Blake's driveway had blown Beal's cover. He saw her in the car and several times later.

"Libby, why is your mother hiding in the parking lot? My parents are concerned."

"I don't know, Blake." I did know, I just wanted to hide the reality of my situation. It didn't stay hidden for long.

Greenups Belles and Brides was a bridal and formal wear staple in downtown Louisville. Trinity's prom was approaching and Beal took me there to find a dress. She had a particular fondness for Greenups. They had assisted many Junior Miss,' back in Beal's pageant days. A posh boutique with a grand staircase that reminded me of Tara in *Gone with the Wind*. All the sales ladies were required to wear black and the service was impeccable. This was NOT a store where you browsed the merchandise. After you were led into an elegant dressing room, dresses were selected for you. "Miss Dickie" was also a staple. She had been a sales lady longer than I had been alive. She was wonderful and brilliant at her job. I described what I had in mind and she quickly disappeared up the staircase. More often than not, what you had in mind and what "Miss Dickie" selected were two different things. I was brought down two dresses. I thought I wanted a fuchsia colored dress but when I saw the lavender gown with cascading ruffles and the beautiful bustle in the back, I knew she had made the correct choice for me. It lay over my hoop skirt perfectly. All that was needed were matching dyed shoes. "It's very flattering on you!" Miss Dickie said as I made a 360 degree turn in the three-way mirror. Beal beamed with pride. Beal was happiest with me when she took me shopping. I was happy for the dress. She was happy for the compliments. I was her show dog.

Beal was in the backyard surveying the newly tilled garden plot. I was flipping through the latest Seventeen Magazine on the family room sofa. The doorbell rang and it was Blake. He unexpectedly had stopped by to see me. I don't remember how things went south, but for whatever reason they did. Prom was off and Blake left. I hadn't realized Beal had overhead our conversation. She must have seen Blake's jeep in the driveway and come through the front door. Beal was a stealthy person when eavesdropping was required. "Blake, Blake!" I heard her yelling. My spine went erect. I couldn't get to my feet quickly enough. Running to the kitchen just in time to see Beal chase Blake down, I thought "Oh God!" I knew whatever she was saying was bad. It was bad. I didn't want to go outside after her and add to the scene. I heard her through the screen door. "Blake, I just bought Libby a new dress for the prom!"

Beal acted as if SHE was the one not going, not me. I hadn't mentioned the new dress during our argument. I wasn't in the habit of guilting my boyfriend, but Beal apparently had no issue. Catching sight of my red face in the foyer mirror, I felt so humiliated. I shut the front door and locked myself in my room. Thoughts went dashing through my head. Blake was already aware of Beal's reconnaissance missions. What was Blake thinking after being accosted? My focus shifted to the doorknob jiggling in my bedroom.

"Libby, open this door right now!"

"No!" I shot back. Beal started pounding on the door but I didn't move. I thought she might wear herself out. Obviously, the drama had impaired my thinking. Beal didn't wear out. She stopped pounding on my door but quickly returned with the screwdriver. I watched as the screws fell one by one to the floor, freeing the doorknob. It wasn't the first time. Beal was in!

"Libby, I paid good money for that dress! Why were you all arguing?" Clearly Beal had come in on the tail end of the conversation.

"It's not really your business. That's between Blake and me."

"It is MY business when I buy the dress!"

"Am I not allowed to make decisions regarding my own relationships? The dress can be taken back."

"Oh, the dress can be taken back?" Beal asked mockingly.

"You don't care about my feelings at all."

"Feelings?" Again, she mocked me like I should be ashamed to have feelings. Jumping off the carousel, I stopped engaging. She left and I started crying into my pillow like the forlorn teenager I was. Two days later Blake called and we made up. He never mentioned my mother's guilt trip regarding the dress. I didn't mention I knew. We went to Trinity's prom and surprisingly he kept dating me. I was happy.

I met Alex shortly before I met Blake. We were both at a birthday cookout for a mutual friend from our high school, Eastern. It was Sarah Winston's sixteenth birthday party, an all-girl affair. Her home was a fabulous venue for a birthday. Sarah lived off Rose Island Road, a long crooked, road that winds its way down by the Ohio River. Her contemporary home was set back deeply on the riverbank. Girls grouped everywhere on the lawn and the warm sunny day provided a perfect backdrop. I thought to myself, my drop-waisted dress and Pappagallo flats were a good choice. It was an afternoon party and everyone was well behaved, unlike some nighttime parties. I mingled about with my friends; we traveled in packs like most high school girls.

We celebrated Sarah's birthday until evening and then it was time to leave. She gave out party favors that included a glow in the dark shamrock keychain with "Sarah's Sweet Sixteen" on the back. I loved that keychain for two reasons. It was a clever reminder of Sarah's party and Blake's football team was the Trinity Shamrocks. I met Alex when it was time to leave. Needing a ride home, I don't remember if I offered or she asked, but soon we were driving back to her house. Alex had that All-American girl look. She was fair skinned with dirty blond hair and a killer smile. Sarah's house was about thirty minutes from Alex's so the drive afforded us ample time for girl talk. Clicking right away, I liked anyone with a quick wit and a sense of humor and Alex had both. She also had an appreciation for Virginia Slims Ultra Light's. It was the foundation for a perfect friendship.

Although Alex and I were an unlikely match, she being a freshman and me, a junior, her intoxicating personality was irresistible. We became inseparable and my friends quickly accepted her. She embraced the Trinity culture as well; football games, parties and congregating at the St. Mathews White Castle. Most everyone from Eastern hung out at Mr. Gattie's. Dating Blake introduced me to a new social scene. Blake had football practice every day during the season so Alex and I hung out together after school. It's unclear when Beal became aware of our friendship, but when she did there was harsh criticism and disapproval. Launching an investigation Beal determined Alex wasn't good enough based on the fact she didn't see her coming from a family with means or status, the two must haves to be Beal endorsed. Like Yogi says, it was déjà vu all over again. Alex was the new Nicole and Beal pounced right away.

Beal would never let alone the friendship I forged with Alex. She constantly picked at it like a scab. Her cruel remarks never ceased. I can remember only a few times Alex was in my house. One of those times Alex and I went into the bathroom together to do our hair. Beal started harassing us. "What are you all doing in there? Are you lesbians? Are you kissing each other? I bet you are!" she exclaimed. We immediately started making kissing noises. I had learned to deal with Beal through humor. It wasn't healthy but that was my coping skill. On one occasion I decided not to swallow my daily dose of Beal. Returning from Alex's house, I barely got one foot in the door before she asked me 'how is your girlfriend?" I simply turned around like I was in a revolving door. I got in my car and drove back to Alex's house. Beal was livid. She didn't give Alex's phone a break, calling over and over to me summon me home. "It's your mother again, Libby" Alex said with a roll of the eyes. I got on the phone, defiantly stated I was not coming home until later. I wanted some peace. Beal was having none of it! She was a painfully slow driver, but she made it to Alex's in record time. Alex, her brother and me were the only ones' home. Beal's bangs on the door briefly went unanswered so she brazenly started turning the knob. Alex met her at the door and I wasn't far behind. Her face shone red through the cracked door. "Libby you had no right to leave the house after I told you not to!" I didn't, but wasn't in the mood for her firing squad of words. Alex had no problem standing up to Beal. It made Beal despise her all the more. "Mrs. Henry you can't barge into my house!" Beal pushed one of the double doors anyway and began berating me. I know there were angry words being cast between us but it was what she was doing that I remember. As she was spewing her venom, she was pinching the skin under her arm. Beal was trying to bruise herself. Beal's powder white skin bruised so easily a fly could land and leave foot prints.

During her self-attack Alex's brother, Little Jim, came down their staircase in a hurry to get to work. He worked at "Farrell's, an 1890's themed ice cream parlor. All the employees wore red and white striped vests and straw boater hats. Their claim to fame was every kid received a free ice cream sundae on their birthday complete with a musical serenade. In Farrell's years I was an old woman. Little Jim stopped midway on the staircase by the spectacle Beal was making. He gave

Alex some backup, explaining this was their home and she needed to leave. Immediately. Beal stormed off, pinching her arm until she reached her car. Alex looked at me dismayed.

The ten- minute drive home seemed long. Earl was home when I arrived. How was I going to explain what happened? I wasn't afforded a chance.

Entering the house revealed Beal showing my dad the marks on her arm. "Look what Libby did to me!" Earl was furious. I could smell bourbon. "Libbah did you do this to your mother?" "No! She did it to herself!" she did! Mom tried to push her way into Alex's house and started pinching herself!" "Libbah tell me the truth!" "It is the truth! I shouted. Earl was highly skeptical. He doubted ME! "How can you believe her when she pretends to commit suicide every month and does crazy things to us? You do nothing! You never have!" Earl said nothing and shook his head. Beal kept buzzing in his ear "Earl are you going to let Libby get away with this? Take the car away from her!" Earl demanded the keys and I slapped them into his giant palm with a look of disgust. My actions angered him and he started yelling at me, then Jean started yelling at him as his voice was escalating. Beal loved to push everyone right to the edge and then pull everyone back like the controlling person she was. I believe creating chaos was a high for my mother. Earl and I went to our corners and the evening continued as usual. Nothing was resolved and there were no apologies. Beal made dinner and Earl lost himself in one of his favorite crime shows. I walked on foot to Alex's house the next week.

CHAPTER 3

Waynesburg, Kentucky is barely on the map. It's an insular farming community where Beal's parents lived their whole lives. Their white clapboard house sat on a generous piece of farmland among tired old trees with limbs too high for me to climb. As a youngster the journey to Waynesburg took forever. Once my mother's car left the expressway, we traveled through country town after country town, each smaller than the one before until we completely left civilization. The town I liked was "Harrodsburg," home to "Old Fort Harrod," the first permanent American settlement in the state. Its cabins were reminiscent of the ones I built with my Lincoln Logs.

I knew we had finally arrived when the car tires hit gravel, the road leading to my grandparents' house. That gritty sound awakened me from slumber surrendered to on the long ride. Even today the sound of tires spitting rocks reminds me of the unforgiving place my mother called home. "Sweetie," my grandmother, appeared from the white house the minute we pulled up the rocky driveway. I never felt welcome. I felt like I was trespassing. There was a greeting and then a dismissal that translated into, "Find something to do Libby, and don't be a bother." I was a bother. Beal told me over and over that as a baby I wouldn't let my grandmother hold me. I didn't understand the point she was trying to make. Apparently, my behavior as a baby sealed my fate. I was given a lesser rank. My mother went on to explain that my sister was Sweetie's favorite. "Your sister loved Sweetie as a baby and never wanted to leave her arms, Libby." When I asked why I couldn't be her favorite too, Beal brusquely replied, "You're not a good granddaughter! You do things you're not supposed to do." There were no activities for kids. Everything was a "Don't" in Waynesburg. Don't talk too much. I failed. Don't ask anyone to play. I failed. Don't aggravate the mean chihuahua out of boredom. I failed, but loved aggravating that dog. Don't pee in the cornfield. FAILED MISERABLY. There was no indoor plumbing and I loathed the outhouse. It was a worn-out, wooden structure that housed the dreaded "pit," a well filled with decades of defecation topped off with a splintered wooden hole for a seat. Fly paper strips littered with dead flies hung from the ceiling. The stench was unbearable and I wanted to vomit every time I shut the rickety wooden door.

There was an alternative facility that doubled as a cornfield, which became my option of choice after one of the fly paper strips broke loose and settled on my bare shoulder. I felt the tiny corpses and their last flutters of life. Unfortunately, the toilet paper I hid on one of the stalks gave me away and I earned a switch whipping. It was worth it, every time. A house without a bathroom makes no sense – everybody has one. I asked my mother why my grandparents didn't have one? I asked her a lot.

"Because they don't, Libby!"

"Do they not have money to buy a bathroom?" I kept on.

"My Mother and Daddy are REEECH!!!" Beal shouted as if she were a little girl too.

"Then why don't they have a bathroom?"

"Go pick your switch, Libby!"

I never got an "A" on my Waynesburg report card. I did try to improve my marks and win my grandmother's affection though. It wasn't that she was mean. She wasn't interested. I remember trying to show her the good work I had done on my hair. I had mastered a French braid and was seeking accolades.

"Sweetie, look at my braid."

"Hush up!" She chided as if I were speaking loudly in church. I was not considered a "good child," one that was quiet and invisible. I wanted to sing and dance and play. Those were unpopular activities for a child in the fundamentalist Baptist community where dancing wasn't allowed. Maybe Beal had opportunities to ride a bike, or learn how to swim, or put a ponytail in her hair, but she couldn't do any of those things and I believe she wasn't given the chance.

The high school my mother attended did not allow dances or senior proms. Dancing was sinful. I was confused. Sweetie adored Elvis as if he were sent straight from heaven. I thought if dancing was sinful how did Elvis win her approval? Elvis' moves were scandalous in the 1950's. I guess his gospel singing cancelled out his shaking pelvis. Unfortunately, I wasn't a good singer.

My grandfather terrified me. He was a drill-sergeant. It seemed he didn't like people. When I was around, he gave orders and everyone jumped, myself included. He wore a high-and-tight flat top and was hardly ever without a plug of tobacco. I called him "Paul" because I thought that was his name. Everyone thought I was calling him an endearing "PA," but mispronouncing it "Paul." My mother didn't realize I thought that was his name until I was getting married. Handing her my list for the wedding calligrapher she exploded.

"Libby! His name is not Paul, it's Willis Bradely!" Paul apparently hated his first name so it was never spoken, everyone in Waynesburg called him "B." I never knew his full name. I never knew anything about him other than he was the youngest of thirteen children and grew up fatherless. He father died before he was born.

Oh, I had questions, lots of questions for my mother, but they went unanswered or were met with hostility. I didn't understand and went to my father for answers. Earl said B was just mean. When I was older, Earl revealed that when he was in Waynesburg before I or my sister was born, B had beaten my mother's brother so badly that Earl thought he was dead. I wondered why my father hadn't intervened. Earl went on to tell me B didn't like him, and I think the feeling was mutual.

Earl told me Beal was just like her Daddy, "Libbah, as long as Beal's alive, B will never be dead." I believe that to be true. There was nothing endearing about Paul. He barely acknowledged us when we arrived and if he did it was a grunt or a strange facial expression. The sound he made acknowledging our presence was similar to the sounds he made when he was running cattle or hogs.

I don't remember him speaking a kind word to me, only commanding me to do something. The only times I saw him show affection was to "Chico," the chihuahua I aggravated. He would rub his belly and call him "Little Man." I tried to put my paw on his belly a couple of times and Paul promptly scolded me. "Leave him be!" I did until he was gone and then I went back to aggravating Chico.

Paul did soften up when he wanted me to clean the dirt from under his fingernails. "Harrr," he beckoned with a metal nail file in his hands. I cleaned the black dirt out from under each nail while he listened to his police scanner. He had been a deputy sheriff. I'm not sure what kind of action he was expecting to hear about in Waynesburg. It didn't seem to be a high crime area but he was ready nevertheless.

As I grew older, I accepted my ranking: Virginia, Misty, my first cousin and only cousin on my mother's side, and then me. It wasn't so bad. Sweetie made the most delicious food and worked at an old country store that was the heartbeat of town. Other than a post office there wasn't much commerce. A visit to the country store was the highlight of any day. The sweet smell of cut flowers met me at the screen door, I loved its weathered wooden floors and old-fashioned cash register. Local produce filled straw baskets that lined the back wall, and fresh eggs were always on hand. I didn't like the brown ones and decided they tasted different. I couldn't figure how they were dyed at Easter. Once across the threshold I begged for a box of Bugles and a NEHI orange soda in a glass bottle. Waynesburg was the only place I ever saw NEHI soda. Orange Crush is what we drank in Louisville, but it wasn't nearly so tasty.

The counter supported large jars of pickled eggs and bologna. The bologna looked like a big snake coiled up inside the jar so I kept my distance. Behind the jars was a miniature bleacher display showcasing different kinds of jerky. At the front of the store sat the freezer chest. It might as well have been a treasure chest, or so I imagined; a bounty of ice cream treats lay just beneath the lid My favorite was the orange sherbet Push-Up Pop. Easily spied among the loose treats all mixed together, the polka dot cylinders were hard to miss. Once a decision was made, I took my choice to the counter and Sweetie took money out of her western style wallet to feed the old register. I savored my Push-Up Pop on the walk back to her house. After the last lick it was back to being bored. I wasn't always successful in rousting Chico.

Sweetie and Paul had a large farm apart from the land where their house rested. Sometimes after dinner we would load up in Paul's truck and go fishing. It wasn't because they wanted to share the experience with their grandchildren, they wanted to fish and we were just there. The ride in the back of the pickup was thrilling and frightening at the same time. The hilly, narrow road and hair-pin turns gave my stomach a free fall sensation and I hung onto the sides for dear life, I was scared if I let go, I would slide out the back along with bits of fodder. Paul's truck wound its way deeper and deeper into the woods until we came upon a creek, which had to be crossed to get to the farm. If the water was high Paul parked the truck and we walked across a swinging bridge. That was terrifying. The bridge was made from old wood planks and thin wire cables. There was nothing but cable to hold onto and it had no type of enclosure. Every step made the whole bridge bounce.

Fear was not acceptable. Stalling was met with yells of, "Get across there!" Beal, who was afraid of everything, was fearless on the bridge, which surprised me. Still, she had so many fears! Riding in the car was her worst fear. Earl declared, "I've driven a thousand miles without you Bealo, (Earl's nickname for Beal), but I can't drive a mile with you!" Her limbs flailed in the air during lane changes until she secured a hand on the roof and a foot on the dashboard. It drove Earl crazy.

Once we got across the creek, one way or another, we went to the fishing pond. At first I didn't like fishing, but after hooking a bluegill it became interesting. I looked forward to going to the farm with the pond. It broke up the monotony until the time Sweetie and Paul took me by myself. I don't remember why my mother and sister weren't with us. When we got to the pond, Paul set out the fishing poles on the bank along with a rusted coffee can filled with dirt and worms. Once I started asking questions my grandparents quickly became frustrated. Being a quiet fisherman at seven was hard. I don't remember if I made a catch that day, packing up is all I remember. Paul angled the fishing poles in the pickup and I took my usual place. On the drive back to their house a low hanging tree limb caught one of the poles. I saw it dangling from the tree by its line and I didn't know what to do. I was too afraid to ever let go of the side of the pickup, so I didn't alert them to what happened until Paul turned off the truck in the gravel driveway. I quickly jumped out and told them, "One of the poles got stuck in a tree!"

They both berated me in tag-team fashion. Sweetie barked, "Libby, you should have pecked on the window!" Paul was shouting so loudly between tobacco spits that Beal heard him and came out the door. She didn't defend me, even if I was her daughter. In Waynesburg, Paul was the supreme leader and his authority wasn't questioned. He ordered me back into the truck and we went off to locate the pole that had been lifted.

I felt betrayed by my mother. There was barely any day remaining, darkness had fallen quickly on the way back to the farm. The tree covered road made it feel like we were driving through a tunnel. I heard the rhythmic sounds of crickets and bullfrogs along the roadside. I looked at Paul and his mean face and I was scared. He kept grilling me over and over. "Was it here? Was it here?" I didn't know. He knew I couldn't know, but he was downright mean. The truck came to a halt. The pole was lying in the middle of the road. It had been run over but the reel was intact. The truck door squeaked as he opened it and he retrieved the reel. He never spoke on the way back. I was sent to bed when we got home. I could hear my mother and Sweetie talking about me from the bedroom.

"She could have pecked on the window, Beal."

"I know Mother, she should have." I felt bad. I had disappointed everyone.

When I hit my preteen years, I made some friends so it wasn't so lonely down there anymore. Making friends helped me escape a loveless environment. I was thrilled when one of the girls asked me to sleep over. Finally, I got to use an indoor bathroom and take a shower. I didn't have to use a metal tub dragged in from the yard to the kitchen. I'm sure I wasn't missed.

Paul was emotionally dead. When it was time to leave, Beal told me to hug my grandfather. When I wrapped my arms around him, he stiffened. I might as well have been hugging a stranger. The stranger might have given me more affection.

Sweetie favored my sister, my Aunt Faye, her family and my Uncle. My Uncle didn't have any children, or so we thought until 2007 when Beal summoned Virginia and me to her house to give us a long-winded and detailed story about how her brother and some woman had a tryst down by the creek that resulted in a love child whose identity was kept from us for twenty plus years. It was disturbing how Beal described their encounter. "They did more than wash their cars that day!" and then she laughed like a high school girl trying to be cute. It was such odd behavior coming from someone who viewed sex as vulgar. She then declared, "There's Misty, Virginia, Libby, and now Francy." We didn't have relationships with anyone from Waynesburg as adults. I don't know what kind of reaction we were supposed to have. I wanted to know how washing the car fit into the story. I couldn't imagine washing a car in a creek. It made no sense but neither did Beal. Virginia and I looked at each other, absorbed the information about our new cousin and left. Earl by then was a hostage and could no longer drive and get away. Endless hours of her talking about the new development probably lulled him into his daily nap. What a blessing.

CHAPTER 4

The Trinity vs. Saint Xavier game was high school's biggest football rivalry in Kentucky. My best guy friend, Graham, Alex, Renee and I made plans to go. Collectively, it was decided I would be the driver. It was my turn. Earl never liked when I drove his car to football games.

"Libbah, the kids today vandalize the other team's cars!"

"Dad, they won't vandalize the car."

"The hell they won't! The last time they ran a key down the side of the door! You put those damn shamrocks and crepe paper on MY car and those Saint Xavier boys took a key to the door!"

"Dad, I won't decorate the car."

"See that you don't, ya heah?" Hmmmm. I was going to have to take my supplies to Alex's house and decorate the car there.

"Libbah, no shamrocks!" he admonished, his voice trailing off as he walked down the hall. Earl was highly suspicious as he should have been. Of course, I was going to decorate the car. I wasn't going to drive a naked car to the biggest game of the season. Promptly I tiptoed out with my green poster board and crepe paper and locked it in the trunk. Fortunately, there was no surprise inspection.

Graham and Renee were already waiting at Alex's house. I quickly handed out shamrocks to affix to the car. When we were done making Earl's car look like a clover patch, we headed out to the game. The fairgrounds where U of L played its football games was packed. Neither high school could hold this large a crowd at their own stadiums. I chose the first available spot to park. Hopefully Earl's car would be returned scratch free. Even a door ding would earn a harsh sentence. It was more than just a car. This was his personal sanctuary away from Beal. Once in a while I saw Earl around town sitting in his car. I would park and watch him a bit. He might have a newspaper or just sitting there staring out the front window. I knew he was just passing time as always before he went home.

Earl was a natural salesman. He was so good at selling that his day might be finished by early afternoon. I knew this because I would drop in at his office and his secretary would say with a grin, "Earl's done for the day and I'm stuck working on all the life insurance policies he sold!" My dad's charm and ability to relate to all types of people won him endless top seller trips around the world. It was a treat hearing his stories about Paris, Spain or Africa, the trip he liked the least.

"Libbah, there was hairs on the bacon and they had us sitting around a damn bowl that we all were supposed to eat out of with our hands!"

"Dad, did you eat out of the bowl?"

"No Sir!" he said one eyebrow raised. He existed on peanut butter and crackers that he stashed in his suitcase whenever he traveled abroad. You never knew what they might serve in a foreign land. Earl was always prepared. Always.

Practically everyone we knew was at the game. Trinity lost but we still had a great time mingling with the congregations of people; we were high-schoolers after all. I'm not sure when or why I decided to let Graham drive us to the after party. There was no good reason. It forever has become one of the mysteries of the evening. In stop-and-go traffic, my only memory is butchering Madonna's "Material Girl" at the top of my lungs before Graham slammed into the car in front of us. For a moment it was silent, and then I realized Madonna was still singing while smoke rose from under the hood. I looked around to see if everyone was okay. They were. Graham jumped out to check on the car he hit. Thankfully they were okay too. Renee ran to a steakhouse across the street to call the police. None of us had been drinking. That's because we hadn't made it to the after party. I guess Graham was distracted by my superb performance.

The reality of the situation was sinking in quickly. Earl's car was wrecked and I wasn't driving. There was absolutely no way I could tell him I wasn't driving. Beal the Baptist would accuse me of being drunk and Earl would have a hard time disagreeing with her. Why else would I let Graham drive? Earl *had* recovered evidence of drinking from the car before. "Libbah, I found a liquah bag in the car!" I had found a few of his myself. I tried telling him it was a brown bag from the gas station, but he frowned and challenged me. "Libbah, I know what a liquah bag looks like!" Well he did have field experience with "liquah bags." Beal wouldn't let him bring a drop into the house, so Earl kept a small bottle under his seat for a quick nip before he came inside.

The police had arrived. Alex and Renee called their parents and I had to call EARL! After a conference with my fellow passengers it was decided that I was driving the car. The passengers in the car Graham hit were an adult couple and weren't aware who was driving, plus they were hit from behind. Graham only asked if they were okay, he never said he was the driver. Yahtzee! I could take responsibility for the accident. Earl wouldn't be happy, but it would be a lot less painful than to say I gave the keys to someone else.

The plan was hatched. Dialing my number on the phone felt like it was in slow motion. The hostess from the steakhouse was right next to me and made me nervous. I didn't want her to overhear my conversation.

"Ah, Hello," Beal answered.

"Mom, can I talk to Dad?"

"Earl, Libby's on the phone!"

"Libbah? What's the problem?" Earl knew I wouldn't be calling home unless there was one.

"Dad, I was in a car accident. I rear-ended the car in front of me."

"Was anyone hurt?"

"No," I replied.

"Where are you?"

"I'm on Crittenden Drive in front of the Fifth Quarter Steakhouse."

"Alright, Libbah," Earl said exasperated. "Your mother and I will be there as soon as we can." Great, he was bringing the sheriff.

Now I saw the police lights. I walked over and gave my account of the accident. Alex's parents had arrived too. They were relieved no one was hurt and consoled me about the accident.

Taking the blame was easier than I thought. Earl and Beal arrived in record time, going against the traffic leaving the game made for a quick commute. I cringed when I saw them roll into the parking lot. We all had our stories straight on what happened. I was driving and the car in front of me stopped abruptly and I rear-ended it. Case closed. Earl stepped out of his car and walked past me straight to the officer.

"I'm her father," he said and went over the report.

"Libbah, you say you looked to the left to talk to Graham? Was he riding on the side view mirror?"

"I meant right, Dad?" Case open. I couldn't believe the police officer didn't ask questions like Earl.

"The man you hit says Graham walked up to the car to see if they were okay? You walked up after he did? He also said no one claimed responsibility for the accident?" God! Earl was poking holes in my story! It's like he knew I wasn't being truthful. Earl was right. We only made sure the people in the car were not hurt. We didn't linger. Only Earl would reconstruct the accident.

The officer told my dad no one appeared to be drinking. Relief. The sheriff wouldn't have to lock me up at home. I don't remember where or what Beal was doing. I find that amazing because when there was drama Beal was like a moth to a flame. I know she wasn't just sitting in the car. "Libbah, let's go!" Earl said. The officer handed him the report and instructed him to contact his insurance company.

"Hell! I'm in the insurance business! I'll contact myself!" The officer laughed but Earl didn't. When it came to money Earl didn't make light. Ever. I watched as the tow truck hooked up Earl's car. I walked over to say goodbye to everyone. Alex's parents had driven their tiny RX7 sports car so there was barely room for three people in the back. Graham was tall and lanky so he had to lie down on his back in the trunk space and let them close the hatch on top of him. I was not able to control my laughter when I saw him – he looked like a specimen trapped under glass.

I was jarred back into the reality when I saw the tow truck man walk up to Earl with the stack of shamrocks we had put on the car. "Sir did you want to keep these?" I sucked my lips. I didn't think to strip them off after the accident. Rookie mistake. I thought he might have forgotten with the matter at hand.

"LIBBAH! Now!!!" Sheepishly I walked over to the car.

"Here!" Earl pushed them into my hands. "I said no damn shamrocks!" I took the fifth. It was complete silence on the way home since nothing I could say was going to do me any good. Beal must have been ill. Once Earl had parked in our driveway, I quietly took my shamrocks and went to my room. Earl was too quiet. Beal wasn't. She got on the phone immediately to call some of her church buddies and regale them with the dramatic crash. "The car was on fire!" I heard her tell the unsuspecting soul who unfortunately answered the phone. The car was never on fire. There was some smoke but no fire. By the time Beal finished retelling the story we were all trapped and had to be pulled out by the Jaws of Life. I let her have her fun. I wasn't in a position to correct her.

The shower felt good, and it gave me a place to think about Earl's line of questioning. He wasn't buying what I was selling. I really didn't know how he managed to hone in on those details, but I knew one thing, when Earl sank his teeth into something he didn't let go. "Stick to the story," I said to myself.

I woke up the next morning to Earl talking to his insurance co-worker and friend, Frank. "Libbah wasn't driving that car I tell you!"

God, I had Columbo on the case. There was no hope, the inquisition would start the minute he hung up the phone. I went to the kitchen table to turn myself in. Earl's breakfast was perfectly laid out on a paper towel next to a half a grapefruit; two strips of bacon, and one sausage patty. I made some toast and sat at the table. Beal was in the shower, getting ready for church. At least I wouldn't be double-teamed. She could yell at me later. As predicted Earl came straight for me after he hung the phone up.

"Libbah, I'm going to ask you one more time, who was driving MY car?"

"Graham was driving," I replied.

"Why in the hell was that damn boy driving my car?" I know I gave him some reason but I don't remember. The next thing I do remember is calling Graham with Earl towering over me. Earl needed insurance information. He was giving me a litany of questions to ask Graham and I suppose maybe I got confused or intimidated and didn't pose the questions correctly. For some reason Earl got the idea Graham didn't have a license. No one knows why. Graham did have a license. Whatever the reason, convinced there was no license, Earl bellowed so loudly the walls shook, "THAT DAMN BOY WRECKED MY CAR! BETTAH HAVE A LICENSE!" From that day forward whenever I received phone calls and wasn't home Earl made a list. It read like this:

Phone calls for Libbah:

Renee

Alex

Kim

Damn Boy

Jackie

John

Jennifer

Earl was mad for a long time and rightly so. I didn't get to drive for months. He forgave me, but he never forgot, and Graham was forever "The Damn Boy" who wrecked his car.

CHAPTER 4

I left for college at summer's end. My parents unceremoniously dropped me off, put my things in my dorm room and left. A feeling of relief and sadness swept over me. Secretly, I envied tearful goodbyes witnessed between daughters and their parents. I quickly switched my feelings off and focused on getting settled. Renee and I were roommates. As young girls we had mapped out what our lives would look like. We would go to the same college, get married, and live on the same street so our kids could play together. We laughed that we had fulfilled the first leg of our planned journey through life. That night I had a fleeting thought as I lay in my dorm room bed. I had no plan. Living day to day was my normal. Chasing a good time was always my goal. Anything that was fun and got me out of the house was my daily bread. Beal clipped my wings and I had no idea how to take flight. I left home like a piece of Swiss cheese, full of holes. Reflecting back on what was said during orientation earlier that day, I was relieved that being undecided was common among freshmen.

Settling into college life was an easy transition. I loved my newfound freedom. The best part was that I could manage Beal. The phone rang differently when a call came from off campus. If I thought it might be Beal, I could choose to ignore it or have Renee tell Beal I was in the shower. I was the cleanest coed at UK that year. And to my surprise I liked my classes. I didn't know I was dyslexic – I just thought I wasn't smart. College classes were daunting, even the idea of class was daunting. I had shut down academically in eighth grade when the war began between Beal and me. When I explained that things didn't make sense, she didn't listen. "Libby, you are just looking for an excuse! I don't want to hear it Libby." If I had had the inclination to ask for outside help, I'm sure I might have found a sympathetic teacher, but I didn't. I learned to squeak by. Unfortunately, I had no emotional insight either. I needed help to process what I had been through at home, but I didn't know it at the time. I continued to cope the way I always had, through humor. Humor had always served me well and college was no exception. I had a great freshman year and I did well in school too. Beal backed off and we shared calm waters.

Things continued to ebb and flow between Beal and me until the summer after my freshman year. Earlier in the school year I had been at the Damn Boy's fraternity house for a Halloween party. I was dressed as Cleopatra and enjoying the house wine they were serving, keg beer. Thumper and The Plaid Rabbits were playing; they were a college band favorite. I was dancing in puddles of spilt beer when I looked up and met eyes with a guy dancing wildly on a sofa and singing into a hairbrush. His costume was not identifiable, it appeared he was just wearing a trash bag. Well, I thought it *was* a perfect costume for a frat party. It was appropriate as well as functional. I was immediately attracted to the tall sandy blond-haired guy with a stupid grin on his face. He was baby-faced and almost too pretty to be a guy. We continued exchanging glances through the evening but that was the extent of our communication. I was hoping we would connect but "Walk Like an Egyptian" started playing. My reign was short so I wanted to make the most of it and began my walk through the house. I danced my way to The Damn Boy who identified my mystery guy as "Benny," and said he was from Louisville. I learned four weeks later that Benny left school and had gone back home. He also left quite an impression on me.

It was May and I was back at Beal's. I was going through my clothes and trying to purge unwanted items. Beal was a hoarder so I had to secretly get them out of the house. She would always say she would donate the clothes herself but that never happened. I would find them, sometimes years later, stuffed away in various closets. I was just about to camouflage my donations in my college laundry bag and act as if they were some of Renee's things that got mixed up with mine when the phone rang. Earl got to it before me. "Libbah, a young man is on the phone for you." It was Benny. The phone call came out of the blue. "This is Benny Livingston." My heart started pounding. I was nervous. "Oh, hi! How are you?" We briefly made polite conversation and then he got right to the point. "If you aren't busy do you want to go out Friday night?" It wouldn't have mattered if I was busy, I was going. "Sure, that sounds great." "I'll pick you up at seven, then," sounding excited. I gave him my address and told him I would see him Friday.

I knew he had heard through the grapevine that I was interested but I never thought it was mutual. I was stunned. Friday couldn't come soon enough. I ran out of the house with my laundry bag in tow and threw it in Beal's car. I turned up the AM radio jam, she didn't have FM, and drove to Goodwill. I thoroughly enjoyed all my mundane tasks that day.

Friday came with much anticipation. By that day I had bought a new dress and gotten an ample amount of vitamin D out in the sun. I was always running late but I had managed my day well and had thirty minutes to spare. I sat ready and waiting at the kitchen table. Beal was at her favorite perch, washing dishes at the front window. She would stand there for long periods of time peering up and down the street looking for anything out of the ordinary. A goodnight kiss was hard to steal when Beal was on the lookout. The minute headlights hit the driveway here she came and watched until I was inside. Out of nervousness, I started to break the green beans she had picked from the garden. It gave me something to do while I waited for Benny. Beal asked, "Where does he live, Libby?" I told her I didn't know because I didn't.

"What do you mean you don't know where he lives?"

"Because I don't know, that's why."

"Well I don't understand why you didn't ask?"

"Why does it matter where he lives," I replied.

"Libby, that's enough!" That was Beal's way of not answering. I felt tension building and I could tell she was taking it out on the pot she was scrubbing. I became amused. In high school The Damn Boy came to pick me up one time, and Beal was hard at work on the pots. Beal liked The Damn Boy and he was the master Beal-charmer. He enthusiastically made conversation with her every time he came over to pick me up. I don't know what got into him one particular evening but as we disappeared into the entry hall to leave, the Damn Boy stuck his head back in the kitchen and took a liberty I hadn't ever seen anyone take with Beal. "Looking good Beal! Looking REAL good!" She started furiously scrubbing her pot just like she was doing now except on our way out we saw her crack a smile. She wasn't smiling now. No one but The Damn Boy could have gotten away with a remark like that.

"Libby, where is he? It's seven o'clock."

"I'm sure he'll be here soon, Mom!"

"Well in my day a boy picked you up on time!" Beal said in a disapproving manner. Yeah, I bet Beal and her pleasing personality had all kinds of Waynesburg courtiers. I don't think she had a "day," I just think she had my dad.

"Well, he's here!"

"His car's not much to write home about." Oh God, Beal was displeased. Too bad Benny was a gentleman and came to the door, I would have settled for a quick honk once I saw Beal's expression. I opened the door to the baby-faced singing wonder. Nervously, I led him to the kitchen to meet Beal. Earl was on a fishing trip so there was no buffer. Benny was the epitome of a mannerly southern boy. He immediately tried to engage in polite conversation. Beal was having none of it; it was so embarrassing. Benny was asking all the questions and Beal responded with one-word answers. "How are you Mrs. Henry?" "Fine," she replied. It was role reversal. Beal should have been asking all the questions but instead was irritated by his very presence. It was the car. Benny's car was a beater, a far cry from the candy-apple red sports car the guy I dated before had driven. I knew what she was thinking. The only question she asked Benny was, "Where do you live?" Benny lived fairly close by except he literally and figuratively lived on the wrong side of the tracks according to Beal. I knew the minute he uttered the name of his neighborhood Beal would disapprove. It was ironic. The self-proclaimed Christian who grew up with no indoor plumbing was judging Benny by his car and his address. Her eyes moved up and down Benny, finally resting on the holes in the knees of his jeans. All the college kids were wearing distressed jeans and I was no exception. Beal knew it was a trend but she wanted to make Benny feel uncomfortable. Beal might as well have put him on a slide under a microscope for closer inspection. The awkwardness was mounting so I quickly ended the introductions. "Mom, we're going now." "Libby, don't be out late! I have to get up early for church!" Sunday, the one day of the week Beal morphed into the faithful follower of Christian teachings. "Judge not, that ye be not judged," was the verse I hoped the pastor emphasized in his sermon the next day and every Sunday after that. Beal was the ultimate religious hypocrite.

Benny and I meshed right away. I don't think we made it to the first stop sign in my neighborhood before we were laughing. Next to The Damn Boy, he was the funniest person I had ever met. He took me to a fraternity party on the University of Louisville college campus. It's cliché to say it felt like we had known each other forever, but it did feel that way. Our infatuation with one another was intense. It was so intense that the party only served as a backdrop while we got lost in conversation. The pulsating music and the shrill of partygoers were just white noise. We were deeply engrossed in one another, forgetting about the hours passing. I didn't want to go home. Of course, I was late and the warden was waiting. Benny hit the driveway and Beal hit the window. Benny told me what a great time he had and I reciprocated. I was anxiously waiting for Benny to kiss me. He leaned in and Beal turned on the front porch light. My long awaited, lengthy kiss turned into a quick peck. Beal was turning the light on and off to signal me inside. I didn't give a damn. Benny asked me out again. "Yes, call me." Responding with a smile.

I ran inside and Beal was on my heels.

"Libby, I said for you NOT to be late!"

"I'm sorry, we lost track of the time."

Beal mocked, "What were you doing?"

"Talking," I replied.

"Hmmm Mmmm, I bet you were talking! Nice girls don't stay out late!"

That's rich I thought. What do nice girls do? Have an affair with a married man and live happily ever after. I kept that thought to myself and climbed into bed. I imagine Beal prayed for my soul the next day at church.

That summer I remained in a state of fervent longing for Benny. He rented more space in my mind than anyone I had ever dated before. Beal knew it too. Every day, she made degrading comments about Benny.

"Why did he leave UK I wonder? What does his father do for a living? He must not do much because you never answer the question?"

Truth was I didn't know why Benny had left school or why he never talked about his dad, and I didn't ask. I figured he would tell me when he was ready. Beal wasn't satisfied and continued to dive into Benny's background. She relentlessly peeled Benny like an onion, layer by layer. Undeterred, Beal finally uncovered the truth about Benny's family. One of Beal's gossipy friends knew Benny and his family from the ballpark. She informed Beal that his father was a drunk who hadn't worked in years. The informant went on to tell stories of how Benny was berated publicly by his father if he struck out during a game when he was younger. This might elicit outrage in most parents, but not Beal. Instead she used her newly acquired knowledge against Benny. Benny was well aware of Beal's disdain, but chose to take the high road and tolerate her bad behavior. A tall order for a nineteen-old boy saddled with family problems. By the end of the summer, Beal had gotten so bad she would holler "Stupid Ole' Benny is on the phone," when he called. Benny didn't blame me for Beal's cruelty. He felt sorry for *me*. Everyone has his breaking point though and Benny was no different.

It was late July and one of Benny's fraternity brothers was having a pool party. Everett couldn't have picked a better night. It was a balmy ninety- two degrees, and the humidity was suffocating. I was working long days at an amusement park that summer, and was held hostage by my overly starched nautical uniform. I constantly maintained a film of sweat. Everett's pool party was the pinnacle of my week. Friday came, and I rushed home to get ready. Benny was off that day so I knew he would want to make the most of it. I needed to be quick. I was never quick! My feet hit the driveway and I ran into the house, slamming the screen door behind me. "Libbah, what's all the racket?" Earl chided.

"Sorry Dad, I'm in a hurry."

Earl was starting on the appetizer portion of his meal, beer cheese and crackers. Earl loved all cheese and passed the gene to me. We were both mice. I jumped in the shower, scrubbed off the park scum and did a Wonder Woman makeover. I was going to be on time. I used my last minutes before Benny arrived to sit down at the table and hog down some beer cheese, I didn't need a cracker I loved to circle my finger around the container and lap up the cheese! Earl was never amused. "Libbah, get your paw out of that cheese! That's what crackers are for." I laughed and Earl shook his head and lifted one eyebrow. Try as I might, I couldn't master the one eyebrow lift. I was enjoying my time with Earl until Beal came in from the garden. She was in a mood. Earl always ate raw onion with every meal, so Beal had gone to the garden to fetch one. I heard the utility door slam and in she came. She slung the green onions in the sink as if she was slinging a doll around by its hair.

"Bealo, what's wrong with you? Why are you in such a bad humor?"

"Earl, there's nothing wrong with me!"

"Libbah, where are you going?" asked Earl.

"I'm going to a pool party."

"With Stupid Ole' Benny!" Beal interjected.

"Beal, let's keep the peace!" Earl pleaded. Earl's plea went unheeded. She just kept ranting. I was used to Beal not liking people but she simply loathed Benny.

"Libby, I drove by his house, and if you continue to date someone like him you'll end up in a house like that!"

"Mom!"

"Don't Mom me! Keep dating Stupid Ole' Benny and you'll see." Beal kept on. Beal had broken Earl years ago. It was horrible, but Earl never intervened – he just preferred to stay out of the line of fire. I could have used a functional father, one that stood up to Beal, but Earl wasn't that man.

I kept bobbing up and down in my chair. Benny had long stopped coming to the front door, so I looked for him through the kitchen window. He pulled up in front and I ran to the door.

"Libby, have a good tiiiiime with Stupid Ole' Benny," Beal sarcastically called out.

"Mom, you have serious problems!" I yelled back, running out to Benny's car.

"Oh, I have serious problems, do I!" I heard the screen door slam. Beal crossed the yard like a furious twister.

"I don't have any problems! YOU and Stupid Ole' Benny are the problem!"

"Mom!" Benny's window was cracked so he could hear everything. Benny had had enough. He got out of his car and stormed towards Beal. His face was red and I could see little drops of sweat beading over his brows.

"Mrs. Henry, I do not appreciate you calling me names!"

"You don't do you?" Beal replied in her most condescending voice. "Your father is a drunk, and I drove by your house and you're nothing but white trash!"

Beal loved knowing Benny's weak spot and delighted in bringing it up with him for standing up to her. I knew Benny wanted to slap her. I know I did. It was the cruelest thing she could have said, because it was true. Benny's mother worked as a nurse and carried the weight of raising four boys on her own.

"Benny! Let's go NOW" The pain of Beal's remark had stunned him; he stood there glassy eyed and frozen.

"You're a bitch! You are a stone, cold bitch!" Benny said and turned abruptly and got behind the wheel. Beal kept talking but I turned my back on her and shut the car door. Benny hit the gas hard and we drove away.

"I...I'm so sorry."

"Libby, I have never spoken to an adult that way and have never had one speak to me like your mother just did." He gripped the steering wheel and his knuckles shone white. "Your mother is sick!"

"I know Benny." We drove to the party holding hands in silence. When we arrived Benny smiled and said, "I'm not going to let that woman ruin my good time, are you?" It occurred to me Benny had developed the same coping mechanism I had. "Turn your feelings off and carry on." We both got smashed that night in spite of the conversation that still vexed us. My new pick-up and drop-off spot became the stop sign at the end of my street.

Somehow Benny and I kept dating. When summer ended I went back to school and Benny stayed behind in Louisville to work. We were crazy in love so I wasn't worried about the distance between us. It was such a relief to be back at school. Benny came up and visited without Beal's interference, or so we thought.

Beal measured people by how much money and status they owned. I remember some of my friends declaring, "Beal likes me!" as if they had earned a stamp of approval. They were my wealthy friends. My friends who came from modest backgrounds fell into Beal's dreaded reject bin. If you were wealthy and challenged Beal you immediately dropped rank as did a friend of mine who questioned Beal on why she hated Benny so much. "Sarah sassed me, and I'm going to call her father." Sarah, who was twenty years old, had asked a question everyone but Alex was too scared to ask. Benny was a thoughtful person who always put others first. Everybody loved Benny – everybody but Beal. She never did call Sarah's father because she knew he was a straightforward man and wouldn't suffer her opinions. He would have been proud of Sarah standing up for Benny. Beal always thought to call somebody. She loved enlisting reinforcements.

Beal was hoping the relationship with Benny would play itself out. I really believe Beal thought I would realize that Benny had nothing to offer. As time went on, Beal came to the realization that Benny and I were getting more and more serious. She couldn't stand that he bypassed her and headed straight to Lexington to see me. Surprise visits became the new norm. Beal showed up without notice in hopes of catching Benny in my apartment. It wasn't a secret. She wanted me to know it was her right to come unannounced. "We pay for your school and I can sleep there if I want!" Beal did show up one time when Benny was there but she had no idea because my roommates hid him in the other bedroom until she left.

The longer we dated the more desperate Beal became. I came home for Christmas break and Beal relentlessly made fun of Benny every day. The pleasure she took in hurting someone I cared about was diabolical. Benny took me to Kunz's, an upscale restaurant, for Christmas. He gave me a gold bracelet and a sweater. I loved them both. When I returned home, Beal came into my room and caught sight of the gifts, judging them cheap and tacky. The next morning, they were gone – she hid them from me. I finally found them along with no less than forty notes I had written in grade school. She wrapped everything in one of her old nightgowns and put it in a drawer. I don't know which was more horrifying, Beal hiding Benny's gifts, or the collection of notes passed between friends a decade ago. There was no acknowledgment of the theft. She was silent when I confronted her. She gave me the silent treatment for days. When I gave Beal her Christmas gift, a pair of nice running shoes, she picked them up, examined them and threw them back in the box in disgust.

"Yuck! Why did you think I would like THAT color, Libby?"

She would have liked them if I was dating a rich boy. I had given them to her early because she was going to Florida with my dad right after Christmas. I thought it would give her a chance to exchange them if they didn't fit. Beal refused to take them back. "Mom, if you take them back, you can get a color *you* like." "Libby, I'm not taking them back and that's enough!" It was enough. I took the shoes back to the store. Beal later complained, "Libby didn't bother to get me a Christmas gift."

Holidays in general made Beal angry. It was obvious that whatever fire burned between Beal and Earl had been extinguished years earlier – not a single ember glowed. I never saw my parents show affection towards one another. No hugs. No kisses. Holidays accentuated this fact. Earl dreaded buying gifts for Beal. She wanted a diamond for her gold wedding band like his first wife had. Beal lobbied for years. "My sister is dripping in diamonds, Earl!" In the divorce settlement Earl had given everything to his first wife. Earl had also reinvented himself. The lifelong dairyman made a career switch to the insurance business. He didn't like to part with a dollar, and every holiday Beal wore a face of disappointment after opening unwanted gifts from Earl. Beal finally got her diamond years later after Earl enlisted the help of my sister, who was working in a jewelry store. It was too late. She knew it wasn't a token of his love and affection He had gotten a good deal.

Beal's crusade against Benny continued. She made threats constantly. "Libby, I'm not going to buy you any more clothes if you continue to date Stupid Ole' Benny," or, "The car is going to be taken from you!" It never stopped. Once Beal sank her teeth into something, she wouldn't release it until her goal was achieved. This time her goal was to get Benny out of my life. Beal's unyielding behavior was starting to take its toll on Benny. I had returned home again for the summer. I was talking to a friend on the phone about *Thirty Something*, a popular show about relationships between people in their thirties. Beal, ever the eavesdropper, was listening and heard me talk of marriage. Thinking I was speaking of potential matrimony with Benny, she was enraged.

"Libby, you are NOT going to marry that trash!"

"Mom, Benny is not trash, and I was talking about characters on a TV show! Wouldn't your time be better spent on something other than listening in on my conversations!"

"Sure, you were, Libby," Beal said in her usual sarcastic tone.

"You know, you're right, Benny and I want to get married." Of course, I was being sarcastic but Beal took my words as fact, and ran with the ball.

"I'm going to tell your father!"

"So?" I replied. I unlocked horns with Beal long enough to get ready. Benny was taking me to The Old Spaghetti Factory and I wanted to be at the stop sign on time. Beal never stopped talking while I was getting ready. Outside the shower I could hear her ranting about my inability to navigate life in the proper direction. Those weren't the words she used.

"You had a boyfriend that was going places and you settled on poor Stupid Ole' Benny! I guess you don't have the sense God gave you."

"God?"

As I lathered up my hair, I wondered why he gave me Beal as a mother. Beal never wound down. The more I ignored her, the more agitated she became. I always was amazed at her endurance. I kept getting ready despite her efforts to re-engage me in battle. Normally I would fight back but now that we had a Neighborhood Watch, I thought Benny's waiting at the stop sign might raise eyebrows. I felt a sigh of relief when I heard the utility room door shut. Earl was home. Good, a diversion. Every night the same scene played out. Earl came in the door and Beal started nagging about whether or not he had a drink before he came home. This had been going on for years. It was white noise to me now.

"Earl, you've been drinking!"

"Beal, get off my back and give me some peace."

The minute Earl said, "I do," he forfeited his peace. There would never be peace with the crazy chaos-maker. I can still hear her high-pitched crow, "Earl! Earl!" as she trailed behind him while he tried to decompress after work. Tonight was no different. I felt guilty for being relieved that Beal had switched targets, but I was relieved. I was putting on the finishing touches of my make-up when I heard Beal yelling, "You don't care if she marries that trash?"

"Beal, I have had enough of that mouth!" Earl hollered back.

Beal came out of the bedroom with a gun.

Beal had threatened suicide for years. When I was younger, I looked to Earl to address the situation, but addressing the situation meant he had to do something, so he didn't. I was afraid to call the police, I didn't want to endure Beal's wrath. Earl chose to believe she would get better, but I never knew his reasons to support that belief. He didn't talk about the situation. We co-existed silently with an elephant in the room.

"I'm going to kill myself and then you will all be sorry!"

Earl just stood there with the familiar stock-still look he always had when Beal threatened suicide. I didn't understand why he kept guns in the house anyway. "Dad, what are you going to do?" "I can't change her, Libbah." I watched as Earl sat down at the kitchen table with his beer cheese and crackers. He dressed each cracker with beer cheese and set them on a plate. The catfish Beal had fried was sitting on grease-soaked paper towels. I rescued the remaining pieces that were drowning in the cast iron skillet. "Dad, do you want me to heat these up for you?"

"No, Libbah, that fish isn't worth a damn now."

He was right. Cold fish wasn't worth a damn."

"Just hand me some cold cuts and bread and I'll fix up a sandwich."

I got out the package of cold cuts and bread, letting Earl go to work. I looked up at the harvest yellow clock that hung above the stove. It was time to start walking. I didn't want to be in the strike zone when Beal came home. I wanted Earl to leave too, for good. That was magical thinking. Gone were the days when I thought my dad would leave and take my sister and me with him. No, he looked away, subjecting us to Beal's aberrant behavior. "Dad, I'm going to dinner and will call you in an hour." He nodded his head and I quietly left.

Benny was parked below the stop sign. Walking down the street, I wondered what to say.

"My mother, who called you trash, has threatened to kill herself. She's riding around Louisville with a gun."

I didn't want him to think I was trying to garner sympathy. My mother had never taken off in a car before. After I had caught Beal spitting out pills and pretending to be dead, she turned to guns. My dad kept them in his closet. There was a wide assortment: my half-brother's high-powered weapons from the Vietnam War rested in the back corner, while Earl's pistols lay on a shelf. Beal would lock herself in her bedroom for hours with the guns and then come out when she had regained the will to live again. It angered me Earl didn't keep the guns out of the house somewhere. I didn't understand, and I didn't question him on it.

Benny leaned over his seat and opened my door. I decided to explain. Instead of being hateful about Beal, which was well deserved, Benny showed concern.

"Libby, should we call the police?"

"No, I'll get in trouble when she gets home."

"You don't think she's serious?"

"She's been threatening to kill herself for years. My dad doesn't want to call the police. He ignores her." Benny didn't know what to do any more than Earl or I did. As we drove to the restaurant, I made idle chitchat. I was a master at compartmentalizing.

The restaurant was crowded. Benny gave his name and we took our place in line. "Harriman," the hostess called out to the crowd. I didn't pay much attention until Mr. Harriman tapped me on the shoulder. "Hello young lady!" Mr. Harriman was a gregarious older man who worked with my mother. He was one of the happiest adults I had ever met. When I went to the school where he and Beal worked, he greeted me as if he had known me for years. I wondered if he ever had a cloudy day.

"Hello Mr. Harriman! How are you?"

"I'm dandy! Who is this gentleman?" He inquired.

"Oh, I'm sorry, this is my boyfriend, Benny." Mr. Harriman introduced us to his wife. "This young lady's mother is Beal Henry. "Well, it's nice to meet you both," Mrs. Harriman said. Mr. Harriman loved my mother. "How about you two join us for dinner?" We couldn't say no. How ironic that Benny and I were going to sit through dinner with a man who loved my mother but had no idea who she really was. I wondered what he might have said if he knew at that very moment Beal was driving around town with a loaded gun, looking for the perfect place to kill herself. Beal was a million different people. He knew one person, and Benny and I knew someone else.

Unlike my mother, Mr. Harriman wanted to know all about Benny. He engaged him right away. It was surreal. While we ate spaghetti, Benny made small talk with the Harriman's and all I thought of was suicidal Beal. I couldn't take it anymore. I needed to make the call home. Excusing myself I searched the bottom of my purse for a quarter. The phone was in use. Damn, the lady on the phone was having a conversation like she was on her home phone. I stepped a bit closer hinting she needed to wrap it up.

"Well, someone is waiting to use the phone – I'll call you when we get home."

"Hell, why did she even bother going out for dinner?" I thought.

I made my call and waited. "Ah, hello?" Beal used the pleasant pitch she always used when answering the phone. If it was someone she didn't like her voice quickly lowered. Being a coward, I hung the phone back on the receiver. I didn't know what to say. I knew on Monday she would find out that Benny and I had dinner with Mr. Harriman and his wife. God, she was going to have a fit. I could already hear her berating me for going out to eat while she contemplated suicide.

I returned to the table and rejoined the conversation. The Harriman's were oblivious. They didn't know about the mad woman with a gun. Mental exhaustion overcame me, and I was relieved when dinner was over. Neither of us was prepared for the Harriman's. They enjoyed their meal and commended us on being such a fine young couple. When I got home, Beal was ironing clothes in the family room while Earl watched one of his favorite detective shows. As usual, it was as if nothing had happened. It was quiet that night. I watched TV in my bedroom. I might have called my sister, but unfortunately, we weren't close. This was a time I needed her to lean on.

Benny and I continued dating, but it was a struggle. Beal's unyielding interference slowly sucked the life out of our relationship. My friends and Benny's knew Beal hated him, which was hard to grasp, because everyone loved Benny. We were all aware of his circumstances, his non-working alcoholic father, his hard-working mother who worked long hours as an RN, and that Benny and his three brothers all had jobs to help make ends meet. Benny never complained and was recognized for his sunny disposition. Beal had big plans for her daughter, but Benny and his family were not the ones to flesh out those dreams.

Alex was still in high school and singing in a talent show. I made plans with Benny to meet in Louisville and go support her. Benny and I sat in the audience holding hands while Alex sang her rendition of "Anything For You," by Gloria Estefan. After the show, we went to Alex's house to hang out and celebrate.

We hadn't been there any time at all when headlights appeared in the driveway. Alex's mom pulled the curtain back in the dining room, "Libby, your mother's here." How Beal found out I had come from Lexington is still a mystery to me, but she had her spies everywhere I guess, and she wasn't going to let me get away with it.

Beal was knocking on the front door. I didn't know what to do. Alex's mom attempted cordiality when she opened the door, but Beal would have none of it.

"Libby, you lied to me! You said you were going to the library to study, but here you are with Benny."

"I came to see Alex perform at the talent show…," I replied before Beal interrupted.

"Libby, you lied to me and I hate a liar."

"Mom, this is exactly why I didn't tell you!"

"We pay for your school! You're supposed to be studying, not gallivanting around with Benny. You get in the car, NOW Libby!"

I wasn't about to and the argument escalated. From nowhere Big Jim (Alex's dad), gave me a hug and said, "Libby, we love you." I was shocked. I lay my sword down and stared dumbfounded. My parents never used those words with each other or me, it was unexpected. It didn't deter Beal. "Libby, you come on NOW! Do you hear me?"

I didn't leave with Beal. When I left later with Benny, I hugged Alex and her parent's goodbye. I would take my licks from Beal later. Riding back to school was sad and uncomfortable. Like Benny and I knew, Beal was going to destroy our relationship. Benny had stood silently in the foyer at Alex's house as Beal exceeded all bounds of decorum, and now we were trying to force conversation. I saw the weariness in his face and turned on the radio to take the pressure off the awkward conversation. I rolled the window down and hung my hand out, making hills in the wind.

Sometime later we were at Benny's fraternity when one of Benny's friends took me aside. We were all a little drunk, maybe more than a little, which is probably why he felt it appropriate to approach me. "Libby, we're all worried about Benny. Maybe it would be better if you stopped seeing him?" Beal's insidious ways were taking a toll on Benny, and though I wasn't to blame, our relationship was becoming untenable. There was a cloud and a gathering storm that worried at Benny, and Beal, in her relentless way, was succeeding in breaking us apart. At the same time, she was breaking my heart.

I spent the night before the Kentucky Derby at Alex's house. We holed up in her room and laid out our plan for the next day. Our destination, "the infield," (the drunk fest inside the track.) We were underage, and that meant devising a clever way to sneak in "the alcohol." A successful entry was as much of a victory as picking the winning horse. Calls were made to the rest of our clan for input. My niece, Patty, came up with an ingenious idea that we all agreed upon. She would wear one of Beal's old skirts to disguise two bottles of Bacardi 151 duct taped to her thighs. Brilliant! She knew Beal kept everything, so finding something would be a cinch. Coolers would be searched extensively by security but they weren't going to ask a young girl to raise her skirt. That happens after you get in the infield. With our plan in place, Alex and I watched a movie and went to bed. Derby was a big day. The next morning, we were awakened by Alex's dad. "Y'all better get up and get going, you'll be stuck in that traffic all day! I'm going to run to the store get some breakfast." I loved Alex's dad. Everyone called him "Big Jim" and his son was "Little Jim." He put everyone before himself. Everyone. I cannot remember one time he wasn't doing something for someone. Incredibly selfless. "Thanks dad! I love you" Alex called out to her dad. "Hmmm Mmmm," That was always his response. It could be an endearing "hmmm hmmm" or a disapproving "hmmm hmmm" according to what he thought we were up to, which was a lot. "Girls, I got your breakfast, c'mon down!" Big Jim said with urgency. The way he said it you would think it was the first day of school and not the The Kentucky Derby. I did "c'mon down," I needed as much of a base as I could get before the marathon drinking commenced. Laughingly I said, "You're right Big Jim it *is* a big day!" He was trying not to laugh and right on cue responded with his "Hmmm Mmmm." I scarfed down my base and headed for the door to set my plan in motion. Patty would be at my house awaiting her costume change. Beal and Earl had already left for Churchill Downs, so there would be no interference. Just thinking about Patty donning one of Beal's outdated skirts made me laugh out loud. "Alex, I'm leaving, I'll call you when I'm on my way back…stopped in mid-sentence by a loud voice outside. "HELLO MARSHALL FAMILY! HAPPY DERBY TO YOU!" It was The Damn Boy! He lived one street over from Alex. They had known each other for years before I would meet either of them. "I SAY HELLO MARSHALL

FAMILY!" The whole family and I filed out onto the front steps. They loved The Damn Boy as much as I did and we could hardly contain our laughter. There he was, The Damn Boy, holding a beer bong in the Marshall's front lawn! They lived on a busy street so passersby got to view "The Damn Boy" in all his glory. His derby infield attire was a t-shirt donning Buckwheat, from the *Little Rascals*. and red doo rag on his head. "GOOD MORNING MARSHALL FAMILY! AND THE LOUVE," which he always called me. "A DERBY TOAST TO YOU FINE PEOPLE!" With that he demonstrated his special beer bong technique. It was 10:00 o'clock in the morning. We all dissolved into laughter. I could tell it was going to be a day to remember. And it was.

After the demonstration, I quickly jumped into my car and headed home. As expected, Patty was waiting. Once inside, she began sifting through Beal's old clothes. Her selection revealed a below the knee, seventies style wrap skirt with an ugly floral pattern. Once I was ready, I masterfully duct taped the Bacardi bottles to Patty's things. She wrapped Beal's skirt over her shorts and waddled to my car. I picked up Alex and the rest of our clan and we were off to the infield. Impossible to find a parking place remotely close to our destination, we settled for one two miles away. It was an arduous walk for Patty trying to conceal the precious cargo, but she knew her mission. The anticipation grew as we neared the gate. Security checked everywhere except under Patty's skirt.

Victoriously we entered the tunnel leading to the infield. It was dark and I had people invading my personal space, sweaty people who clearly didn't think personal hygiene was necessary. I was relieved to literally see "the light at the end of the tunnel!" As we walked up the ramp into the stew of drunks, one of the bottles hiding under Patty's skirt smashed onto the concrete. Loud cheers on both sides of ramp rained down from above us. Patty answered the crowd by ripping off Beal's skirt to reveal she had a back-up bottle. More cheers. One inside, the infield gave us exactly what was promised, rowdy drunks, long bathroom lines and no hope of catching a glimpse of a horse. My only indication I was at the derby was a roar coming from the stands once in a while. No one gave a damn. We were living our best life. My only complaint was when an attempt was made to throw me into a baby pool by strange men on my way back from a port-a-potty. They failed. I wondered "How the hell did a baby pool make it through security?"

By the time "My Old Kentucky Home" was sung, our clan was feeling no pain. The drunken crowd became sentimental, swaying to Kentucky's National Anthem. It was memorable because as Alex swayed, she lost her balance, stumbled and landed her foot in our cooler of jungle juice. Her new white Tretorn came out like a purple dyed Easter Egg. I suggested she might as well dye the other shoe. After the winning horse, (whoever that was?) crossed the finish line, we made our way out with a sea of other people. It had been a hell of a day and I wouldn't know it then, but it was going to a hell of a night! Everyone had a wild tale to tell at the after party. I was anticipating the arrival of The Damn Boy, his was surely to be the best. Anyone starting the day with a 10:00 am beer bong would be top teller in my book. The Damn Boy had been MIA all day. There *had* been sightings, but the "white whale" had evaded me.

The Damn Boy was dating a girl named "Cricket" We had become friends and she was staying at my house for the weekend. Cricket was wild as a buck. She was the biggest excitement junkie I knew. I liked her right away. Disappointed they never showed at the party, I would have to hear their story at home. The day finally caught up with me. I was fading fast. Ready to collapse into my bed, I unlocked the door to find Earl waiting on the other side. He was wide awake with a grimace on his face.

"Libbah! That Damn Boy and his little girlfriend let the dogs out and HE was in my house! DRUNK!"

"What?" I asked confused.

"I'll tell you what! He grumbled. "That Damn Boy and Cricket let the dogs out! The dogs were circling the house waking up the damn neighborhood!" Now that had to sink in for a moment. Beal joined the conversation. "Well, what they were trying to do was sneak Graham inside this house!" I had so many questions but none of them were going to get answered that night. Earl shut off the lights and I was ordered to bed. Cricket looked unconscious and was laying diagonal on the mattress, I would have to choose a corner for the night. A full report would be expected in the morning.

Beal's voice awakened my barely rested body. You never get a good night's sleep after putting in a full day's drinking. I had put in a full day. Beal was not even trying to talk in a hushed tone. She wanted us up! I would wait her out. Nothing came between Beal and church. Earl was a wild card, he also attended regularly, but he would have no problem sitting out a service if that was warranted. When I heard the door slam and the shower running, I knew Beal was off to Sunday School and Earl was going to church. "Get up Cricket!" It took several attempts to roust her. "Cricket, get up!" "I'm up," she said in voice husky enough to pull a dog sled. "We have to go now! My dad is in the shower so we only have a short window! Whatever you and Graham were trying to pull off last night was obviously a mistake! Earl was not amused!" Cricket started smiling. "No smiling! Put on a t-shirt and shorts and let's go!" I implored. "Go where? She groaned. "We're going to pick up Graham and go eat, you all need to give the details of last night's misadventure!" She started laughing. "No laughing!"

Twig and Leaf was and still is one of Louisville's favorite vintage diners. With its old steel barstools, a light blue clock holding at 8:16. and the neon sign outside bearing the name, you felt like you had stepped into the fifties. The Twig had the best grease and we needed grease. After the waitress set down the laminated menus, it was time for my interrogation.

"Alright you all, start singing!" The Damn Boy took the conversation by the reins.

"Well, I was almost IN until Cricket let the dogs out, and let me say McDuff (our Carin Terrier) was most unfriendly.

"Wait! you all were really trying to sneak into MY house? Where Earl and Beal live? MY house where Earl owns many guns and stands behind Kentucky's Castle Doctrine?" I questioned. Beal was right! I imagined she was regaling the story to the church goers as The Damn Boy was telling me. The Damn Boy continued… "Cricket got in through the kitchen window and unlocked the side door, that's when McDuff and Rugby (our Golden Retriever) made an escape. I quickly apprehended him (He proudly emphasized "I"), but Rugby was crafty and got away from Cricket. Then HE appeared! It was Earl, in his kimono robe!" Earl owned a robe with Asian details, I assume it was a gift from my half-brother, when he lived in the Philippines. "He was like an apparition. There I was in your utility room holding Earl's dog! I was caught! There was no running away!" "Earl shouted 'DAMN BOY,' WRECKED MY CAR, IN MY HOUSE, GOT MY DOG! GIMME THAT!" Then he pushed me outside with his giant palm, slammed the door and turned off the lights." I could hardly contain my laughter. "Sooo you all thought this was a good plan? Even if your 'well thought out plan' hadn't gone sideways, how were you going to escape the next morning?" I pointedly asked Graham. "There was no plan, just action!" he said grinning. "I'm trying to imagine Earl's wrath if he had caught you in his house the next morning. Your life was spared!" The Damn Boy knew. We paid our checks and left. It was a Derby to remember, unfortunately for Earl as well.

Now "The Damn Boy" was "The Damned Boy."

CHAPTER 5

B eal's attempts at breaking apart my relationship with Benny failed. She interfered, she insulted him, and she belittled him, all to no avail. Years ago, Beal had set up a secret meeting with Alex's mom to end our friendship and now she set up one with Benny. They met at White Castle. I never knew exactly what transpired, but Benny became distant. Finally, he came to my apartment at Two Lakes in Lexington. I remember him being tense, sitting on the edge of my twin bed. A lot had happened, and I could tell he was nervously trying to tell me something, but I wasn't catching on. But then I was: he was breaking up with me.

"Your mother said, "Her father and I will no longer pay for college if you all continue to date." Hearing those words made my heart bleed. My eyes filled with tears, I knew what was coming, a myriad of emotions: desperation, heartbreak, sadness, and anger. It were overwhelming. I think Benny was relieved it was over. I would be too if I had been in his shoes.

The next couple of months I binged on soap operas and made-for-TV movies, anything to escape the storm going on in my mind. When I did go out with friends, I always hoped to catch sight of Benny. I hadn't seen him in months. One night I finally did see him. I was maneuvering through the dance crowd at a bar with a drink in each hand. My friends had set up office next to the band. I almost made it through the sea of people with both drinks intact when an elbow knocked one to the floor. Like any broke college student, I reached down to salvage what was left in the cup. When I popped back up with the empty cup there was Benny dancing with another girl, looking so carefree and happy. It wasn't so long ago that it had been me dancing herself dizzy with Benny. Now he was dancing with someone else. I was just some girl he used to date, someone with a ruthless mother. His partner had poker straight hair to her shoulders. Her face was shielded by moving bodies and I was grateful.

Slinking back to the office, the pain was unbearable. "Libby, let's do a shot!" one of my girlfriends yelled. We could barely hear one another with the band playing so loudly. "Yes, let's do," I yelled back. I wanted to feel nothing. "Nothing" never felt so bad the next morning. I needed Mexican food and a giant coke STAT. Seeing Benny ended up being a good thing, it was time to step back into life. I was floundering in school while Roman rescued Marlena from the sinister Stephano… again on Days of Our Lives.

Months passed, and by summer I was dating again.

August 29, 1991, was a hot summer evening. It hadn't rained for weeks, the air was still and the grass was sparse. A sea of kids, boosters and rabid Kentucky fans poured through the entrances, noise echoing off the grandstand in waves. A bluegrass band added to the buzz while the wild cat danced, pumping up the crowd. The Big Blue Bash was gearing up to kick off football season.

I only half-paid attention to Delia, "Lib, listen. One of Neil's fraternity brothers wants to go out with you. Ted House." This was the first time I heard his name. "The four of us could go together," Delia continued enthusiastically. I scanned the ocean of revelers in search of some friends. Several drinks later we decided to move to Cheapside, our favorite bar. I was relieved. Every inch of grass had been staked out and jostling our way through the crowd, people kept spilling beer on my dress.

CHAPTER 5

The patio at Cheapside was sprinkled with clusters of people. It was refreshing to feel the evening breeze after sweating like a hog. Delia and I joined some friends from the Bash. She wasn't far into some girl gap when her boyfriend, Neil sauntered over with a giant of a friend. He was introduced as Ted House, undeniably good-looking, well over six feet tall, and handsome.

"I'm Ted, nice to meet you."

"I'm Libby," I replied.

We talked about our classes. We talked about our classes a lot, even though Ted seemed disinterested. It was just a way to keep the conversation going. I took long drags off my cigarette and watched the smoke spiral off into the night air. I was buzzed and hungry.

"Last call!" the bartender yelled. I had nothing left to contribute as Ted went on about the syllabus, I was ready for Tolly-Ho, the greasy spoon where we and other UK students ended up for late night feed.

Four days after the Bash, Ted left a message on my answering machine. He asked me out on a date with Delia and Neal, "This is Ted House and I was wondering if you might want to go out with me Saturday night. Delia and Neal are coming too. Give me a shout if you want to go, and I'll talk to you later." Immediately calling Delia, she already knew about the message.

"Lib, if you say yes, we are all going to dinner at A la Lucie's."

"Delia, are you trying to bribe me with French food? Who is going to be the fourth if I say no?" We both laughed.

"C'mon, Lib, it'll be fun."

"Ok, but he better talk about something other than the history syllabus!" more laughter. Calling Ted back, I accepted.

The four of us sat in a booth patterned with leopard spots. Having been there before, I loved the ambiance. The restaurant's décor was over the top but in a shabby chic sort of way. Brightly colored posters, paintings and framed match collections covered the bistro walls.

"What sounds good to you?" Ted asks.

"The snapper special sounds good," Delia chimed in, "and the stone crab claws are wonderful!" I loved stone crab claws but I wasn't

77

about to order the most expensive appetizer and I didn't want threads of crab hanging from my teeth either. First dates are awkward enough.

Ted ordered the crab claws and the special as well and the bartender kept the drinks coming. After a couple of Makers Mark and cokes, the awkwardness began to vanish. Ted wasn't talking about the history syllabus anymore. He was intoxicatingly charming and funny. The night was turning out to be more than expected. Clearly, I misjudged the person talking to me at Cheapside, and I certainly was interested in THIS guy. We capped our night off at a popular bar, but not before I completed a full dental exam in the restroom. By the end of the evening I was hoping Ted and I would go out again.

It wasn't long before Ted and I were an exclusive couple. It was autumn, and the happiest of times. Aren't relationship beginnings always the sweetest? Everything old seems new again – dinners in Lexington, football games and Keeneland, the beautiful racetrack we both adored. With Ted, I felt like I was experiencing them for the first time. Sweeping me off my feet, he catered to my every need and those of my friends. One of my friends became our third wheel. Not only did he make sure she was included, he never let her pay for anything. She called him, "Daddy Warbucks," and Ted liked being that guy. I thought him amazingly generous. A big man with a big heart, that's how I saw Ted. The first time he told me he loved me, I thought how lucky I was to have someone like him, never thinking that he might be the lucky one to have someone like me.

My parents met Ted for the first time at a UK football game. I hadn't given Beal much background on Ted because I knew she would launch a background check. Ted wasn't poor like Benny. He came from a wealthy family. Both his parents were from Indiana and had moved to Anchorage, Kentucky when Ted was nine. Anchorage has long been home to some of the area's wealthiest citizens and some of those citizens went to church with Beal, so it seemed inevitable that given Ted's background she would be bragging at church about her daughter's new boyfriend. I put off acknowledging Ted as my boyfriend, but now that things were serious it was time for introductions.

The game was the perfect venue. Football would dominate halftime conversation and Beal wouldn't be able to do her "trapper keeper," thing as I called it because she "trapped" and "kept" unsuspecting people in conversation that was mind-numbingly boring. People just don't want to hear endless gabbing about growing up on the farm and who's who at church, her two favorite topics. No matter what the topic, all roads lead back to Beal when Beal hijacked a conversation. It's painful and embarrassing to remember how people wiggled their way out.

"A twenty-minute halftime is just long enough," I thought to myself as we approached. Literally the clock was ticking. Introductions unfolded just like I planned. Earl and Ted immediately made a connection. Beal chimed in, but the clock ran out and there was no time left to kidnap the conversation. Ted was impressed with Earl. Earl was impressed with Ted, and Ted had no idea my mother had issues. Perfect. Now I could slowly spoon-feed Ted little bits of Beal when I felt comfortable.

"That's a good-looking boy Libbah, and he knows football. And Libbah, that boy has some size on him. Did he play basketball?"

"Yes, Dad, he played in high school."

"He seems like a nice young man." Earl either liked you or he didn't.

"Earl, Earl, I need to talk to Libby!"

"Libbah, your mother wants to talk to you." Sigh.

"Ok dad, I'll talk to you later."

"Libby, where does Ted's family live?" I knew there was no going back.

"Anchorage."

"Oh, well I'll have to ask Betty Ann Johnson on Sunday if they know the 'House' family."

Eye roll. Inevitable. I never got asked, "Do you really like him?" or "Are you happy?" My feelings were always dismissed.

I met Ted's father first at a UK football game, and his mother at a dinner in Louisville. My first impression of Ted's father was a congenial man, who genuinely seemed interested in getting acquainted.

Deeply involved with the Democratic Party in Indiana, Ted's parents were going to a private fundraiser, and Ted informed me that we were going too. We would even be meeting Evan Byah, the Governor of Indiana. Evan's father had been a close friend of Ted's grandfather, Wilson House. The closest I had ever been to politics was making some extra bucks working at the polls one election.

That day I had a late class and was cutting it close; sixty miles from Lexington to Louisville where the dinner was being held. Once I did arrive, horrified at discovering three runs in my white pantyhose, I grabbed some clear nail polish and slapped some on the runs to prevent them from traveling down towards my ankles. I sat in the car until the polish dried.

I walked up to the imposing wooden doors with oversized wrought iron handles that reminded me of a medieval castle. I rang, and anxiously waited. A guest, still in conversation, opened the door. Sliding in I found myself in a foyer surrounded by strangers. Feeling completely out of place, I looked for Ted who was nowhere in sight. By now the nail polish had hardened like scabs on the back of my thigh. I asked the first approachable-looking woman where the restroom was.

The bathroom was nicer than most people's dining rooms. Perfectly placed golden accessories adorned Damask wallpaper. Seemingly royal, soft lighting and fragrant candles gave it a cozy feel. I lingered as long as I could. Examining myself in the mirror, I fiddled with my hair until I heard a knock. Quickly, I ripped the scabs of nail polish stuck to my pantyhose and opened the door. I saw Ted, scurried across the room through a throng of guests, and tugged at his arm.

"Hi, I made it!"

"Well, hello!" he replied. "Let me introduce you to my mother."

"Great," I said. Ted barely got past introductions before we were called to dinner. I assumed we would be seated with his parents. I assumed wrong. People seated at our table were Ted's parents' age with the exception of an attractive thirty-something woman, much younger than her husband. Political chitchat swirled around me. When Evan Byah stood up to deliver his campaign speech, all eyes turned to him. After the

Governor finished, small talk ensued again at our table but was curiously interrupted when the attractive thirty-something slumped face first onto her plate. That grabbed everyone's attention, and much to my relief, idle conversation came to a halt. Her husband and the man seated next to her swiftly lifted her head up. I looked away to compose myself. She had wild rice stuck in her hair and on her face. I don't know if she was drunk or medicated or both. Ushered away from the table she disappeared into the night and the evening continued as if nothing had occurred. These people were pros. I wanted to let out a big belly laugh. It was too much. It was all too much! I thought of very sad events to stay composed. I caught a break when dessert was served – it gave my mouth something to do. After dinner I talked with Ted's parents. They were nice enough but I didn't get to talk with them very long. They still had guests to attend to.

Ted and I made some light conversation before excusing ourselves. We needed to get back on the road to Lexington, but we did no such thing – we headed to Spring Street, a bar in Louisville, to have a drink. I was grateful. I had been "on" long enough. I just wanted to relax.

Towards the end of college, I had dinner with Beal and Earl. Earl had just had knee replacement surgery, and wasn't yet cleared to drive. Beal called to say they were coming to take me to the grocery store. I preferred doing my own shopping but she insisted on coming with me. She insisted on doing many things together that I could have done for myself and should have. Beal took me on shopping sprees, too. I loved getting new clothes, however, Beal made me promise I would call the modeling agency in Lexington. "Libby, I want you to call!" I never did, and we danced the same dance time and time again. It was all about control. Years later, my sister told a similar story. Beal bought her clothes at an upscale boutique, Especially for You, in Louisville but made her pay on the ride home.

"I want you to know I have holes in my underwear and I don't have ANY clothes!" Beal yelled at Virginia.

I met Beal and Earl at the grocery store. Earl waited in the car, resting his leg while I walked the aisles with Beal. She was in a particularly sour mood.

"Hurry up Libby, I don't have all day!"

"Mom, if you all would just deposit money into my account, I can do my own shopping."

"Libby, we absolutely will not do that! If you don't shut up, your tuition won't be paid!" I did shut up, not because I was afraid my tuition wouldn't be paid, but because fellow shoppers were staring. Making valid points was futile; Beal's threats simply ended conversation. After loading my groceries, we went to grab a quick dinner before they drove back to Louisville.

I followed in my own car. Once we arrived at the restaurant, I watched Earl struggle to get out. Obviously hurting but not one to complain, he hobbled to the door and we were seated immediately. Dinner ordered, I asked Earl how he was feeling. He gave a response I had heard so many times before, "Fair to middlin," which meant "slightly above average." Hijacking the conversation, as usual, Beal expressed her disapproval of a man running around on a good friend of hers whom I had never heard of before.

"It's just awful what he has done to Helen! Just awful!"

I loathed it when she talked about someone having an affair. I never understood how she judged others when she was guilty of the same. Earl never participated in those conversations.

"Who's Helen?"

"She's my GOOD FRIEND!" Beal sharply shot back.

I swiftly tried to redirect the conversation back to Earl, but Beal over-talked and kept going on and on about the indiscretion. Earl and I exchanged glances, each understanding the other. I finally had to stop her diatribe.

"Mom, let's talk about something fun!"

Earl decided to get a little dig in before Beal could respond.

"Libbah, you know Bealo likes to tell a story or two."

That seemed harmless enough but not so to Beal. Her face went tomato red and she demanded Earl let her out of the booth.

"MOOOVE!" she shouted in a low baritone.

He did his best to slide out.

"Mom! This is ridiculous! Dad's just kidding and he's just had surgery!"

She didn't care. She stormed out. The food came and we ate our dinners quietly while hers grew cold.

There wasn't much to say. I thought she would come back but she didn't. Earl thought so too.

"Libbah, I know your mother was hungry."

I asked the waiter to box up her meal because she wasn't feeling well. I felt bad for my dad because I knew what was waiting for him in the car. He knew too but would never say.

Earl paid and hobbled back out the door with me close behind

"Dad, Mom's car is gone!" Earl scanned the parking lot.

"Libbah, she wouldn't leave."

"I don't know Dad, maybe?"

I never knew what she might do. We stood there, looking around until I spotted her car in a parking lot that served an establishment behind the restaurant. She turned her headlights on to alert us where she was. It was clear she was going to punish Earl.

"Dad, I can't believe she is doing this to you! You've just had surgery!"

"Libbah, let's not worry about it."

I walked with him to the car. She didn't move an inch. As Earl approached, I imagined her berating him the entire sixty miles home.

"Goodbye Dad, thank you for dinner."

He turned to grab the door handle, but he barely had his hand on it when Beal sped away. Standing in the drizzling rain, with his signature fedora and raincoat, Earl was like a lost child.

"Libbah, she wouldn't leave."

"Dad, let me take you home! This is crazy!"

I couldn't convince him to come with me. Beal drove back and stopped in front of us. Earl again grabbed at the handle and Beal moved the car forward, then abruptly stopped. Earl walked up to the door and practically fell into the seat. Beal demanded he apologize, or else she wouldn't move the car. He did, and it went right through me. At that moment, I hated her. I didn't realize at the time, but I was witnessing a preview of a future when Earl would no longer drive. He would become completely dependent on her. Watching the car disappear, tears streamed down my face.

Ted and I had been dating almost a year when he started talking of moving to Indianapolis after college. My roommate, Christine, and I had talked of moving to Atlanta to become flight attendants for Delta. That never got beyond talk because Ted's parents wanted him to move home and look for job prospects. I didn't want to move to Indiana, but I loved Ted, so I was going. Logically, it seemed like the next step.

We stayed a final summer in Lexington after graduation and planned to move in August. That was the best summer. I worked at an apartment community, and Ted worked at a pawnshop called, The Castle. Some of his friends worked there too and they made good money. Ted loved The Castle, and his employers loved Ted. He was a natural salesman who loved to haggle. Ted could sell anything. I thought he was joking when he talked about pink ice rings he sold. I didn't know there was such a thing. "It's rose quartz, Libby!" he laughingly told me, "and I sell them all day long." Once I got a look at the selection, I told him not to sell one to himself because they weren't my style.

We did anything and everything. That sweet summer slipped by on road trips, lazy days by the pool, and evenings at Hall's On The River. For the Fourth of July we planned a road trip to Hilton Head. The weather was perfect and we had many friends working there to visit. I loved Hilton Head. This was our last hoorah before getting serious about the future, which meant getting a job and getting married. I wasn't thinking about a long-term career, I wanted a family, a normal family. I would have been better off with the long-term career.

Our trip was quite a bit different from the last time I went to Hilton Head. Several years before, my boyfriend, Mike, planned a trip to Hilton Head with his friends for the Fourth. I had no plans until once he got there, he called and said I HAD to come. I was sitting outside my parent's home. They still had a wall-mounted phone and I could pull the cord just outside the screen door. Speaking in undertones, I dodged

Beal's eavesdropping hobby, which made private conversations nearly impossible. I caught her often. She would forget to turn a light off and her cartoon shadow gave her away. When I did catch her, she became extremely defensive "What are you trying to hide, Libby?" Sometimes I just answered, "everything!"

Years of her nonsense had upped my level of sarcasm. When I was younger, she wouldn't hang up the phone, but would stay on the line, which wasn't always noticed. My girlfriend and I would be talking "girl talk" when a strident voice came out of nowhere, "Your father has cancer and is dying! Get off the phone!"

Earl did have cancer, when I was eleven and two other times, years later, but he didn't have cancer then, nor was he dying. I went to school crying the next morning but then I figured out it wasn't true, so it became "The Little Beal Who Cried Wolf."

Mike was telling me how much fun we would have in Hilton Head, and it wasn't a hard sell. I rounded up two other girls for a long weekend and we finalized our plans. Knowing Earl would never agree to let me drive his car to Hilton Head, I told him I was going to Cincinnati to see the fireworks. For all the times I was absolutely up to nothing and the target of Beal's accusation, this was the time she missed the eavesdropping opportunity of a lifetime.

The day before we set out in Earl's car, an old friend called from out of the blue. Maybe we talked every few months, sometimes it was longer than that. I told her where I was going, but failed to inform her my parents didn't know. I never dreamed she would call again while I was down there having the time of my life. She told Beal to have me call her when I got back from HILTON HEAD, not Cincinnati. Imagine the euphoria Beal felt when she knew I had lied. Beal loved a good "catch." I called the next day to check in. Earl answered the phone. Letting me go on and on about the fun time I was having in Cincinnati, deeper and deeper I dug. Finally questioning me about the fireworks show,

"Libbah, how were those fireworks?" I replied,

"Oh, they were great! We all sat on a hillside and watched. They were really spectacular!"

"They were, were they, Libbah? You must have damn good eyesight to see them all the way from SOUTH CAROLINA!" I froze. Caught with nothing to say, I felt Earl's fury through the phone. Before I could utter another syllable, he roared "GET HOME NOW...WITH MY CAR! NOW!" Click. Apprising my friends of the new development, everyone gathered their things and we hit the highway. We made it about an hour and half outside of Hilton Head when dark smoke started rising from under the hood. The oil light was lit up on the dash. I had failed to notice.

The smoke forced me off the road, and soon the engine was on fire. Earl's car was dead. I had killed it. My two girlfriends and I got out and started walking. Having no idea where we were, we didn't get far when a silver Mercedes pulled over and backed up. Stepping out the driver asked if he could take us to the nearest garage. He, his wife and her sister, were ethnic, maybe Lebanese. Extremely attractive, everyone was covered in gold and diamonds as if they had come from one of the stories in the Arabian Nights, and what had been nightmarish turned dream-like.

We accepted the ride, and the beautiful people took us just as they said. I can't remember where we were but it was nothing more than a dusty forgotten-looking town with not much around. Everyone I saw wore a film of sweat. The man at the garage let me call Earl, collect, to deliver the blow. This is karma I thought to myself. I killed Earl's car and now he's going to kill me. Delivering the news was the harrowing experience I thought it might be. I think the only words Earl heard were: Car, Engine, Smoke, Fire, everything in between was white noise.

"Libbah, let me talk to the garage owner!"

Between the two of them, they worked out a plan to retrieve the car and decide its fate. My two friends and I sat on a bench in the greasy garage like kids in the principal's office.

Sitting there forever, we waited for the tow truck to bring the car in. I knew the car was gone but waited for the mechanic to declare it dead. He did. "Mr. Henry, it's a complete loss," I heard him say. "I'll need the title." Earl sold it over the phone. Motioning for me to come over, the garage owner said,

"Your father wants to speak with you." I bet he did. Earl got straight to the point.

"Libbah, I just had to sell the damn car because of your adventure! There wasn't a damn drop of oil in the engine! Why the hell didn't you stop when the oil light came on?"

In my defense, I wanted to suggest a possible electrical problem but I knew Earl wasn't buyin'.

"I didn't notice the light, Dad," I responded, bracing for impact.

"You didn't notice the DAMN LIGHT! What the hell did you see?"

I'm sorry." I was out of answers.

With the interrogation over, Earl wanted to know how we were getting back to Kentucky. I told him we could call friends still in Hilton Head to see about catching a ride home tomorrow.

"Tomorrow?" It was as if Earl knew that I and my cash-strapped friends had no money for a hotel room.

"Oh Hell!" Earl said, while I'm sure he was shaking his head. I told him there was a Holiday Inn within walking distance. He instructed me to have the front desk call him when we arrived. Earl paid for the room over the phone. My friends and I did get rides back to Kentucky.

I went back to Lexington, and then waited two days before going home to Louisville. I was buying time before I had to do time. I was afraid to go home. I knew Earl was lying in wait for me. I'm surprised I ever got another car. I had been terribly irresponsible. When Earl died, I thought of that story and many others that tested his ability to give second chances, and thirds and fourths. He did though, and he didn't rehash every poor decision I made since preschool like Beal did. I regularly atone at Earl's gravesite.

Ted and I had a great vacation. We grew closer, and I knew I was with the right person. The trip ended drama-free for me AND Earl. A month later, Ted and I moved to Indiana but not before Beal looked me dead in the eye and said, "You and I both know you'll never amount to anything!"

Ted and I moved to Indianapolis in August and I got a job as a leasing agent at an apartment community. A great perk was being able to live on site for a reduced rate, however, my apartment was not ready, so I stayed with Ted's parents. It was awkward staying at their home, even though I stayed downstairs in a walkout basement. It had a family room, a bedroom, a beautiful bathroom, and a walk-in closet unlike any I had ever seen. Everything was custom made, separate drawers for jewelry, and racks for shoes, a place for ties, and lots of room for hanging suits and shirts. Like an upscale men's store, it was clever, spacious, and nicely appointed. Part of me was trying to acclimate to a new place and another part was scared about Beal. I didn't want Ted's parents to know about her, at least not right away, so I was trying to hide Beal from them. I overheard Ted's mother ask him why my mother never called. That was fine with me. We didn't have the kind of relationship. Things would go along a lot smoother if I could get to know the House family better before introducing them to Beal.

That summer I experienced the first of many health issues. Driving a potential renter around the property in the company golf cart I felt a sharp unbearable pain. Describing my symptoms to my gynecologist, she felt I should have a laparoscopy, a surgery that uses a thin-lighted tube through an incision in the belly to look at the abdominal organs or the female pelvic organs in order to see if cysts or adhesions are present. I left, nervous and worried. Three weeks later, I had the surgery, and it was confirmed that I had endometriosis, a painful condition in which tissue that normally lies inside the uterus grows outside the uterus. My doctor explained that, while she had removed the lesions there was no guarantee I wouldn't have issues again in the future. The worst news was that it can cause infertility. The recommended treatment to buy time until we were ready to get pregnant was birth control pills. I couldn't tolerate birth control pills; they made me nauseous. I spent the rest of the month obsessing about my reproductive future. I had always thought of myself with children. Get married and have children; that was the plan. I wanted to create a "normal" family, something different from my background. The scenario of a life without children played over and over in my head. During the day, I was going through the motions at my job but I really wasn't doing it well. I just couldn't concentrate. I gave notice not long after the surgery. Needing a change, I wanted something different.

Ted's father had strong government connections, which helped both Ted and I land state jobs. I took a government job at the Indiana Department of Insurance, and Ted got a job working in Land Acquisition for the Department of Transportation. Ted quickly moved up the ladder, and soon was heading the Department. My job as an administrative assistant was an ill fit for me. I can't type worth a damn. I'm a people person, so I had my eye on jobs in human resources.

My first three months in Indianapolis were consumed by wedding events. Ted's brother was engaged, and set to marry in October. It seemed every weekend there was a wedding shower, a barbecue, or a dinner party to celebrate the upcoming union. I didn't know anyone in Indiana other than Ted and his family so it kept my otherwise open calendar busy. The "I do's" were exchanged on Halloween, and three weeks later the House family was back in the wedding business.

Ted proposed to me two days before Thanksgiving in my apartment. The words were said nervously while he was giving me a hug; he wasn't the type to declare his love in a momentous way. Accepting, he slid the ring on my finger. I was overwhelmingly happy. Ted's parents bought tickets to a symphony performance the next evening to celebrate. We weren't classical music enthusiasts, but that night I fell in love with the violin. Its emotive sound made it seem like it was weeping. After the last note faded, we drove to Louisville to spend Thanksgiving with my family.

The Seelbach is a historic replica of a grand old-world hotel where my family enjoyed Thanksgiving dinner every year. It's from another era, and the ghosts of Al Capone, Lucky Luciano, and Dutch Schulz walk the hallways. You might see FDR or Woodrow Wilson in the study, or the Rolling Stones at the bar regaling old times with F. Scott Fitzgerald.

I loved eating at the Seelbach. Once you walked through the stately doors, you felt transported into a different world. The grand hall was massive with matching stairways that curl their way up into the heavens. As a young girl, nothing was more exciting than to dress in my most fashionable clothes and step into the elegant lobby trimmed with fresh evergreens and garnet bows. The Christmas tree adorned with period ornaments dwarfed even the tallest patrons. Upstairs awaited a feast fit for royalty. First, I made my way to the ice sculpture at whose feet was a cascade of ice in which sterling trays floated, crammed full with oysters on the half shell, plump shrimp and my favorite, snow crab claws. Next trip was for turkey with all the trimmings and finally to the dessert table. Earl liked to take that trip with me. I picked pumpkin pie, piled high with whip cream, while Earl selected a generous slice of chocolate cake. Once I got in my teens, my niece Patty and I surreptitiously ordered champagne. Earl did some surreptitious ordering of his own. Ordering a bourbon would put him on Beal's radar, and he surely didn't want that. Those were some of my fondest memories, and now I had a fiancé with me to make more of them.

I let Earl drive a few miles before I made my announcement. "I want to tell you all something, I'm engaged!"

Beal turned around in her seat and examined my ring. "Ooooh look at that ring, that is beautiful Ted."

She was elated and impressed.

Earl said, "Ayyyy that's good news!"

He genuinely liked Ted. There was no pretense. I felt like I had finally done something to make them proud of me. It had only been a little over a year ago that Beal had told me I would amount to nothing right before I moved.

We arrived at The Seelbach Hotel. I stepped out of the car feeling like a different person. I wasn't really different, though. I was the same person concealing the hurts from the past with a ring on my finger.

Beal enthusiastically helped plan the wedding. I didn't mind either. I knew we didn't have an authentic mother-daughter bond but it was easy to feel that way when she set out on the road with me to the alter. Filing away the horrific arguments and fights of the past, I carried on as if nothing had happened. I was used to doing that. Alex pointed that out to me years ago. I had picked her up, but left behind directions to a party and had to go back home. When we arrived, Beal and I started battling about something in the driveway while Alex sat in my car. Eventually I jumped behind the wheel, eager to get going. Alex, looking befuddled, asked, "Libby, how do you do that?"

"Do what?" I was just as confounded as Alex.

"Ignore what just happened and put a smile on your face."

"I have to or I would never have any fun!" I turned the key, and off we went.

Beal knew etiquette as well as she knew her bible verses. The Amy Vanderbilt Book of Etiquette proudly sits on the bookshelf. My mother went out of her way to educate herself socially. I have to admit I learned how to be properly mannered from Beal. With her many personas, it was Sophisticated Beal who was the wedding planner. Country Beal, Fragile Beal, and the one I saw at home the most, Unstable Beal, she must have stuffed in the closet with all her other junk. Like a chameleon, the company she kept decided the persona.

Sophisticated Beal made a good mother of the bride. I knew it couldn't last forever, but it was a welcome change. I was grateful for her hard work and I told her so, but it never failed that when she got angry, the laundry list of "what I have done for you!" came bubbling out. The list went back to kindergarten and I never knew which misadventure would make an appearance. Beal felt everyone had let her down one way or another. Her parents had let her down, Earl let her down and my sister and I let her down. The truth is that in Beal's mind others are in charge of her happiness – she has no control of the wheel. That means every time she's disappointed, someone is hurting her. Every time something doesn't work out, someone has intentionally used her badly. There's no personal accountability, and she only feels happy living vicariously through others.

We spent hours registering for gifts around town. Beal knew every serving dish, fork and towel set that would make for the perfect home. In some way, in her mind she was the bride and was using this opportunity to give herself another chance to a life fulfilled. I guess she forgot I grew up in her house, but it really wasn't about me anyway. Nevertheless, I enjoyed this happier person.

Like any other soon-to-be bride and groom, Ted and I had our share of typical showers and engagement parties. One engagement party was not so typical. The Sturgeons, longtime friends of Ted's parents from Anchorage, gave us a party a week before the wedding. I loved this family. Their youngest son, Will, was one of Ted's best friends and his sister, Amy, was close to Ted as well. The whole family had auburn hair, freckles and an English last name. By appearances, though, I would have sworn they were Irish.

The Sturgeons had comedic talent. They had so much fun together it was contagious. If you didn't have fun with these people, you didn't have a pulse. So, it was only fitting that "The Unfortunate Incident," happened at their house.

Shopping all day for the perfect outfit, I found it at Shay's, a local boutique with unique clothes. After many try-ons, I chose a black and white striped tank with matching palazzo pants. The outfit was very sheer, and the silk tank had a star stitched on the front. Looking back, what I thought looked cute probably resembled an umpire's uniform. It was on sale, and probably for a reason.

It was the perfect summer night for a party. The air was warm, with zero humidity. I hate humidity. My thick, curly, hair that I straighten every day resembles a shrub when it's humid. Tonight was the night I would have good hair. Ted and I arrived fashionable late to the party. We were always fashionable and always late. The Sturgeon's ranch house sat to the rear of a deep lot, with a pool in the back. Mr. Sturgeon built pools, so his was especially nice. Walking up to the tiki-lit walkway to the back of the house, Ted and I joined the party.

"The happy couple has arrived!" hailed Mrs. Sturgeon. Seeing so many people I loved in one place felt special. Ted and I looked forward to this party because it wasn't a shower where we had to open gifts. Good friends and family, good bourbon, and good food were the gifts we went to enjoy. I caught sight of Earl already enjoying a fine Kentucky bourbon, while Beal had caught someone in her talk-trap. Even when

9575558

Beal was around, there was always someone willing to slip him a nip. I was one of those somebody's.

Sauntering up to my girlfriends congregating beside the pool, I soaked up the relaxing atmosphere.

"Hey girls!" "It's Libby!" they sang in unison.

We girl gabbed about everything from my dress to Seinfeld headlining in Louisville that night. I heard Ted cackling in the background – he had a booming voice, and when he laughed, he made a raucous sound. I looked over and our eyes met. I made the "I would like a drink gesture with my hand."

He loudly remarked to his friends, "My Honey-Do list has begun!"

I crowed, "It sure has, and you better saddle up! It's gonna be a long ride!" We were all laughing.

The girls and I settled onto a nearby patio. Gabbing about this and that, one of the girls abruptly stood up and pointed at the pool "Look, there's a frog hopping across the pool!" For some reason, I needed to see this frog. I'm sure it wasn't the bourbon cocktails I had been drinking. I jumped to my feet and hurried over to the pool, only I didn't make it to the pool. I took about eight steps and found myself neck deep in water. Stunned, I looked around and couldn't process what had just happened. I knew I hadn't misjudged the distance to the pool because my friend, Marty, was standing by the edge.

"Libby! Libby!" she cried, "Are you okay?"

"Marty, I don't know? I'm still holding my drink so I guess I'm okay. Am I in some sort of fish pond?"

"No, Libby, it's a hot tub. There was a candle but it must have burned out. Didn't you know it was there?"

"No, I didn't know it was there, of course I didn't know it was there or I wouldn't be IN HERE!"

By this time all of the girls were staring down at me, stunned and desperately trying to hold back their laughter. They were all asking if I was hurt.

"I think I cut my arm but otherwise I'm intact…except my pride damnit!"

I started to survey my surroundings. Most of the guests were inside. I saw people laughing and drinking through the large picture window.

"Why was everyone inside?" I wondered.

"What are you going to do Libby?" Marty asked.

"Well, I don't know. I didn't come with a Plan B in case I found myself neck deep in water!"

"Okay, smart ass!" chuckled Marty.

"I think you all need to know something else about my present situation," I said. "I'm wearing Christmas underwear that reads 'Joy to the World' across my butt!!!"

Staying at Beal and Earl's house the night before, I had forgotten to put my clothes in the dryer. The Christmas underwear was all I found in my dresser. One of the girls laughed so hard her drink came out her nose.

"Carmen!" the other girls shrieked

"Get her a napkin," I commanded from below. Marty, barely able to talk between laughs, got out "Libby, you look like a head without a body directing us!"

Our laughter soon blew my cover, and my plight spread through the party like wildfire. Ted's mother quickly came on the scene with Mrs. Sturgeon. Like the others they were concerned I might be hurt, when it was apparent I wasn't, they too had a hard time not laughing. When I got out of the hot tub my sheer outfit stuck to my body like wet toilet paper. "Look," someone shouted, "Libby's butt, 'Joy to the World'" I don't blame them for laughing as it was totally ridiculous. I spent the rest of the evening in an ill-fitting gray sweat suit and no shoes.

I slept in my nephew's nursery the night before my wedding. My wedding day was going to be full of mixed emotions. In a freak tractor accident, Renee's brother had been killed earlier that week and the funeral fell on my wedding day. Making a decision that I would forgo our wedding brunch, I planned on attending the funeral. I remember packing my clothes in Indiana, thinking how unfair life was. Renee's family must be going through hell. I didn't understand God. I threw my black linen dress in my suitcase and zipped it up. Driving to Louisville, my mind wandered to those long ago slumber parties at Renee's house. We were in sleeping bags, planning our lives and future weddings.

"Libby, we are going to be roommates in college, be in each other's weddings, and live on the same street!"

"Yes, we are!" I seconded. Then we discussed our wedding dresses until we drifted off to sleep. Renee's aunt had made a one-of-a-kind dress for Renee's Barbie doll, and mine was going to look just like that. I loved that dress and always tried to make a trade for it every time we played.

My childhood friend who I had mapped my life out with was not going to be at my wedding. She was going to be burying her brother.

The clock was ticking before I put my feet on the floor. The rehearsal dinner had proven to be a long evening, and I was moving slowly. The sun was shining, filling the whole room. The nursery walls, painted a shrimp color, were blotched with sunshine. Laying across a rocker was my dress from the rehearsal dinner. A herd of stuffed animals stared down at me from a shelf. Stretching my arms and legs, I clenched my fists and hurried myself out the door.

Who goes to a funeral on her wedding day? Renee's brother had been killed on Wednesday, the funeral was today, the day I was to marry Edward Needham House. Jumping into my shorts and t-shirt, I stopped by McDonald's to get caffeinated, and headed home.

I woke up in the nursery at Virginia's because Aunt Faye, Sweetie, and my cousin, Mitsy, were all staying at my house. Never close to Beal's family, I still felt like that rejected little girl in Waynesburg. I wasn't upset that they were there, though years later Beal claimed I wanted them to stay in a hotel. I just didn't feel comfortable with them. Beal's persona-of-the-day demanded that we be a close family, so she was infuriated that I stayed at my sister's. BUT, this was my day and I was asserting myself. If I didn't want to wake up at home and pretend we were all so close then I wasn't going to. The truth is Beal's family never cared much for the girl with boundless energy who sang and danced, and who was always seen and heard.

When I got engaged, Beal's Aunt Flossy, from Waynesburg, broke her arm and unexpectedly died from an infection that was treated too late to save her. I was sitting in the waiting room next to Sweetie before she passed. Sweetie said, without turning her head to look at me, "Your mother said you and Ted are getting married."

I decided that could be an invitation to speak. Sweetie loved china so I began to tell her about my china pattern. She had different china plates that adorned the bulkhead around her kitchen so I figured we were on common ground. I was grateful to have something to talk about to keep an uncomfortable silence at bay. I was wrong. She didn't want to hear about my china pattern.

"Sweetie, my china is double banded with..." She interrupted, "You're getting forty dollars just like Virginia Lee and that's all I WANT TO HEAR ABOUT IT!"

For some reason that made me think how Beal had pressured me and the wedding coordinator regarding Sweetie's needs at the reception. Beal demanded a separate punch bowl be set out for Sweetie, apart from the bar. I told her that a bottle of punch would be kept behind the bar and poured upon request (I was ready to give her a punch.)

"Mother isn't going to walk up to a BAR!" Beal squawked.

"Mom, this is a country club not a saloon!"

"Libby! She doesn't want cheap punch!"

"Mom!" I was getting embarrassed and angry at the same time, "I'm not saying it's going to be a big can of Hawaiian Punch! I'm sure they can make something homemade!"

The wedding coordinator, sensing an argument, assured Beal something could be made. I wanted to look Sweetie in the eye right then and there, in the hospital waiting room and say, "You're getting Hawaiian Punch in a beer mug and that's all I WANT TO HEAR ABOUT IT!" I didn't dare.

"Libbah, where have you been? You bettah get a move on! You need to get to the church on time!" When I pulled up, Earl was cleaning up the yard, and he didn't mean be at the church on time for my wedding, he meant be at the church on time for Michael's funeral. Glad it was just

Earl and me, Beal, Sweetie, and Aunt Faye had gone to the salon to get their hair done. Quietly, I got ready in silence, which seemed appropriate.

Tiffany, Alex, and I parked near the church. Tiffany and Alex were two of my bridesmaids, and both knew Renee. We stood together with the others in a semi-circle in front of St. Michael's when a hearse and a long line of limousines pulled up. Renee and the immediate family got out of the first limo, and our eyes locked for a moment and hers got big as saucers she was so surprised to see us. Limo after limo emptied as friends and extended family came to pay their respects to the young man taken too soon.

The darkness of the funeral and the brightness of the day and my impending wedding all felt like a surreal juxtaposition. We followed into the wide expanse of the church where everything was golden and aglow. I chose a pew in the back so we could leave unnoticed. The priest talked of Michael's life, but I saw the despair, torment, and grief in the eyes of Michael's mourners and how unacceptable Michael's death was in this place in spite of anything the priest said. When the congregation rose to sing, my bridesmaids and I, with the exception of Renee, slipped out through the great oaken doors. Feeling guilty leaving Renee mired in grief, I had to prepare for my wedding across town.

Mentally, I tried to switch gears. I was getting married in four hours, and needed to focus on that, but Renee was never far from my thoughts. "Life is unfair" was damn right.

My dress was at the church but my veil wasn't. Rushing back to my parent's house I thought Renee was probably burying her brother by now. It was difficult to refocus.

Pulling into the driveway, I was again relieved that Earl was the only one home. But why was Earl the only one home? I was running late, but Earl didn't run late. Earl's cologne permeated the air; I loved that smell. Earl took pride in his appearance, call it vanity, but the outcome was always an impeccably dressed man. He was my father and I'm biased, but he was a good-looking man. Believing in a crisp, clean look, right down to your shoes, his generation took pride in how they looked. I loved watching Earl shine his shoes. It was a process. Stage one: get out an old razor back undershirt, a can of Kiwi, and apply. Stage two: let them dry for twenty minutes. Stage three: buff the shoes to a high shine with a horsehair brush. He also did my shoes when I was young.

"Where's your nickel, Libbah?" I laughed.

He told me back in his day you got your shoes shined for a nickel.

"Yeah, I bet you did, dad!" I said sarcastically and he raised an eyebrow. Earl had definitely taken appearance cues from his father, Earl Sr. Earl said Granddaddy wore a suit and tie every day when he wasn't working at their dairy, and I knew that to be true. When he and my grandmother came to visit, he always wore a suit and tie. Everyday. I loved my Granddaddy. He'd wait for me to get home from school and we played "Stay Alive," my favorite game. He had the game set up on an ottoman before I walked through the door, and the minute I got off the school bus, I ran inside, went to the family room, pulled up my rocking chair and play commenced. Grandaddy played to win, if I died, all the better. I'm deeply grateful for that memory. It's a far cry from memories of cleaning out dirt from under Paul's fingernails.

Earl walked into my old bedroom while I was gathering the last of what I needed for the honeymoon. We were going to St. John's in the Virgin Islands. It was supposed to be a surprise but one of my bridesmaids, not aware it was a secret, let it slip the night before. I didn't care. I was going to know at the airport anyway. As I was reaching for my straw hat and bathing suit, Earl patted me on the back.

"Libbah, I want to give you this," and then he choked up before he could finish.

He handed me a white, pebbled leather bible with my name engraved in silver. I had asked for a bible, as I always admired the worn bible at my grandmother's house with all-important family events recorded in the back. It held the Henry family history, so I thought I would start my own recordings. I had never seen Earl get choked up before and never did again.

Putting my bag of essentials in my car, I followed Earl to the church. I was grateful for a quiet fifteen minutes. As I came closer to the church, I saw the steeple poking up through the canopy of trees.

"Here we go," I thought to myself.

Flower arrangements were being carried in when I drove up. Worried that I might run into Ted, I parked on the side of the church and quickly made my way to the bridal suite. My bridesmaids were buzzing around in their white column dresses. A beautiful tray of food was sitting on the coffee table. Good! I was hungry. I scarfed down three chicken salad sandwiches and a generous portion of pasta. I needed a good base.

My dress was hanging in the church bridal suite. It was the first dress I tried on, and it fit perfectly. I had seen it on the cover of Vogue but never thought that would be my dress. I figured I would find a knock off, but to my surprise it was at a wholesale warehouse in Cincinnati. I quickly slipped on the dress with its thick lace bodice and full tulle skirt. My niece, Patty, handed me some champagne when Beal wasn't looking. The whole day I had been rushing, but now, now, I could relax.

Everyone says your wedding day goes by so quickly that you barely remember anything, and they're partly right. I remember how pretty my bridesmaids looked in their white dresses holding English bouquets. I remember standing with Earl before we went down the aisle, thinking I was lucky to have my seventy-five year old father still with me. I remember how nervous I was at the altar, and I remember the shuttle for the wedding party breaking down on the way to the reception.

I watched from my limo as the bridesmaids and groomsmen spilled out onto the street. Two lanes of traffic were now blocked. There was a shopping center on the other side of a chain-linked fence. I'm not sure who was leading the formally attired group, but it was decided they would all climb the fence to safety. It was funny to see the girls hoisted over in their long dresses with bouquets in hand. Ted and I were out of the limo by now. Passersby were honking and we cheered back to them. The driver of the shuttle radioed the company to send another shuttle. In the meantime, assessing the situation, we decided the prudent thing would be to take the limo to a nearby liquor store to buy some beer that would ease the suffering of the wedding party. Around the World Liquor Store was happy to accommodate a wedding party in their time of need.

The employees laughed as I shopped in my wedding dress. They even threw in three free bottles of champagne. I will never forget how they stepped up.

Returning, we quickly watered our dry wedding party. They were going to make it. Forty-five minutes later, the new-and-improved shuttle arrived. The funniest thing about the whole incident was that our videographer was behind us, capturing every moment. It certainly adds flavor to an otherwise boring wedding video.

Arriving noticeably late to the reception, we saw the food stations had been opened as hungry guests could wait no longer. I didn't blame them.

From that point on the rest of the night is a blur. The last memory I have is of Ted yelling from the limo at Earl that he wanted some sausage patties when we got home from our honeymoon.

"FIX SOME SAUSAGE PATTIES, EARL!"

"I hear ya, Ted!" Earl responded. It was a beautiful last moment!

Our honeymoon in the Virgin Islands was wonderful. We had a memorable time, and when we returned, I was overjoyed to be "Mrs. Edward House."

CHAPTER 6

W e lived in a blue clapboard home in Zionsville, Indiana. Zionsville is charming, with a village-styled downtown area. Main Street is done entirely in brick. Small shops, boutiques and restaurants draw many tourists. For me it had a movie set-like appeal. Walking down the street always made me happy. Ted and I frequented a restaurant called The Friendly Tavern, and it was. It was cozy and just the kind of place you would want to eat at after a day of shopping or to just hang out and have a beer. As a couple we didn't have much of a social life. Ted had a childhood friend from Anchorage living in town, but I didn't know anyone outside of work other than Ted's family.

Ted and I were only married a month before my endometriosis returned. Since I couldn't tolerate birth control pills that staved off the disease, I was left with few options. It was depressing to be newly married with a disorder that made sex painful and that also might render me infertile. I felt like damaged goods. Experiencing married life as a couple without children for a few years is what I had in mind. In my married fantasy, we were adventurous and made memories that I artfully plastered in frames around my home. I would have proof that I was in a happy marriage, unlike Beal and Earl's, but fantasies are just that...fantasies. The real world had other plans.

I had naively decided that I was cured after the first surgery. I didn't want to believe that, at twenty-three, I had something that could rob me of children. Back then none of my friends had ever heard of endometriosis. No one related. I finally met a woman at work who had the same condition, and her horror story sent me spiraling. She had tried to get pregnant for ten years with no luck. She was thirty-two. When she revealed she had a hysterectomy to end the chronic pain I wanted to vomit. I never asked her about her marriage and didn't want to know.

The surgeon told me after my second surgery that getting pregnant immediately would be a good idea since a substantial amount of adhesions had been removed. We had only been married two months and were faced with a decision. Heed my doctor's advice and try to get pregnant, or roll the dice, wait and possibly be childless. There was a silver lining. I could take a drug called "Lupron" that would throw me into menopause, (stopping periods meant stopping endometriosis from growing). The side effects were every newlywed's dream: hot flashes, night sweats, nausea, depression, mood changes, increased growth of facial hair and my personal favorite, loss of interest in sex. Those were the common side effects! Ted would become a monk and I would be Chewbacca with no sex drive until we decided to procreate. We decided to procreate right away and I got pregnant two months later.

As an adult, my visits to Waynesburg consisted of Christmas dinner every two years and the occasional family reunion I felt compelled to attend. Anyway, Earl needed back up. At the reunions, I never knew who anyone was. Sweetie was one of twelve children, and Beal acted like I should know who everyone was and what had happened recently in their lives. I can hear her saying, "Vestal was in the hospital." She said it like it was someone I knew. "Who is Vestal?" I asked in an I'm so not interested sort of way.

After years of hearing about illness and death on a daily basis, I had become desensitized. Beal went into a long diatribe against me for being disrespectful. I never understood why Beal was so obsessed with death, anyone's death, even strangers. Beal loved to comb the obituaries looking for a connection with someone's passing. When there was a connection, it's all we heard about for days. Beal was in heaven when a local TV station started airing obituaries. She sat on the sofa and watched as they scrolled down the screen. It was her favorite show.

Truth is I didn't have a relationship with any of Beal's immediate family, let alone her extended one. Beal remained in denial about this. When I asked her who so and so was at the reunions she snapped.

"Libby, that's your second cousin!"

There was a sea of second cousin strangers. As wave after wave hit the reunion, Earl leaned over and said, "Libbah, these aren't your people!" He wasn't joking, and to me they weren't my people. Having the same blood running through our veins didn't make them family. No bonds had been formed.

The reunions were held under a pavilion at a local park. Food was everywhere, delicious country food. These people could cook. Trays of buttermilk fried chicken, beef brisket and barbecue covered long portable tables. Cracklin' cornbread with pork cracklin's, casseroles, bacon greased green beans, Mac 'n Cheese, every type of potato, and desserts that rivaled those of commercial bakeries were an endless train, each car more enticing than the next. I had no problem eating myself into a food coma.

Each clan staked out their spot amongst the weathered picnic tables, others formed circles of chairs in a grassy area. The clans mingled but no one talked to us. We might as well have been behind glass at an exhibit. We were the "Louisvillians." I knew by then my mother had an affair with a married man who was older than her own parents. It was like a page out of Nathanial Hawthorne's *The Scarlet Letter*. Beal shamed her family and was treated accordingly. It was a different time, and affairs were scandalous. She and Earl had been denied permission to marry at the Double Springs Baptist Church in Waynesburg, and so they were forced to wed in another town where they weren't known.

Sweetie had told my sister how shocked she was when she found out she was younger than her son-in-law. I can relate. Earl hid his license from me growing up and never revealed his true age. That bothered me, and I was shocked when I realized my father was older than my grandparents. Years later, after Earl's death, I discovered his age was incorrect on both my birth certificate and my sister's. I can only speculate.

I sat next to Earl at the picnic table. I found myself peering around, looking at my family of strangers while I ate their marvelous food. The highlight of the reunion was the best cake contest. One year, my mother won the contest with her coconut cake. Her frothy cake was one of my favorite confections. When no accolades for her were forthcoming, a sadness overcame me. I had conflicting feelings for Beal. At times I felt sorry for her, and this was one of those times. I despised hearing her brother tell childhood stories at the table about my mother.

"Beal always had her nose in a book! All Beal wanted to do was play school!"

I thought, "How criminal of her!"

Really wanting to be a smart-ass, respect and fear warned me not to smart-off in Waynesburg country. It wasn't hard to see Beal was the odd child out. She thirsted for an education, and was the first to attend college. After earning an associate's degree at Cumberland College, she transferred to the University of Kentucky. These accomplishments were never acknowledged by her family since the perception was that Beal's desire to better herself meant Beal thought she was better than everyone. Sadly, Beal never received the four-year college degree she sought. During her senior year at UK, Sweetie informed Beal she had to drop out of college because she needed the money for an operation. Beal dropped out, but Sweetie never had the operation.

I'll never know the real story, but I feel confident Paul made Sweetie tell my mother she had to quit. Paul didn't subscribe to the belief that parents want a better life for their children. He was controlling and abusive to Sweetie. She didn't even have a driver's license though she had gotten her permit twice. He wouldn't sign for Beal to get a license either, so Beal tricked him into thinking he was signing for an ID card.

Sweetie babysat us when my parents went abroad, and Paul demanded she get paid. That always upset Earl; he didn't think a grandmother required payment to spend time with her grandchildren.

Paul and Sweetie weren't poor. Paul had done very well for a man with an eighth grade education. It was all about control and property. He wasn't going to spare Sweetie without compensation. I wonder if payment was necessary for her to attend my sister's wedding? He, of course, was absent.

I believe after college there was no way my mother was going back to Waynesburg. She took a job in Lexington as Earl's secretary. He was her ticket out of an oppressive family. I think it's sad that my mother almost crossed the finish line only to have the rug pulled out from under her. What's hard to comprehend is how she abandoned her strict moral code and started an affair with a married man. She was young and beautiful and certainly could have attracted someone age appropriate. Whatever the reason, a match was made in hell and my sister and I paid dearly. All of this knowledge made sitting with "our clan" incredibly awkward.

When the award ceremony was over another stranger stood up and asked the family who had traveled the farthest? Earl leaned in again and whispered, "Libbah, any distance is too far!" Touché!

I enjoyed two weeks of pregnancy bliss before I was mugged by debilitating nausea. I fought a biting cold wind as I walked from my car to work. Indiana winters are tough but the winter of 1994 turned out to be particularly unforgiving. My face was completely lost in a scarf, with only my eyes peering out over the wool as I walked down the sidewalk. Within ten steps of the door without warning, I threw up right on the sidewalk, having barely enough time to unravel the scarf around my face. People stepped around me, obviously no one wanted to catch what I was carrying.

I wanted to scream, "It's a baby! I'm pregnant! Thanks for your concern!"

I made my way inside and headed straight to the bathroom.

"Good God!" I thought, "This isn't the way I thought morning sickness would be."

I was thinking along the lines of nausea relieved by soda crackers and Seven Up. The nausea didn't relent. What started out as morning sickness became all day sickness. I had to leave work. It was January. I returned in May.

The sickness turned joy into fear. I became so ill I could no longer drink or eat. Gripping nausea consumed my every waking minute. Seven days later I was hospitalized for severe dehydration. My doctor explained I had hyperemesis gravidarum. My first thought was I had a horrible disease. He went on to explain it was a condition characterized by severe nausea, vomiting, weight loss, and electrolyte disturbance. All symptoms I exhibited. What troubled me was there was no absolute cause and it could last throughout the whole pregnancy. Again, no one related. None of my friends were married or pregnant, and most everyone thought it was morning sickness and I would just get over it. I didn't. I became a regular at the hospital for extended periods of time. IV's were the only way I could stay hydrated and receive nutrition. While at the hospital no food trays were supposed to enter my room because all food smelled like spoiled milk. Sometimes the dietary staff accidentally overlooked the sign on my door and brought in a food tray.

Nausea sent me dashing to the bathroom. As the weeks passed my 5'8" frame plummeted from 122 lbs. to 109 lbs. That was the most miserable time. One day melted into the next. By April my nausea began to subside and I was released. The seasons had changed while I was lying in a hospital bed. I remember leaving the hospital and being surprised that everything was green. The world was in technicolor. I looked at Ted and said, "I missed winter!"

When we pulled in the driveway multi-colored tulips we planted in the fall were blooming. Everything smelled fragrant. It had been our first planting project, and I was proud. Once inside the door I noticed Girl Scout cookies piled on the dining room table. One day I bravely sampled a Do-si-dos. I kept the cookie down and rejoiced. Something finally tasted good. Ted kept me stocked with cookies and I put a hurtin' on a box daily. We used to joke our baby was going to come out square dancing.

At five months pregnant life slowly returned to normal. A rubber band trick accompanied my expanding belly. I threaded one end of a rubber band through the other end, securing the band to a button hole and used the rubber band as my new button hole. Voila! I now believed it was all happening. Both of my sisters-in-law were pregnant too, so it made for an exciting time. My oldest sister-in-law Katie was due in June, followed by Holly, due any day, and me, due in September. Three babies in six months, the House family was going to be busy and blessed.

Life slowly returned to normal. For three weeks in the spring and three weeks in the fall, Lexington's racetrack draws the best thoroughbreds from around the country. We made plans to go over the weekend. It was the first time I was able to go anywhere in months. The day of the races I dressed up a tailored cream-colored suit with a matching Audrey Hepburn style hat. I was so happy. Ted was too. The past months had taken a toll on him as well.

Close to the end of April, I was reading *What to Expect When You're Expecting*, a bible for pregnant women. I was engrossed in the chapter pertaining to my pregnancy status when the phone rang. My friend, Sheryl, was on the other end. I voiced a concern about how disenchanted I was with my doctor – he was so cold and abrupt. I didn't believe he found any joy in delivering babies. Perhaps proctology would have been a better fit for him. I wanted more than one ultra sound, considering I was categorized as high risk, but my doctor claimed it was unnecessary.

"Sheryl, I have been too sick to challenge him, but I read in a magazine that some OBGYN's will accept new patients far into their pregnancies.

My sister-in-law, Holly, raved about her doctor, so I called her office and they agreed to see me! I was thrilled to get an appointment. I told Sheryl I would call her back afterwards. We hung up and I curled back up with my book and a sleeve of Dos-si-dos.

I woke up Monday morning to the buzz of the neighbor's weed eater. Mr. Remsdale annoyed the hell out of me. He weeded for a bit and then hid his weeds in our Day Lilies. Ted and I watched him in the act from our kitchen window. We resisted the urge to peck on the window to alert him of our awareness. He scurried back and forth like a squirrel hiding nuts for the winter. I poured myself a generous bowl of Raisin Bran and ate while observing him. My patience was wearing thin. I wanted to acquaint him with "the trash bag." I glanced at the clock and quickly washed down my cereal with some orange juice. I would have to handle Mr. Remsdale later. My appointment was in an hour.

I arrived at Dr. Leema's office ten minutes early. Holly had talked about her so much I felt like I already knew her. The waiting room was warm and inviting. Bright colors, a children's play area and up-to-date magazines were in sharp contrast to Dr. Zimmerman's forbidding office. When the nurse called me back, I popped up eagerly. After the usual weigh-in the nurse was shocked. "You haven't put on any weight?" I explained to her I had been suffering from hyperemesis gravidarum.

"Oh honey, we've seen so many cases, patients tell me it's just miserable."

"It's horrible! I'm so glad it's behind me. I eat everything now"

She took down my history and said she would have Dr. Leema request my records from Dr. Zimmerman. When the blood pressure cuff released its grip, she led me into the examining room. Once she left the room, I looked around and noticed pictures with funny sayings on the ceiling and oven mitts on the stirrups. Dr. Leema had a sense of humor. I heard papers rustling outside the door; Dr. Leema was familiarizing herself with my chart. She bounced into the room with childlike enthusiasm. Dr. Leema was petite, with a stylish bob haircut. Her fashionable shoes and beaded fetal scope were unconventional, and I felt comfortable instantly. I was used to Dr. Zimmerman's chilly bedside manner and orthopedic shoes. Sometimes he had to check the chart to remember my name.

Dr. Leema looked at my last name and said, "I bet you have a sister-in-law named 'Holly?'"

"I sure do!" I replied.

As she was thumbing through her nurse's notes, I explained why I left Dr. Zimmerman and my concerns about not getting a current ultrasound. She understood and said, "Let's check this baby out!" I had to ask about her fetal scope.

"Dr. Leema, I have never seen a beaded fetal scope."

"Oh, it's my favorite! I volunteered at an Indian reservation and one of the women did this as a thank-you gift," then she held it up so I could get a closer look.

"That's amazing. You donate your time?"

"Well, I do well, and I believe in giving back."

I liked her even more. Dr. Leema put the fetal scope on my belly and listened for a moment. She hung it back around her neck and said, "I would like to do an ultrasound now."

"Oh wow, I didn't think I would get an ultrasound today. I can't wait to see the baby!" She smiled benevolently. The nurse came in and showed me into the ultrasound room. I thought, "Too bad Ted is going to miss this." He was out of town on business. The tech came in and prepped me. I could hardly contain my excitement. I knew I could find out the sex of the baby.

I blurted out, "I don't want to know if it's a boy or a girl!"

I'm sure she was used to overzealous mothers-to-be. She nodded. Dr. Leema entered the room and the tech began. My eyes were fixed on the monitor. While the probe was sliding across my belly, I started asking questions

"Where is the head? Is that a hand?" She rolled her stool away from the monitor and walked over to my side

"Do they call you Elizabeth or do you have a nickname?"

"Oh, they call me Libby!"

"Libby," Dr. Leema said in a soft voice, "Libby, we don't have a heartbeat."

"I'm sorry," still smiling, "What?"

"Libby," she put her hand on my shoulder, "the baby has died. I suspected as much in the examining room, I couldn't pick up a heartbeat."

Dr. Leema's mouth kept moving but I couldn't hear her anymore. My ears were ringing. I got up and walked to the bathroom. I didn't need to use the bathroom, I just wanted to hide. I didn't even turn on the lights. I just leaned on the wall in the dark. I have no idea how long I was in there, but it must have been a while because Dr. Leema knocked on the door.

"Libby, are you ok? Can I help?"

I couldn't breathe. My ears wouldn't stop screaming. I didn't want to open the door. Dr. Leema continued gently knocking. I opened the door and sat in the closest chair. She asked if there was someone she could call. I told her "No…." and asked, "Was my baby a girl or a boy? Why is my baby dead?"

She told me the baby was a girl and died from a cystic hygroma, a giant cyst that had obstructed the airway. In other words, my baby had been strangled. She explained to me that it occurs as the baby grows in the womb. Rage built up in me.

"If Dr. Zimmerman had done an ultrasound would my baby be alive?" She said he would have definitely seen the growth since the hygroma, pointing at the monitor, is bigger than the baby's head. I was having trouble forming pertinent questions. Dr. Leema took the lead and told me that I needed to deliver the baby.

"We need to do an autopsy, because the baby could have a chromosomal problem."

Vomit built up in my mouth and I ran for the bathroom. I threw up, washed my face and started walking, wanting to run, out of the office.

"Got to get home. Got to get home," kept running through my head.

I was stopped by the lady at checkout. She asked, "Can we call someone for you?" Again, I answered "No."

Everything else I nodded yes to without hearing a word. I drove home in silence with my window all the way down. I wanted to feel the wind on my face. Tears filled my eyes, and soon my vision blurred. Violent crying forced me to pull over into the emergency lane. The dam had broken.

When I got home, Mr. Remsdale was still working in his yard. Quickly I slipped into the house. Nothingness was inside. I had walked out of the house full of hope and excitement. I walked back in fruitless and hollow. There was no way of getting hold of Ted. He was on the road. I called my in-laws, but the phone was busy (later I found out my mother-in-law was taking a nap and the phone was accidentally knocked off the hook). I finally got hold of my sister-in-law; crying, I uttered the words, "My baby is gone."

I was barely audible. I don't remember more conversation; I doubt there was much.

My brother-in-law was the first to arrive. I was sitting on the kitchen floor inconsolable with grief. Ted arrived sometime after his brother. I don't remember how long after. Time stands still after tragedy. Clouds had settled in my mind and I was unable to recount to Ted what Dr. Leema had told me. Later that evening, Dr. Leema called and spoke with Ted and me together on the phone. She introduced herself to Ted and conveyed her heartfelt condolences. I had only known her for thirty minutes, and now she was having to explain how I would deliver our dead baby on Friday. I imagine the hardest part of her job were situations like ours. It was Monday. My mind started racing. I was going to have to carry the baby all week? She said we would need to wait a few days because I needed to have seaweed sticks inserted into my cervix to dilate it. I put down the phone. My emotions had swallowed me up and I lost what composure I had left.

I flopped down on my bed and sobbed until there was nothing left. Three hours had gone by and I hadn't slept. Terrifying thoughts came to mind.

"My baby is gone. All that's left is her lifeless body rotting inside me. How will I emotionally handle labor and delivery?"

These thoughts churned the normally calm waters of my equanimity. Worry stole my sleep; I hadn't slept in two days. My body finally conceded after day three.

I spent those black days leading up to the delivery in the short white cotton nightgown purchased for my growing belly. I smoked cigarettes in the guest bedroom and stared at the ugly green walls left over from previous owners. I'm sure there were conversations with friends and family, but I don't remember. I wasn't showering because I didn't want to see my naked body. When I did, I avoided the mirror. I didn't want the image of me carrying my dead baby girl seared in my mind.

Friday arrived. Ted and I drove to the hospital in silence. What was there to say? I was angry and spoken words wouldn't mitigate the anger and grief I felt. I needed my anger, my companion. She would get me through the delivery.

Ted and I walked into the hospital and headed for labor and delivery. Waiting in the registration area fueled my friend, Anger. She held my hand and turned her dark eye on those around us. There was joy all around and then there was us. We were in the same ward where other mothers were to deliver healthy babies. I thought it was cruel. That wasn't logical but neither was I. Anger demanded a secluded labor and delivery ward from happiness.

The registrar's smile quickly faded when I gave her my name.

"Oh, I'm so sorry."

When I was done with the arduous registration process, she led us into the ward. The warm environment was nothing like the sterile hospital facility I expected. Modern colors, wood accents and soft light felt like a decorating concept for a home not a hospital. I suppose it put women in labor at ease. I wasn't at ease. The registrar introduced us at the nurses' station. I got the same reaction, the nurses struggling to make eye contact. I felt like a leper. While Ted was filling out some paperwork, two women in labor were lapping the nurses' station. My eyes followed them with envy. As I took in the rest of my surroundings, I noticed a gigantic chalkboard on the wall behind me. In pink and blue chalk were the names of all the women in the ward. Beside each woman's name was her room number, date of conception and due date. Beside my name was my room number, date of conception and "stillborn/fetal." My personal tragedy was on display. (Today that chalkboard would certainly violate the HIPAA Privacy Law.) I felt tears bubbling up inside me. My companion, Anger, abandoned me, and Sorrow grabbed my hand.

My thoughts were abruptly interrupted when a nurse named Pam introduced herself. "Hello, my name is Pam. I'm going to be your labor and delivery nurse."

"Ok," and a nod was all the conversation I could muster.

"Please follow me." We followed her into an LDR (labor and delivery room). It looked like an extension of the home-like ward. The spacious room had a family room-style area: an armoire, rocking chair, plaid love seats and end tables with brass lamps. A hospital bed and baby incubator anchored the other end of the room. Paralyzed by the agonizing fact that the incubator would remain empty, Anger built up in me again. I thought, "Couldn't they have at least removed the damn rocking chair and incubator? They aren't nailed to the floor!" My emotions were taxed, and I didn't know if I was going to explode or become a puddle on the floor. Before my emotions kicked in my nurse, Pam, spoke.

"There's nothing I can say that will ease your suffering, and I'm not going to try. I don't want to minimize your loss. What I will say is that I am going to help Dr. Leema get you through the delivery." I appreciated her candor. When she left the room so I could change into a gown, I burst into tears.

Later, I remember my sister sitting the rocker while I was waiting for the Pitocin to start labor. I felt like I was going to break down and kept reaching for my Anger, keeping it all together. Everyone was watching, as if I was singled out, and whispered in hushed voices, "That's her, she's the one!"

I know now they were only walking on eggshells due to the delicacy of my situation, but who can be rational in times like these? First, I got pregnant right away because the endometriosis might prevent me from starting a family. Then, I got hyperemesis gravidarum, which required hospitalization and disappeared when my baby died. If the world wasn't judging me, I felt they were. That's always been a problem and a key to who I am. My emotions are generally formed by my understanding of how I feel I am viewed by the world.

Beal always said, "They're talking about you. Everybody says…," and "They think…."

Who is this governing body, and why AM I always on trial?

I lay in the bed looking at the opposite wall as another nurse started my IV. She explained how Pitocin would cause strong contractions; I didn't even try to listen to the rest. I knew how it worked. Dr. Leema was very thorough at her office. Instead of projecting my anger onto an innocent nurse doing her job, I shook my head in acknowledgement and let her escape. Ted was sitting on the sofa staring as if he was in shock. He probably was. We were operating in our own spheres of reality: abbreviated conversations of simple questions and one-word answers.

Hours passed and no action. I had not dilated one centimeter. I was so relieved when Dr Leema walked in. She had a calming effect on me. I think Ted was just as relieved.

"How are we holding up?"

Dr. Leema didn't wait for an answer, she rubbed my hand instead. After examining me she put the sheet back in place and told me disappointedly that I was not progressing and she was going to attempt manually dilating me. I thought, "What the hell does that mean?"

She explained it meant inserting mechanical devices inside my cervix that expand while they are in place. It sounded horrifyingly painful and it was. Even with the pain medication the nurse shot into my IV, I felt unimaginable pain. The sweat running down my forehead into my eyes blurred my vision. Pam quickly wiped my brow.

The attempt was unsuccessful. Dr. Leema told me I was hitting a brick wall because my uterus wasn't ready or ripe enough. "I'm going to give the Pitocin some more time."

By this point, exhaustion had overcome me. I couldn't imagine pain worse than what I had just experienced. I was wrong. Dr. Leema left to attend another patient while I waited and waited to dilate. My screams had exhausted Ted as well. He seemed to be just as drenched in sweat as I was and aimlessly walked around the room pulling his shirt from his chest. Ted was the kind of person who could faint at the sight of blood or anything else that caused the body pain, and he wasn't holding up well. Holly arrived and provided much needed support. As she and Ted began talking, I closed my eyes and started to drift.

Sweet sleep was abruptly interrupted by strong contractions. Holly rushed to my side to help me with my breathing; she had gone through labor herself three weeks before. Dr. Leema reentered the room and determined my contractions were irregular and I had dilated only one centimeter in nine hours. She increased the Pitocin. It's hard to say when the unbearable contractions started. All I know is that when they did, I sprang forward like I was being ejected from the bed. Holly had returned home to breast-feed her newborn, so Pam was trying in vain to comfort me, but it was futile. The contractions became so excruciating I started vomiting on myself. Ted paced back and forth, demanding, "Somebody do something!"

Pam and another nurse cleaned me up and got me a new gown. I didn't want them to touch me, I was in so much pain. I begged for an epidural. Pam tried to explain an epidural would slow things down. "Please, please! I can't take it anymore!"

My pleas turned into blood-curdling screams. I felt like I was passing out between contractions. Dr. Leema was back, wearing a physician's coat over the top half of an evening gown. She told Ted that she never thought I would be in labor this long. Ted had reached his limit, "I can't watch this anymore!" he said. Dr. Leema calmly told Ted the anesthesiologist was coming to administer an epidural.

"Unfortunately, Libby has barely reached two centimeters; we are going to have to perform a C-section in the morning. I'm truly sorry, we just can't seem to get her there."

Pam was echoing Dr. Leema's words to me until Dr. Leema took over. "Ok!" I cried, "Please get the anesthesiologist and stop the pain!"

Stop the pain! That was all I could think about. Once the epidural took effect, I wilted like a dead flower. The C-section was scheduled for 8:00 a.m., and Dr. Leema cleared the room so Ted and I could sleep. The last thing I remember before the lights went out was Ted pulling the covers over himself on the sofa bed. I awoke to the sensation of something pushing itself out of my body. I knew it was the baby. After hours of grueling labor, I had my baby in the dark alone. Ted was out cold. I just lay there for a while before hitting the call button, knowing it would be my only time with her. Once I hit the button, they would take her. They did.

In the week that followed, cards filled my mailbox and flowers arrived steadily at the door. I vacillated between anger and despair. Adding insult to injury, I had delivered my baby two days before Mother's Day. To the horror of my best friend, Renee, her arrangement showed up in a whimsical vase that read "Happy Mother's Day!" I knew it was a mistake, but Renee said she unleashed her fury on the florist. I wouldn't have enjoyed being on the receiving end of that call. Unfortunately, I didn't have close friends in Indiana, as most my friends lived back in Kentucky or other places. Ted conducted life as usual while I sat at home alone in the ugly green room. I couldn't understand why he wasn't there for me emotionally.

I was grieving. Why wasn't he? I felt completely disconnected from Ted. After weeks of trekking upstairs to the ugly green room to stew and smoke, I grabbed the book the social worker had tried to give me the day after delivery. Full of anger and not wanting visitors, I had instructed her to leave the room immediately. It was too soon for me. Later, I felt badly about how I treated her. She was just doing her job. *Empty Arms* was a guide offering support and guidance to bereaved parents. It touched on everything I was feeling. I identified with the author's story. The book explored the stages of grief and how differently couples grieved.

I finished the book the same day. My mindset changed. Hearing someone else's story put me on the healing path. I wish I had the book before the delivery. I might have made different decisions, like creating a place where I could go to lay flowers and remember. The healing path was rocky when I stepped out publicly. I went to an event in Kentucky where not everyone knew what had happened. I was hurt when people assumed I had the baby.

"Libby! Did you have a boy or girl?"

I felt bad for them when I told them my baby died. We were all inexperienced twenty-somethings, and it was beyond awkward. I put them at ease. I did heal and to my surprise, quickly became pregnant again the following July.

We stayed with Earl and Beal when we came to Kentucky. I walked into my parent's kitchen and Earl and Ted were sitting at the table having breakfast. Earl loved Ted. He related to him in ways he never related to me or my sister. Life was different once I married. Beal's chaos all but disappeared. I'm not sure what life was like for Earl – he didn't say.

CHAPTER 6

I was now able to eat anything I wanted, and I did. Nothing was safe. Biscuits, bacon, sweet cantaloupe and pancakes found their way to my yawning stomach. Earl kept putting the inside of his biscuits on my plate. He never liked the "stuffing" as I had called the layered center as a child. Earl liked the ends, and he liked them well done with honey. He liked everything well done except his steak, which had to be medium rare, period. I laughed when he ordered a burger with fries and so did the waitress or waiter. "I'll take a hamburgah, medium rare, and burn those fries, burn 'em!"

It was a gorgeous spring morning, and it was going to be a gorgeous day. There is nothing like horse country in the spring when the countryside seems brand new with a promise of life reborn as dogwoods, red buds, and crab apples promote new growth and blossom. Tulips and daffodils push their cheery faces vivid from the earth, and the bluegrass grows so fast and thick you can almost watch it grow. But most exciting of all are the newborn foals stretching their legs alongside their mamas as they frolic in the dew and the early morning sun. It's an exciting time, and I felt reborn, too. I was ready to rejoin the world.

The autopsy of my baby girl revealed her cystic hygroma was a fluke. She also had the appropriate number of chromosomes. Dr. Leema thought my baby might have Turner's syndrome. She explained cystic hygromas often were a complication of the syndrome. I was terrified of the same outcome, but she assured me that would be like lightning striking twice. I was sick again, but it wasn't remotely comparable to the first time. I was in the high-risk category, so my pregnancy was closely monitored. I made weekly visits to Dr. Leema's office and had one outpatient visit to the hospital for IV fluids. That was fine with me. I wanted to hear the heartbeat every week. I wanted a fetal scope of my own. Dr. Leema laughed, but she knew every week I held my breath until she smiled and said, "Everything looks great and we have a strong heartbeat."

Dr. Zimmerman should have been as thorough. I was offered the chance to sue, but I declined. I didn't want the money. I was leaving nothing to chance and didn't need the stress of filing a suit. In the springtime, Dr. Leema delivered a healthy baby girl and we named her Kennedy.

Kennedy's arrival brought joy and fear. I imagine most mothers have that "Oh my God! What if I drop the baby?" What if the baby contracts a terrible illness? And the biggest fear, SIDS!"

Thankfully none of my fears came true. She was a thriving baby girl with a rare talent, sleep robber. My life began to ebb and flow like any other person. I welcomed mundane daily tasks. I felt like Ted and I could finally catch our breath. It was nice for us to have dinner and take Kennedy on a walk through town. The downtown area of Zionsville was perfect for strolling a baby. The wish for friends may have pointed to something missing in my life, a void I wasn't ready to explore or validate. It was like a door cracked open, and the little kid dares herself to take a peek at the darkness on the other side.

Perhaps, trips back and forth to Kentucky were an attempt to fill the void, or maybe an effort to ignore impending troubles. I missed my friends, and Ted and I proved to be better suited in their company. Kentucky made up for the void.

My family life improved when I married Ted. It calmed the troubled water running through Beal. She was thrilled I had married someone from a wealthy family, not to mention they had lived in Anchorage where many of her church friends lived. Deep down I knew (as far as Beal was concerned), I was only as good as whomever I was with, but the broken unhealthy part of me enjoyed her approval.

Kennedy brought more calm water moments. Beal was a good grandmother. She was nothing like the mother I had known. I wondered if she was trying to make up for the past. Our relationship still had its peaks and valleys, but it was different. Ted and Kennedy provided a buffer between us. I convinced myself that I was living a normal life. It wasn't that hard since I had never known normal.

Ted and I adjusted to our new life as parents. Kennedy was a good baby. Getting her on a regular feeding schedule happened with relative ease. While on maternity leave, I sought out daycare for Kennedy. Every mother knows it's gut-wrenching to think of leaving your whole life in the hands of a stranger. We agreed upon an in-home situation and paid a holding spot deposit. No sooner than the non-refundable check was cashed, Ted came home with news. Big news. He had been offered a job in the mortgage industry back home in Louisville. It would be a new endeavor for Ted. He loved anything to do with real estate, so I thought it would be a good fit. I was thrilled. I was going to leave all our misfortune in Indiana and start fresh. I'm a liar. That was only partially true. Ted was quick to anger, so I was hoping that going home would turn him down from high heat to simmer. My Friends provided a distraction for me, and most of them were back in Kentucky. We quickly moved into a condo in Louisville until we sold our home in Zionsville. Ted started his job. I got a job at a paging company, and Kennedy was in daycare right up the road. Life was falling into place, and happiness for Ted and me was right around the corner.

Sprawled out on the sofa, watching mind-numbing television, my big toe went numb. By next morning, pain had grabbed hold of my lower back. It wasn't a familiar feeling, but I wasn't overly concerned. I thought I had strained it somehow. When three days passed and the pain wouldn't release its grip, I called an authority.

"Dad, my back hurts and Advil doesn't help."

"Libbah, come get some Doan' pills."

"Is that the green bottle with the man holding his back?"

"Yes sir!"

Earl had medications and a local remedy he swore by. Doan's pills for back pain, BFI Antiseptic powder for cuts, and bourbon for just about everything else.

"Libbah, put some bourbon on that baby's gums, it will stop that teething pain in its tracks!"

"Dad, I cannot put some bourbon on Kennedy's gums!"

"Well, why the hell not?"

"Moose put it on mine."

"You started early, Dad."

"You're damn right," he said, laughingly.

I never consulted Beal about health issues. She had no empathy. None. She pretended to outwardly, but privately she snapped at me, "Libby, there's nothing I can do about it!"

Beal didn't like that I had health issues. She had staked out that territory as hers long ago. I felt like she competed with me. As sick as I was with our first daughter, I was not going to die. I was incredibly miserable, but modern medicine was not going to let that happen. Growing up, she repeatedly told me that she almost died having me. I believed her until she came to make an obligatory visit when I was hospitalized for hyperemesis. I had volunteered the information to Dr. Zimmerman, thinking it might be something he needed to know.

"Your mother almost died in childbirth?"

"Yes, but I don't know any details."

Beal had the misfortune of being in my hospital room when Dr. Zimmerman made his daily rounds that day. I introduced her to Dr. Zimmerman. He wasted no time asking her questions about her birthing experience.

"Well, I was put to sleep and ..."

"Excuse me, Mrs. Henry, your daughter said you almost died in childbirth?"

"I was put to sleep and the next day all I wanted was eggs," Beal said with disturbing glee.

I chimed in "Mom, you said you almost died having me!"

Clearly irritated she snapped back, "Well, I did." Dr. Zimmerman was not satisfied.

"Mrs. Henry, is it my understanding that you DID NOT almost die during childbirth?"

He sounded like an attorney cross-examining a witness.

"I was put to sleep to get fluids."

"So you were given fluids during your first trimester?"

"Well it was at the beginning, but I could have died...they put me to sleep and I wanted eggs!"

Dr. Zimmerman was growing impatient. Beal told the story as if she was put in an induced coma for months and then miraculously

120

awoke healthy and hungry…for eggs! Her story was crumbling under cross-examination, but it didn't keep her from trying to convince my doctor she almost died. I personally believe she was probably told in the hospital that people can die from dehydration during pregnancy and did, before IV infusions. Although she wasn't in danger of dying, she ran with the possibility and the "I almost died having me story" was born – a story to be passed down through the generations. Dr. Zimmerman turned his back on her in mid-sentence and focused on me. Clearly, he wasn't going to waste his time listening to Beal's ridiculous fabrication. If I wasn't so sick, I would have cared more, but I was, so I didn't.

I never did give Kennedy an early nip of bourbon. I did drive to get a supply of Earl's Doan's Pills. The pills never worked. It wasn't long before an MRI revealed a severely degenerated disc in my spine. The news was stunning. I was just beginning to exhale from my past misfortune. I felt cursed. It didn't help that Ted was marginally supportive.

"Great, something else is wrong with you, Libby!"

I could understand his frustration, but the cutting remarks brought back the feeling of being "damaged goods."

I tried everything to alleviate pain: medication, physical therapy, cortisone shots, praying and bourbon. Nothing helped, but the bourbon lifted my mood. I could see why Earl endorsed bourbon's medicinal purposes. It would take the edge off the pain for a while. Earl needed to take the edge off more than pain. He had become Beal's new chew toy since I left the house.

I had back surgery in July of 1996. Dr. Day called it a microdisectomy. The way the procedure was described made it sound like he would be using knitting needles. "Minimally invasive, and I believe it will alleviate your pain Mrs. House."

I was all in! Dr. Day never called me by my first name even when I insisted. He reminded me of an old-fashioned kind of doctor, the kind who would slam the patient's chart shut and tell them to let him do the worrying. My biggest worry was that Kennedy was only thirteen months old and wouldn't understand why mommy wasn't able to pick her up for a while.

I awoke to pain from the surgery, but the pain that had dogged me for months was gone. I was given pain medicine in recovery and introduced to the "pain pump." I pumped a lot. A month later, Dr. Day declared the surgery was a success. Two months later, I collapsed to my knees. I was picking Kennedy up out of her crib, and the pain was so fierce my legs turned to spaghetti. Luckily, she fell back in her crib. I knew the surgery had failed. My body was screaming and soon so was Ted. Kennedy was crying from being dropped so abruptly.

I shouted, "Ted! Ted! Can you come up here?" But he would only respond by shouting back, "What's the problem, Libby?"

"Ted, can you just please come up here?"

"What the hell is the problem?"

"Don't yell at me in front of Kennedy."

He repeated "WHAT! IS! THE! PROBLEM?" with a long pause between each word.

Ted had bet on one of the college games and was busy quarter-backing from the sofa.

"I don't know, I just know something is wrong."

"Something's always wrong with you!" He grumbled.

"I need you to take Kennedy down with you." Ted complied and I crawled onto the twin bed in Kennedy's nursery. I lay there until I gained the strength to walk downstairs.

Dr. Day wanted to do a spinal fusion, a major surgery that would permanently change the anatomy of my spine. A friend's mother had recently had a fusion in her neck and insisted I see her neurosurgeon, Dr. Welty, for a second opinion. She told me Dr. Welty was well known for being one of the most gifted neurosurgeons in town. I did my homework and she was right. I did just as she said and made an appointment. Dr. Welty was nothing like Dr. Day. He was loud and bursting with personality. I liked him immediately. He looked at my films, looked at me and told me Dr. Day was an idiot!

"The procedure he performed on you is outdated just like Day. It was a guaranteed failure with a disc as compromised as yours. Fucking idiot!" Good God, I had never heard a doctor say "fuck."

We talked for a while. He was generous with his time, and he laid out a plan for me. He was referring me to an orthopedic surgeon who he hated and said I would, too.

"Dr. Justice has no bedside manner and you'll hate him!" but conceded he was the most competent in a sea of apparently incompetent doctors. I didn't hate Dr. Justice. I liked him, and he liked me, too. He went through my films, slapped them on the examination table and asked me if I had ever had a moving X-ray?

"No, what's that?" I replied.

"Miss Elizabeth, you have a lot of sophisticated tests here, but a moving X-ray can pinpoint an instability."

"Where do I need to go to have a moving X-ray?" He smiled, "Across the hall." Ten minutes later, the moving X-ray confirmed Dr. Justice's suspicions. Dr. Justice and Dr. Welty performed the surgery. The two kings of their field came together to help me, but once the surgery was complete, they sat back on their thrones. They couldn't agree on a recovery plan, and each insisted his was superior. I cherry-picked from both plans and began my recovery. Sometimes I laid on the floor with a heating pad for hours. It irritated Ted. He made sarcastic comments. "Libby, you're going to wear a hole in the carpet! Do you think you could get dressed today?"

Some days I was hurting and getting dressed was an effort. Other days I would exhaust myself during the day and pay for it at night. I carried a tremendous amount of guilt around for not being able to pick up Kennedy for months. Ted's comments didn't help.

We were celebrating New Year's Eve at Azalea's, a local restaurant, when Kirk, one of the guys, laughingly asked me if I ate Bon Bon's and watched Oprah every day. I was stunned and tried to play it off, but my red face and tear-filled eyes gave me away. Swiftly walking to the restroom, I made it there just in time to close the stall door and sob until I composed myself. By the time I came out, the check had been paid.

Ted claimed he berated Kirk for insulting me, but years later I was told HE had been making fun of me and my back for some time. I suppose that's why Kirk felt free to take liberties.

We moved to Prospect, Kentucky soon after my surgeon removed the rods and screws from my spine. The fusion was successful, but it left my back stiff as a board. The hardware had served as scaffolding while the fusion healed and was supposed to remain in my back for a lifetime, but as bad luck would have it, mine caused chronic back spasms. I waited two years until the fusion was solid enough for Dr. Justice to remove what I had called the "clamp." When I was free from its grip, I almost felt like I did before I had ever heard the words "spinal fusion." Dr. Justice warned that degenerative disc disease was the cause of my instability, and that I might need more surgery in the future.

"How far in the future, Dr. Justice?"

"Everybody's different, but I'm hopeful you will get twenty years. I also suggest swimming and working out with weights."

I was a step aerobics girl, but that was over now. Dr. Justice was against the jumping.

"You need someone qualified to work with, someone familiar with your limitations," he added.

I didn't like the word "limitations," and it obviously showed on my face. "Miss Libby, I made you a nine out of ten, don't screw up my work!"

I smiled and as he left the room, he turned back, smiled and repeated, "Don't!"

Dr. Justice proved to be a caring doctor, and he had my number. Shopping a couple of weeks later, I met a girl whose son went to school with my daughter. We were both trying on Derby dresses. I came out to look in the three-way mirror and she was already doing the same in the same dress I had chosen. We laughed, and it sparked a conversation.

"Derby?" I asked her,

"No, I'm going to the Oaks."

"Perfect! I'm going to the Derby; we won't run into each other," I replied. In Kentucky, your Derby dress is almost as important as your wedding dress, you want yours to be one of a kind. Our conversation led us to discover our children attended the same school. We were also members at the same country club. She introduced herself as Mary Sundley. I'm not sure when we stumbled on the subject of weight training, but somehow we did. Mary told me she had a personal trainer. I told her about my situation and that I was looking for someone to work with me. "Tim is great, you'll love him!" she praised. I took down his name, thanked her, and bought the dress.

The next Monday, I started my workouts with Tim. In six months, I was stronger than I had ever been.

We were able to do considerable work on our new home. Ted's business, Advisors Mortgage Group, was thriving, and we bought the house at a good price. Ted and I shared a love of house renovation. House projects were the only area of our life together where I felt like we were a team. Ted truly could have been an architect. He understood construction as well as any contractor. He told me all the years his mother toted him around to home designer appointments must have rubbed off. I didn't know where my love for decorating came from. As long as I can remember, I had loved to decorate anything. I felt on track.

When I was a preteen, Earl, who didn't want so much as a thumb tack pressed into the wall, was not pleased to uncover my newly-converted closet. I had turned it into what I called my "mini make-up room." Using left over contact paper from my "Young Authors" book cover as wallpaper, some of Earl's leftover paint and an old school desk a neighbor gave me as the vanity, I had created a beauty sanctuary. I set my lighted makeup mirror on the vanity and assembled my young girl cosmetics. I was proud as punch. Earl was not.

"Libbah, what the hell did you do to the closet?"

"I made a mini makeup room!"

"I hope you didn't spill paint on the carpet, and what are you doing gettin' into my paint?"

"I needed it for the trim work!"

"Hmmm!" Earl grunted and shook his head as he went to change out of his work clothes. I followed him, explaining it would keep the bathroom cleaner. Earl liked "clean," so I used that as motivation for creating my mini room. Earl was onto me.

"Libbah, I know you didn't mess up that closet to keep the bathroom clean!"

He was right; I just loved to decorate, and the closet was a blank slate just begging for some imagination.

"Libbah, what's done is done. Now scram!" I scrammed. Today the closet remains the same.

I never questioned the leap in lifestyle Ted and I were able to afford once we moved into Bridgepointe. We had always lived more than comfortably. Ted came from a wealthy family, and he worked hard. Advisor's Mortgage Group had brought more prosperity than the year before. There was more good fortune when Pinnacle Entertainment Inc. and Full House were awarded a gaming license to build Belterra Resort and Casino in Switzerland, Indiana. Ted's father, Donald House, was the Indiana Partner and he created the Full House Co., giving ownership to Ted's mother, Ted, his two brothers and himself. Donald had been hunting for a gaming license for some time, losing earlier to Argosy Gaming Co. and Stephen Hilbert, CEO of Conseco Insurance (Hilbert was later forced into bankruptcy for borrowing money from the company to purchase personal stock). Adding insult to injury, Stephen Hilbert lived next door to my in-laws. I was mesmerized by his over-the-top mega-mansion that sat on thirty acres. The beautifully manicured grounds touted a 15,000 square foot "sports barn" that is a replica of Indiana University's basketball arena. The front gate guardsmen's house alone qualified as a dream home. I don't know exactly how high the front gates are, but I imagine them to be forty feet tall. At Christmas, the largest and most gorgeous live wreath adorned the gates. The wreath was created in two halves in order to separate upon entry.

I was excited about customizing our new home, every detail mattered. I spent hours perusing specialty hardware shops, fabric stores, furniture stores and antique malls in search of unique ways to decorate. I dropped a sink into an old chestnut dresser I found hiding in an antique mall. I then paired it with contemporary Japanese red and straw grass cloth. Bringing rooms to life was my love. My type A personality craves perfection and decorating satisfied the craving.

Growing up, Beal hoarded anything and everything, useless combs with missing teeth and empty prescription bottles. Earl kept on top of the situation by secretly disposing items one handful at a time until Beal caught him. From that time on, all trash cans were searched extensively, both inside the house and outside. I helped Earl out when I was able to stop by, hiding trash in the car to discard elsewhere.

Finding ways for my creativity to express itself was virtually impossible in my childhood home. Aside from space issues, Earl had little tolerance for glue, glitter and paint, all of which were essential for my creations. Too bad my art projects didn't call for pill bottles and hair combs. Eventually I left my love of decorating behind, until Ted and I owned our own home. Our house was a blank canvas and I could not get a brush to it fast enough. In no time Ted and I remade our house into one that was truly ours.

Ted's thriving business provided me with experiences I never had before. Growing up, our family made one trip a year to Fort Lauderdale at Christmas time. Beal wanted to visit other parts of the country, but Earl would only go to Florida. It wasn't any different from being at home other than the warm air. Earl rented an efficiency, the kind where the owner lives on site and the vacancy sign is always blinking. Beal resentfully cooked meals during the day, and like at home, Earl was off on his own. He was having drinks with his brother, who also vacationed in Fort Lauderdale, or at his favorite watering hole, while Beal waited. No one played with my sister and me. Beal couldn't swim and neither could I until I was nine. It terrified Beal to go to the pool, because she knew she couldn't help if we got in trouble. Earl had no interest in teaching or playing. I have only one memory of Earl in the pool. I was so excited to see him I couldn't stand it. I was hoping he would let me jump into his arms like the other Daddy's let their children, but he didn't. He swam some laps, toweled off and went back to the hotel.

"Libbah, I got some things to do, stop pestering me!"

Once I learned to swim, I did stop pestering Earl. It never felt like a family trip until my half-sister married a man who owned a condo in Fort Lauderdale. They, along with my nieces (we were all about the same age,) were there to hang out with now. It was a blast. My fondest memories always have my nieces in them, and I cherish those memories.

We went anywhere that aroused our curiosity. It was exciting to visit new places. However, I always had to contend with Ted's quick temper. Patience had never been a virtue for Ted. There was always a waiting period after Ted let his temper flare. I had become accustomed to it for a long time. Vacations were no exception.

One time we were driving from Cape Cod to Newport, Rhode Island, and were stuck in gridlock traffic. It was the end of the weekend and everyone was trying to get off the Cape. Ted, like everyone else, became increasingly irritated. What wasn't like everyone else was Ted stopping the car midway around a rotary and stomping around like a petulant child. We had friends in the car behind us and one of them cleverly named him "Ted the Angry Giant," with a nod to Howard Stern's ever returning guest, "The Angry Dwarf." They laughed and I would have, too, but what they didn't know was as soon as I took over the driving, Ted berated me for thinking it not so smart to stop the car in moving traffic.

"Libby! Shut the fuck up and driiiiive!"

I expressed my dissatisfaction with his cutting remarks, but it was useless. Ted didn't care. He was getting mean, and it was not worth rationalizing with the irrational.

That wasn't the first time Ted showed his inability to wait out traffic. One afternoon, leaving Keeneland on their biggest stakes day, traffic congestion proved too much for him. He was liquored up and had lost on every race. When Ted bet, it was no meager amount. I bet long shots and ten dollars was my limit. Ted bet hundreds, and when he won, he usually parlayed it into the next bet. That day, there were no "next bets" and he was fuming. The valet drove the car up, and I could tell Ted was resentful that he needed to tip.

"Takin' every last dollar from Ole Teddy!" he muttered once the valet was out of earshot.

As soon as we shut the doors, he realized it was going to be a long wait. Hundreds of cars were bottlenecking into the exit road. Ted was having none of it.

"I'm gonna put this thing in sixth gear and run over these cars!"

He had just leased a shiny new black BMW, one of the many cars that appeared in our driveway, and he was all about what the "ultimate driving machine" could do. I liked the car but had no desire to run people over with it.

He kept mouthing, "I wish I had a bumper that wrapped around this car!" I imagine Ted must have enjoyed the bumper cars more than other rides at the amusement park. I was jerked to the present when he suddenly drove up on the sidewalk in order to pass the traffic.

"Ted, what the hell are you doing? You're going to kill somebody! I'm getting out unless you get back on the road!"

"Then you better find a ride home!"

He kept driving and pedestrians parted in horror like a parting of the Red Sea. I had to duck down, because I was horrified and didn't want to be identified. "Fuuuuuck you!" he mouthed to the angry crowd. I didn't come up for air until we were miles away.

Ted and I had our share of good times, but the tinderbox just below the surface was ever present, so I made an art of being careful where I stepped. Ted had an emotional barrier that was impenetrable. When we first met, it made me feel loved that Ted was especially possessive. It never occurred to me that he might see me as just that - a possession. Nothing made me happier than being loved by a man. I never had the father-daughter bond that so many articles claim is essential in developing a good self-image. I loved Earl, but he also had that same emotional barrier. I needed him to encourage me, be sensitive to my feelings and take time to hear what I had to say. Earl was unable to be that kind of father. I know he loved me, but I needed more. Blaming Beal for everything is easy, but Earl made choices, and those choices, mainly to stay with my mother forced me to endure her abuse. It gave me a skewed sense of what to tolerate and not tolerate in a relationship.

In my mind, I had a great life. We had a beautiful daughter, a wonderful home, and were able to vacation and enjoy life in ways I never had growing up. Never mind that I was belittled when Ted got angry and that our fights never ended with any resolution. I was broken and didn't know how to have a real relationship. I knew I wanted to be heard, but I never figured out how. I still hadn't dealt with my past and didn't blame Ted for my deficiencies. That wasn't his fault. I was accustomed to sweeping things under the rug. I had been doing it all my life. My rug housed all the hurts from the past, and I was still sweeping. Sometimes, I thought Ted and I were close and other times the divide couldn't have been wider. When I set Ted off, it resulted in humiliation.

One time, Ted and I were at the Pendennis Club for a wedding reception. The band was playing the eternal matrimonial anthem, Kool & the Gang's, "Celebration." It was getting close to the end and my group wasn't ready to call it a night. We decided on Have A Nice Day Café which I referred to as the "Smiley Café," (the sign sported a giant smiley face). It was a hotspot. We arrived late in the evening, and the line was out the door. Some of our group were already waiting. Quickly, Ted parked the car, and we ushered ourselves into the line. Fortunately, the line was moving and soon we were inside. I could hear the dance music and was eager to hit the floor. Ted paid our cover charge to a tattooed woman sitting in a glass booth. He walked while I practically danced my way past the bouncer.

"Excuse me Miss, I need to see some ID!"

Already half-lit, I smiled, "I'm a Mrs.!"

"Well, Mrs. I need to see your ID!"

"I was at a wedding and I changed purses to match my dress," I said in my most charming voice. The bouncer was having none of it, and when I caught sight of Ted's face, it was turning red.

"I have to see your ID or I can't let you through." I tried my best to assure him I was over twenty-one.

"I'm thirty-two years old, surely you know I'm over twenty-one."
Any other time I would have loved being carded, but this wasn't one
of them.

"Either you go get your ID or you are going to have to leave!" I
was no longer smiling at the "Smiley Café," and when I turned around,
Ted was gone. I ran outside and yelled to him. Not even turning to face
me, he yelled back, "Get a ride home!" I was beyond mad. Two more of
our friends were walking up and I told them what happened. They were
gracious enough to cut their evening short so I could have a ride home.

When we arrived at my house, I thanked them and walked around
to the back door. The door was locked, and my license was taped to the
glass. I knocked for fifteen minutes before Ted got up and let me in. I
don't know if he was passed out or not, but he knew I didn't have a key,
and I venture he didn't have my safety in mind. He turned the lock and
walked back to bed. I tore my license off the glass and slept upstairs.
Nothing good was to come from confrontation. I ignored him the next
day, the voice in my head whispering, "Take action, you're sacrificing a
part of yourself." Quelling the voice was easier.

What was so confounding about Ted was that he could be incredibly
cruel and then spend hours helping me in the kitchen. I don't mean
the kind of help a husband begrudgingly does to appease his wife, I
mean rolling out cookie dough, measuring ingredients, or icing a cake
to perfection. I came to realize Ted liked working with his hands no
matter what he was doing, and he had the dexterity of a surgeon. Any
project, inside or out, he mastered with precision. Ted's mother, Scottie,
and I had many conversations about his drive and ambition. "Teddy,"
as Scottie often referred to him, "had it as a child." She told a story of
six-year-old Ted having a clubhouse when he was a child. I imagined
wood 2 x 4s hammered together with big nails and covered with a film
of dust. Apparently, Ted took great care of the clubhouse but saw a need
for improvement. Scottie went on to say that she and Donald went out
for dinner one evening, and when they returned, the clubhouse had
electricity. He had run an extension cord from the house. I loved that
story. Ted would follow that story with one of his own.

"I was in middle school when a man paid me to paint his fence. I paid some young girls in the neighborhood pennies on the dollar to paint the fence for me while making a profit for doing nothing."

"How enterprising of you, Ted, exploiting little girls," I remarked with sarcasm. "You could have run your own sweat shop!" Scottie was not particularly proud, but everyone was laughing as he regaled his early business days.

I loved how Ted contributed when we had a party. His attention to detail was impressive. Girlfriends of mine would joke, "I need a little Ted to rub off on my husband!" Once we gave an engagement party for one of Ted's best friends. He was my favorite friend of Ted's. Everyone loved him. Earl was no exception, naming him "The Ambassador." I would have been suspect of anyone who didn't like "The Ambassador." If you couldn't get along with the Ambassador, in my mind, you couldn't get along with anyone. I was thrilled to give a party for him and his fiancé. It was a summer party, so I had white tables and chairs brought in for the lawn.

Periwinkle gingham tablecloths and blue hydrangeas adorned each table and the buffet as well. Miniature water buckets held the silverware tied with raffia. I hired a bartender and a caterer, and both were exceptional. The bartender, James Clay, was referred to me and he was in his late seventies. Mr. Clay – I didn't dare call him James, and he didn't ask me to either – had Earl's personality and spoke just like him. It was uncanny. Not surprisingly, he used the same expressions. I asked how he was when he arrived and he responded, "Fair to middlin'," meaning better than average. I laughed and explained my Dad used that same expression. He laughed, too, and got straight to business.

It hit a hundred degrees the last three nights, so we brought in giant fans to create a breeze. The day was stifling, and the air felt heavy and stiff. I knew Mr. Clay was hot and he wanted to know where his set-up would be. Ted had set up a bar under a white tent trimmed in white lights. It was equipped with all the appropriate accoutrements. Mr. Clay smiled when he realized he would be in the shade with a fan. We introduced him to the bar, and Ted was about to lay out the liquor when Mr. Clay politely said, "I can take it from here." I whispered to Ted while Mr. Clay arranged his bar, "Ted, I think we are being supervised tonight?" We laughed and continued to set up for the party. When we finished and had dressed, we took a moment to sit at one of the tables together for a pre-party cocktail. It was a sweet moment. The music played in the background, the smell of barbecue permeated the air and the tiki torches were burning. It was as if Ted and I were at a romantic dinner, except our dog, Traveler, was lapping melted ice water from metal bathtubs we had put around, so guests could pull out a quick beer. It was funny, the next morning we were at the same table alone again. Hungover, hair askew, sweaters on our teeth, in our jambos, eating left over country ham sandwiches. Traveler was there, too. It wasn't so romantic anymore.

Gambling was always a favorite pastime of Ted's. When I met Ted in college football season was starting, and I soon became familiar with terms like "the over," "the under," and what it meant to "parlay" one bet into another. I didn't particularly mind, unless the whole night was ruined when he lost. Once I made it clear I wasn't going to be projected on, Ted began to hide his disappointment. Monday night card games with friends and a visit to the casino were a regular part of Ted's life. When Ted's family became part owners of Belterra, it became a place for us to entertain. However, as an owner, Ted couldn't gamble. Gambling could cost an owner their holdings. I saw, for the first time, a glimpse of the troubled side to the relationship Ted had with his parents.

Grand Opening invitations were sent to guests for a sample "Taste of Belterra." Guests were treated to complimentary food, accommodations and, of course, a memorable night of gaming, and it was memorable. The night was in full swing with friends and family scattered about the casino. I was having a great time. After losing a few hands at the blackjack table, I ventured over to the slot machines, a.k.a. "fruit machines," to be kinder to my wallet. Pulling the one-armed bandit with one hand and having a drink in the other made me feel like an old lady on the boardwalk. I could see why they set up an office there for hours. Mindless entertainment. I was in deep when Ted came up behind me.

"Libby, you feeding the machine?" He asked laughingly

"It's ravenous tonight! I need to talk to an owner!"

I was digging deep into my token cup to give the bandit another bite when Ted pulled the arm down. Before I could raise my head, I heard my father-in-law's booming voice.

"What the hell do you think you are doing Ted?? There are cameras all over! Are you trying to ruin everything before it even gets started?"

I didn't move. Ted walked away with his father. I emptied the rest of my tokens into the bandit's gaping mouth until my cup was empty. I didn't care. It wasn't fun anymore.

I didn't doubt that Ted was in conference with his father somewhere. I started looking for my friends. I walked towards the entrance, not expecting Ted and my in-laws to be in intense conversation right out in the open. I could hear them, "Ted, you never liked us!" my mother-in-law was discreetly saying under his chin. I was stunned. I knew Ted was difficult and had a sharp temper but hearing her say he never liked them opened a door I hadn't expected. I looked down for a moment at the extremely distracting carpet, patterned on purpose to keep gamblers stimulated, and then sauntered back to the private lounge. No one was aware of my presence. On the way, I kept turning over in my mind what Ted's mother had said. Scottie had always said, "Teddy has no patience, and he just needs to count to ten when he gets angry or take a walk." It always sounded like special instructions. I realized now there were deeper issues between Ted and his parents.

Ted came through the door of the lounge as if nothing had happened and ordered a bourbon. I said nothing and neither did he. The window was shut as quickly as it was opened, but I've never forgotten that exchange between Ted and his parents. It made me wonder.

Nathan had worked for Ted awhile. We hadn't lived in Bridgepointe very long before Ted made him partner in his company, Advisors Mortgage Group. I liked Nathan, and if Ted said it was a good business move then I assumed it was. The one thing I knew and agreed with was that if Ted were to die, Nathan would buy me out and have controlling interest in the company. Throughout the next year, Advisors Mortgage

Group was thriving beyond expectations according to Ted. It appeared to have been a good idea for Ted to have taken on a partner.

The company's financial gains afforded us more freedoms. One thing we did was travel more frequently. Ted enthusiastically booked vacations, while I purchased corresponding travel guides. I was thrilled when we agreed on a vacation through New England. In Kennebunkport, Ted and I took a touristy lobster cruise. The idea was to watch the crew pull up lobster traps from the ocean, but the real attraction for us was a view of the Bush compound. We bought some lobster rolls sold from a shack right before we boarded. They were scrumptious and worth every over-priced penny. I ate plenty of seafood while we were in Maine. Every restaurant served delicious food. Even clam chowder sold at a local gas station was fresh and a treat.

We brought our lobster rolls and drinks on board and set out for our "Hands-on Lobsterman Experience," according to the brochure. The rocky coastline looked familiar, like those on the blank postcards Beal had stuffed in a drawer. It was just as I imagined, lighthouse and all. The Bush compound also didn't disappoint. We were staying at Cape Arundel, which provided a nice far off view of the compound, but the boat was able to cruise around closer. Of course, the Secret Service allowed boats to only get so close, but it was still a better view. We admired the Cape Cod-styled buildings on the estate and were especially impressed with the Secret Service.

Cruising around on the water, waiting for the big catch, I started thinking of Beal. She always had wanted to visit Maine. Earl won trips to Paris, Spain and Africa to name a few, from his work in the insurance field. Beal wasn't satisfied. Not satisfied, because Earl never took her where she wanted to go, only to places where he had won a trip. I was seeing other parts of the country she had lobbied Earl to see for as long as I could remember. When I was younger, I didn't understand why my Dad wouldn't take her to Maine. When I was older, I understood. If Earl was going to part with a dollar, it certainly wasn't going to be on a trip for two with Beal. There were always other people on the trips Earl won. Without a buffer, Earl would have to spend quality time with Beal, and he knew there would be no "quality," he would just be doing "time." He had already put in enough over the years.

The cruise was fun, but the lobster catch was a bust. We and all the other tourists were waiting for the climactic moment when the lobsterman pulled up the trap from the cold Atlantic bursting with fresh Maine lobsters. The only thing in his trap was one sad grayish-looking crab that was not fit for a snack. I looked at Ted and laughingly said, "The only lobsters we're going to see today are the ones on our buns!" "Slow day at the office," the lobsterman offered abashedly.

We de-boarded and talked about a dinner destination. We settled on Hurricane Restaurant recommended by a friend. On our walk back when we were trying to locate the restaurant, Ted asked a weathered older man for directions. The man paused a second and, looking at us, said in his gruff New England accent, "If ya goin' to that restaurant, ya betta have a big wallet!" If I could have slapped a yellow rain jacket and hat on him and put him in front of a wooden boat wheel, he might have made the perfect Gordon's Fisherman. We did go to "that" restaurant and he was right about the big wallet, but I had the best stuffed lobster ever.

Ted spent money fast. He bought houses all over Louisville to flip, and the ones in the east end I helped decorate. The ones downtown I never saw. He told me it wasn't safe.

"Why do you buy houses in an unsafe area, Ted?"

"I'm trying to better the community."

"Aren't you afraid?"

"I just take off my Rolex and go with Khalid."

"What's a Khalid?" Ted started laughing.

"No, Libby, he's a person! His name is actually Master Khalid Raheem."

"Master?" I questioned. "What do you mean?"

"Libby, he's a kick boxing champion."

"What? Like Jackie Chan?"

"Something like that."

"Well, Jackie Chan is just Jackie Chan, why the 'Master'?"

"Libby, that's his name!"

"Okay, but I don't believe 'Master' is on his birth certificate!"

Ted started laughing again.

"How do *you* know the Master?" I asked sarcastically. Ted replied,

"Nathan met him. We fired the weird loan officer guy, and Nathan took over the files. The 'Master' is refinancing a home."

"Why does he go with you downtown?"

"He knows the area."

"Oh, I see. Too bad about the weird guy, he was nice."

Ted was upping the ante on his gambling as well. He now bet more than his usual half (fifty dollars) on a game, he was betting dollars, which is a hundred dollars in gambling speak. Once his father sold his interest in Belterra, he gambled hundreds at the roulette table. I couldn't pry him away so I went to my room alone as Ted played the wheel until all hours of the morning.

Paul suffered from Alzheimer's disease for quite some time. My sister and I made obligatory visits when he was hospitalized until he passed in 2001. The visits were terribly awkward. Beal talked as if we had a relationship with the man lying in the hospital bed. "Daddy would be soooo happy knowing you all were here." Daddy would be so happy? Yeah, if I had brought my nail file. I loathed it when Beal played fantasy family with us. Beal neither acknowledged her father's cruelty, nor validated my feelings towards him, and she always justified his behavior.

"Libby, his father died before he was born!"

As I got older, I challenged Beal. "So, Mom, are you saying that being fatherless gives a person free pass to abuse others?"

Her response was always the same, "Shut your damn mouth or I'll mash it for you! You were a bad granddaughter!"

Accolades followed in a child-like voice, "My Daddy only had an eighth-grade education, and he is reeech! My Daddy could buy and sell your father-in-law! My Daddy was a Deputy Sheriff!" I thought it ironic, an abusive lawman. She kept vomiting praise until I walked away. None of what she said had anything to do with the issue at hand. It never did.

I did feel bad Paul was suffering. I didn't like seeing the man with the high and tight flat-top lying motionless with his mouth agape. I just wanted Beal, for once, to get real about what had happened. I'll never know the traumatic events of Beal's childhood, but they shaped her behavior in later life. It took years before I realized Beal was incapable of "getting real."

When Paul died, I felt nothing except guilt for feeling no grief. I didn't attend the funeral. I knew he had molded the person my mother had become, and I couldn't celebrate his life. My sister didn't attend either but visited Sweetie the day before. She told me Sweetie wished Paul had been a kinder man. I can only imagine what lay behind those words.

Spring break of 2002 couldn't come soon enough. We were going to Naples, Florida, where Ted's parents spent the winter. I thought the presence of his parents and some warm beach air might temper Ted's attitude. Kennedy's second grade class had just read the book, *Flat Stanley*. Stanley Lambchop was flattened in his sleep when the bulletin board above his bed fell on him. This enabled him to slip under doors, to be flown as a kite by his brother, and to be mailed to addresses around the world. Kennedy's teacher had the children make their own paper Flat Stanley to take for break and keep a journal to document Flat Stanley's travels. Students were encouraged to be as creative as they liked. Kennedy and I went to Target and picked out a special journal and a disposable camera to record Flat Stanley's adventures. The day we were leaving, Earl came to take us to the airport. Earl was ALWAYS early. I packed everything the week before, so we were ready to leave. Ted had gone to run a quick errand. Earl was impressed and skeptical.

"Libbah, I wasn't expecting you to be ready."

"Dad, we have a plane to catch, you know!"

"Libbah, I have shuttled you to the airport many times and shuttled you right back home after you missed the damn plane!"

"Dad that was my high school spring break and maybe once in college!" He raised one eyebrow at me.

"Poodle, whatcha know?"

Earl had names for everyone, and he called Kennedy, "Poodle." Moose, Bunco, Noodle, Punkin,' Budmo, Fuzzy and Dammit (which was me when he was mad), were all family nicknames created by Earl. Earl passed out names like business cards.

Kennedy responded, "A lot!" and got out her Flat Stanley. I explained the assignment to Earl. Kennedy decided to get her camera so Flat Stanley could pose with Grandad Earl, since he was taking us to the airport, kicking off Stanley's adventure. She took the picture and I had a backup just in case. Ted walked in and started laughing when he saw Earl with Flat Stanley.

"Earl, you going somewhere with Stanley?"

"Apparently, we're taking a trip to the airport, which we bettah get to right fast!"

"Dad, we have more than an hour!" Ted settled into the chair next to Earl and the conversation turned to the NCAA tournament. Indiana had made it to the final four in Atlanta and Ted was thrilled. The entire House family was thrilled. I was less enthusiastic. Kentucky had been knocked off by Maryland and I was still licking my wounds. I needed time.

"Oh shit!" Ted yelled in a panicked voice startling all of us. "I read the time wrong, the plane leaves in thirty minutes." Earl slapped both hands on the arm rests of his chair and shook his head. "Hell, you all aren't going to make that plane! You all will be lucky to make it out of the neighborhood!"

He was right, but we went hoping to catch another flight. We threw our luggage in the back of Earl's car and headed to the airport. Ted drove Earl's car so fast, we miraculously weren't slapped with a speeding ticket. Zig-zagging in and out of traffic, we made it to the airport in fifteen minutes. Ted pulled up to the curb; we spilled out and walked as fast as we could. We were afraid to run because frantic passengers running to catch flights were suspicious after 9/11. The last thing we needed was to be detained in the airport clink, though it would have been a spectacular entry in the Flat Stanley journal. As predicted, we missed the plane, but we did not predict there were no outgoing flights available for the next four days.

Ted was irate. The older ticket agent was doing everything in his power to try and find seats, but it wasn't happening. Ted was incredulous and kept at him. "There has to be something! We can go on separate flights! Put my daughter and her mother together, and I can wait and fly out later." He said, his voice rising. "Sir, there is nothing. I can't get you all to Atlanta until Monday. You all and half the country are scheduled to fly into Atlanta or connect from it. You've got the NCAA tournament being played there and thousands of spring breakers."

Ted's face was turning red. I poked at him. "Ted, there is nothing he can do." Ted, undeterred, asked the agent if we could get to Atlanta could he get us on to Fort Meyers? We always flew into Fort Meyers because of its proximity to Naples. The answer was still "no," but he continued to check on all possible routes Ted suggested. This man had the patience of Job. Ted's idea wasn't a bad one; as a matter of fact, it was a good idea. Agent Job finally snagged us three separate seats out of Atlanta to Fort Lauderdale. We could drive to Atlanta, fly to Fort Lauderdale, rent a car, drive across Alligator Alley and land in Naples. However, we had a new problem. Our return flight wasn't through Atlanta. There was no way to retrieve the car.

It wouldn't be the smoothest travel day, but it beat waiting three days. The hard part was getting to Atlanta. Our flight left from Atlanta at six o'clock AM. It was now four in the afternoon. I imagined weighted down mini vans bumper to bumper the whole way. Kennedy, Flat Stanley and I waited at the counter for our tickets, while Ted stepped away to give his dad an update on the situation. Whatever Ted's dad was saying on the other end of the phone put a smile on Ted's face. He hung up and said,

"Libby, my Dad's sending a limo from Belterra for us at nine tonight. The driver is taking us to Atlanta."

"WHAT?"

"A limo is coming and will drive us through the night to Atlanta."

"Just like that?" Ted let out a hearty laugh,

"That's the plan."

"How much does that cost?"

"It's taken care of, Libby!"

"Well, okay!" I told Kennedy Flat Stanley is going to have quite an adventure. I called Earl and jokingly said we were ready for pick-up.

"Libbah, I've been waiting for your call. I knew you all weren't going to make that plane. What the hell took you so long? It's a quarter after 4:00! The Watterson expressway will be backed up for miles!"

"Dad, it took forever just to figure out how to get to Florida."

"No time to tell me now, Libbah, I've got to leave!" Earl wasn't mad, he was efficient. On the ride home, Ted explained how we were getting to Naples.

"God damn, Ted! Your Daddy must know the right people." We laughed. "Well, at least you all won't miss this ride!"

He raised his eyebrow again, conveying skepticism. More laughter. Earl pulled in the driveway and we unloaded our bags. We thanked him and he replied, "Alright! Poodle, you and Stanley have a big time!"

Nine o'clock came soon enough. We were stuffing the last of the pizza in our mouths when the doorbell rang. It was the driver. He was wearing a suit. I was surprised. I thought someone driving through the night might be in loungewear. I guess there were appearances to keep up. He politely introduced himself as Patrick and quickly asked for our bags. Ted and the driver grabbed them and headed to the limo. I was shocked at its size – it was enormous. The tiny lights that ran along its side looked like a landing strip. Kennedy and Flat Stanley were quick to dive in and claim their spot. No need for that, it was spacious enough to accommodate Ted at 6'4", me at 5'8", Kennedy at 3'9" and Stanley at twelve inches. I snapped a picture of Stanley and Kennedy as the limo pulled out of the driveway.

"Ted, I'm glad it's nighttime. The neighbors would think we're weirdos leaving for spring break in a limo!"

He laughed as we settled in for the ride. It didn't take long for us to fall asleep. Being awakened didn't take long either. Our driver pulled into a gas station somewhere in a remote region of Tennessee. "Hey! Hey! Anyonefamousindere?" voices kept rattling off the same words over and over. "Anyonefamousindere?" The voices sounded like banjos and the banjos were now rapping on the window. They looked like twenty somethings and they were obviously out too late.

"Ted, where's Patrick?"

"He's probably using the restroom."

"Anyonefamousindere?"

"Ted!" We were killing ourselves laughing. "Hey Ted, why don't you poke your head out the window? Your wig is looking goooood!" Ted's hair was sticking up all over his head. My hair was askew as well.

"C'mon stick your mug out there and sign some autographs."

We kept laughing and didn't dare open the window. Patrick, back on the scene, quickly dismissed the banjos.

"No one famous in there, just regular folk."

They didn't believe him and kept carrying on. Patrick hung up the gas hose and we disappeared into the night. Kennedy and Stanley never stirred. I was grateful. It wouldn't have been an optimal photo opportunity.

Ted and I fell back into our slumber and didn't wake up until Patrick reached the airport. We made it from Atlanta to Naples without incident, and by one o'clock we were rolling our towels out on the beach. These were the days before Facebook, where everyone chronicled their toes in the sand and posted pictures, but that's exactly what my posts would have looked like. Kennedy was happily burying her cousin, while Ted walked the beach with his Dad. Ted's demeanor changed immediately. His parents had that effect on him. I envied the emotional support Ted's parents gave him and was grateful they gave it to me as well. I couldn't get that from Beal and Earl. It was a great vacation in every sense of the word, although I knew reality was lying in wait for me at home.

Keeneland had opened by the time we returned. The prelude to the Derby had begun in the bluegrass. The whole town was abuzz. I welcomed a month of events to attend. I couldn't figure out what was going on with Ted, and frankly I was tired of asking. I buried my feelings and conducted life as usual. Ted's attitude wasn't great, but the Derby festivities seemed to provide some distance from whatever was causing him stress.

CHAPTER 6

That year we hosted a Derby party after The Kentucky Oaks with some friends. The Derby is on the first Saturday in May and the Oaks is the day before. I paced myself at the track, knowing it was going to be a long day. I had learned my lesson after deciding it would be a good idea to drink mint juleps after spending the day drinking Maker's and Coke. I was found after the Derby race in a random box, eating the unopened bags of potato chips from abandoned boxed lunches. Ted did not pace himself. He was lit. He hadn't been a winner, like the year before when he cashed a $5,000 ticket. He didn't break even either. Farda Amiga had upset his trifecta bet, winning The Oaks over favorite Take Charge Lady. Immediately, he was scanning the entries for the next race.

"Ted, there's no time for the next race if we expect to get to the party at a reasonable time!"

I needed time to wash the day off me and change. He rolled up his program and slapped his other hand with it.

"Let's go then, Libby."

I drove home as quickly as traffic allowed, which surprisingly, was moving well. I caught the brim of my hat on the door frame stepping out of the car into the garage. Ted was quick to grab it and put it on his noggin.

"Libby, how do I look?"

"Drunk!" I grabbed the hat back. "Come on, Foster Brooks." We walked up the back steps to a locked door that was almost never locked.

"Ted, the door is locked, do you have a key?"

"No, I don't have a key. Why the hell is the door locked anyway?"

"I don't know. Just get the key under the flower pot?"

"I gave it to Vicky when she watched Kennedy!"

"Oh no," I said with a sigh. Ted's mercury was rising.

"I'm calling Vicky! Check the back door, Libby!" I knew the back door was locked. I let our dog, Traveler, out right before we left for the track. I checked it anyway as if magical wishing was going to unlock it. I rendered the verdict to a drunk Ted who was about to explode.

"It's locked, Ted."

"God dammit!" I followed Ted to the front yard as he continued to call Vicky.

"Ted! Ted! Let's call a locksmith. There's nothing else we can do! Vicky probably can't even hear her phone, and if she does answer, do you really think she's going to leave and come here?" I was trying to rationalize with the irrational. "Let's just call a locksmith."

Distracted by a passerby, I no sooner turned back to find Ted running towards the front door like a bull at full speed. He went straight through it as if it were nothing more than paper. The door was split and had ripped away from the frame. Jagged pieces of stained wood protruded from every direction. I was stunned. Our front door was gone. Gone. I walked through in a daze. I found Ted eating country ham finger sandwiches I had fixed that morning like nothing was out of the ordinary. He funneled down the sandwiches and then passed out on the sofa. Crumbs covered his starched white shirt. Traveler was more than happy to help with the cleanup. Too bad Traveler didn't have carpentry skills.

While Ted was resting comfortably, I got ready for the party. I figured I was going alone. Fine with me. We were going to the Derby the next day, and then an after party to celebrate. Again, I thought it best not to rouse Ted. The back door was all glass. I had to consider his safety. I called The Ambassador who was hosting with us.

"It's Libby. Ted has broken down the front door and is passed out."

"What?" he questioned.

"I'm serious. We were locked out and Ted broke the front door down, had a feast and passed out on the sofa."

"Nooooooo, he didn't," halfway laughing.

"Oh yes! We are minus one front door! I don't think Ted is going to make it tonight!" The Ambassador offered to come over and assess the situation. Ted was still resting comfortably when The Ambassador arrived and inspected the damage.

"Oooooooh! Not good," followed by the half-way laugh again.

"Stevie, I propped the door back up and called 'Johnny' our fix-it guy. He's a saint! He's going to put on a temporary door tomorrow. On a Sunday!"

144

"Nice," The Ambassador replied.

"Ted's on the sofa, that's as far as he got. Stevie, I'm going to grab a country ham sandwich in the kitchen, you want some? I need a base before drinking again." The Ambassador laughed.

"I'll take a base!" We were polishing off our bases when I heard movement from the family room.

"Hey, big fella! You rested?" Stevie said to Ted, who was now standing in the kitchen.

"I'm up and I know the door is broken, meaning I don't want a lecture."

"I'll call Johnny."

"Oh, Ted, I already called him." He pointed at me as if to say, "you're on it," and went to take a shower. Twenty minutes later Ted was back in circulation and ready for the party.

As it turned out, it was a fun night. Ted's fireman entrance story amused some and shocked others. I was not amused when it happened, but I softened through the night. What's done was done. I hardened back up on Monday when I walked out to get the mail. I met eyes with my neighbor, who was examining the damaged door set out for the garbage men to take. I didn't realize Ted had set it out and didn't dispose of it elsewhere. "Brilliant," I thought. My neighbor was my mother's age and had an inquiring mind. Damn! I couldn't turn back. She wouldn't be the type to find the story amusing.

"Are you throwing the door away?"

"Yes." There was an awkward silence. I knew she was waiting for an explanation. I wasn't in the mood.

"Oh, I was looking at it because my daughter is in the market for a new door. It's a nice door." I thought sarcastically, "It was a nice door."

"I doubt your daughter will want it, it's damaged."

"Oh," she was still waiting for me to spill. "I forgot to let my dog out, nice to see you!"

That was the worst and best excuse I could come up with. Had I known Ted set the door out with the garbage, I would have manufactured a better one. Embarrassed, I scurried back into the house and forced

Traveler out for an unneeded business call. By the end of the week, we had a new and much heavier door. Ted would need an axe next time.

With all the spending, I never knew what we had in savings and I didn't ask either. Ted liked to be in charge of all things financial. I had a checking account and Ted put money in when it was running low.

Looking back, this was the same arrangement Earl and I had when I was in college. Even when I was working full-time, I gave Ted every paycheck except one I used to buy him a fancy bicycle. I didn't even know how financially illiterate I was. I remember going over to my neighbors' house to help out with some decorating. She was holding up pictures to get placement ideas and remarked, "Ugh, I have to pay bills and do our budget." I replied,

"Greg doesn't do that?"

"No, I'm in charge of all bill paying." It wasn't said resentfully. It was said like they were a team and bills were her responsibility. I must have sounded like a 1950s subservient housewife. I guess in many respects I was, and what's worse, I didn't mind. I never gave it a second thought.

By the end of 2002, the comfortable life I led was becoming less comfortable. Ted was increasingly irritable and if I questioned him, his temper escalated.

"Ted, what is wrong with you?"

"I've got work stress, Libby!"

"Ted, you come home angry almost every day! What is the problem?"

"You're the problem right NOW!"

"Very mature, Ted!"

"Get off my ass, LIBBY!"

"Is it possible to have a productive conversation with you? It's not fair to me or our daughter that you come home and take out your work frustrations on us!"

He didn't respond. He walked outside, got the hose and started spraying already saturated flowerbeds. We had a sprinkler system, but when Ted got upset, he watered the flowers anyway. That's the way it was with Ted. If he didn't like the questions, he watered the flowers, sometimes the lawn, but mostly the flowers. I was tired of evening storms, so I did what I always did; I ignored him and waited for a change in the weather.

Maybe I shouldn't have married Ted. Maya Angelou says, "When someone shows you their true self, believe them."

This must be one of the great quotes of all time. Ted showed me his true self long ago, but I didn't believe him. A month and a half before we were married, I came home at one o'clock in the morning without Ted and without my engagement ring. We were in town for Easter weekend, sitting at a bar having a great time with friends. Ted was becoming loud and belligerent.

"Ted, calm down, you're getting too loud," I said laughingly to soften my delivery.

He had had too much of the brown water, and my comment didn't sit well. The more he drank, the more enraged he became. On the way to Earl and Beal's, he berated me. Once we slid into the driveway, he grabbed my hand and pulled off my engagement ring. I didn't even try to talk to him. In his condition, there would be no reasoning. He sped away and I walked into the house.

I still don't know how he managed the two-hour drive back to Indianapolis. Beal opened the door and there I was without Ted, and without my engagement ring.

"Libby, where is Ted and where is your engagement ring?" Beal has eagle eyes.

"We had a fight and he took it from me," I said in a calm voice. Beal quickly spiraled into panic.

"Libby, what did you do? Is the wedding off? Your father and I have put down deposits, the dress can't be returned! Oh my God, the invitations have gone out!"

"Mom, I'm tired, I'm going to bed." I suppose Beal and Earl must have conferred for a while, because an hour later Beal flipped my bedroom light on and continued going over the same material. Earl joined in asking,

"Libbah, what are we going to do?"

"Dad, I don't know. I'm really tired, please let me go to sleep!"

"Okay, okay, Libbah!"

It was obvious Beal had sent him to my room. Earl wasn't the type to get involved if he could help it. It would have been nice to have parents that didn't care if I married Ted, parents that only cared for my happiness and wellbeing. I didn't have those parents. If Earl had independent thoughts apart from Beal, he never voiced them. Earl was in need of a second knee replacement but was putting it off until after the wedding. He would soon be at Beal's mercy again. I imagine after the last knee replacement he wasn't about to cross her. Another hour passed and Beal was back in my room. It was as if I had a concussion and needed to be awakened every hour.

"Libby, you've got to tell me if the wedding is off!"

"Mom, leave me alone!" I refused to respond at all. I went mute. She gave up and I passed out. I felt like I had shut my eyes for a minute and Earl was back in my room telling me I better get up if I was going to make it to church.

"Libbah, it's coming up on eleven o'clock." I sat up in my bed, both my eyes at half-mast.

"Dad, what time is it?"

"It's five after ten, Libbah."

"I'm going to meet you at the Audubon. Audubon was the country club where we were having Easter dinner.

"Well, you better get a move on." Showering, I thought about Ted.

"Is he regretting his actions? Are we still engaged?" I had no idea.

CHAPTER 7

It wasn't long after the Derby that Ted's work pressure resurfaced. It was now interrupting his sleep, and mine as well. He woke up in the middle of the night. That was unlike Ted. I didn't think too much of it at first, and as a matter of fact, it annoyed me, because he would ask me if I was up until I WAS. It reminded me of the old Aspirin and Sucrets commercial where the husband keeps asking his wife, "Barbara, are you up? Barbara, are you up?" and keeps asking until Barbara, clearly irritated, answers, "I'M UP NOW!"

Annoyance turned to worry when it became an every night occurrence. Ted's troubles had permanently taken up residence in his mind. We would lie in bed wide awake at around three in the morning, every morning. I couldn't get answers from him, so I lay beside him quietly, with my hand on his until we drifted off again. Something was off, very off, but I tricked myself into believing his work pressure would resolve itself and life would go back to what I considered normal.

The drive to Kennedy's school took twenty minutes, and from time to time we talked about moving closer. The housing market was good, and Ted kept a watchful eye on any houses for sale in the area near her school. One day Ted came home happy if not downright giddy.

"Libby, I have something outside for you!"

"You do?"

"Yes, come outside!"

"Give me a second, I want to get Kennedy." I was excited. I walked outside and there was a black Toyota Land Cruiser parked in the driveway. He knew I admired the SUV, but I didn't know he was going to get one for me. I was thrilled. That wasn't his only surprise. Ted had found some houses to tour closer in town. This signaled that the momentary storm had passed.

"Wow! What happened at work for all of this to happen?"

"I closed some deals I've been working on for months." Sadly, still tricking myself, I accepted his answer as if the moods that gave me whiplash and nighttime awakenings were normal. I knew zero about the mortgage business, but failure to close on houses didn't seem to warrant Ted's erratic behavior. Ted gave me the keys and we all piled in my new SUV. Taking in the new car smell like everyone does on their inaugural ride, I asked, "Hey, it's close to dinner time, do y'all want to go eat Mexican?" I polled. I got two "yes" headshakes. I remember dinner very well. Kennedy was telling us about school and who she wanted to have for a sleepover while we stuffed ourselves with chips and salsa. It was nice. It seemed normal.

Spring gave way to summer and Kennedy was almost out of school. Having carted her around to activities and practices, I was ready for summer break. Field Day fast approached, and Kennedy was excited. I was too. I couldn't wait for the school year to end, but summer's end, I couldn't wait for it to begin again

It was going to be a busy summer. Kennedy would be swimming for two teams and taking riding lessons. She loved horses. In fact, she loved all animals. She even loved reptiles…reptiles scare the hell out of me.

Her favorite part of the summer was a week at Camp Hi-Ho, a day camp. They partnered with the Humane Society and had this ingenious plan for placing puppies and kittens. Campers are allowed to host a puppy or a kitten that is up for adoption overnight with the idea that they will never return. So when Kennedy came home with Cinnamon, the camp mascot, I wondered why she didn't have a little puppy or kitten like the other kids, even if Cinnamon was on the small side. The reason Kennedy had Cinnamon was that all the puppies and kittens had been hosted and there was a diminishing supply due to the flurry of adoptions.

Cinnamon took to his new family and thought to protect us from Traveler, the Lovin' Boy, our overgrown lummox of a Bernese Mountain Dog. Cinnamon had Traveler scared off, and he wouldn't come into our bedroom, so I'm guessing Traveler was relieved when Cinnamon went back to camp.

What I loved most about those summers with Kennedy were the days with nothing planned, when she played with the neighborhood kids until evening. I kept the door open with just the screen door closed and let the warm air waft through the house. The kids would tear through the door, bare feet slapping the wood floors, hoping to grab a freshly baked cookie or cupcake. It was a great set up, none of our backyards had fences, and the kids had the run of the neighborhood. Sometimes they put on plays; they loved getting dressed up in their costumes. Even Traveler, an unwilling participant, was in costume, even if he just wandered off and sulked during the performance.

Grateful our lifestyle afforded Kennedy opportunities I never had as a child, I tried to share my gratitude with Ted. He didn't like conversations that got too "deep." I tried to have conversations about my childhood, but these made him uncomfortable and eventually angry. I needed someone to talk to and was naive in thinking my husband was equipped to help me process those things that were just starting to spill out.

I started having panic attacks, periods of insomnia and disturbing dreams. Ted didn't like things he deemed "different." The issues I was having were "different," and he considered them a weakness. I found it ironic that I was supportive when he was getting up every night, but he couldn't do the same for me. Making a connection between the childhood trauma I suffered and the physiological symptoms I was experiencing never occurred to me.

One summer evening, I awoke from a nap panicked and trembling. We had plans to go to Avalon, a new restaurant, with two other couples. Ted was getting out of the shower when I approached.

"Ted, I can't do it. I can't do it!"

"Can't do what?"

"I can't go tonight. I'm having a panic attack."

"What the fuck is wrong with you, Libby?" Ted was screaming at me.

"We made plans with these people!"

"Call them and tell them I'm not feeling well, they'll understand."

"It's always something, isn't it, Libby?" Ted wasn't just referring to the present, he was referring to all my medical problems, endometriosis, my back, my pregnancy problems.

"I'm not doing this on purpose," I said. Ted made me feel defective.

"I don't want to hear it! Go get ready!"

I got ready, applying my makeup with a shaking hand, and got in the car. We weren't halfway there before I said I couldn't do it and had to go home. Ted became enraged and started screaming at me, "You fucking freak!"

I noticed a train going by. I wanted to be on that train. I wanted to get away.

I was pathetic. I started crying, apologizing for the way I felt, but it only fueled his anger. "I'm sorry, so sorry," I sobbed.

"You're not sorry!" Ted snarled. His face was turning red. The two couples we were meeting for dinner belonged to the country club. One of them was very wealthy, and we had never socialized with them outside of the club. Ted was highly motivated to cultivate a friendship and was enraged I was spoiling his plans.

I cried the whole way home. He was so furious he wouldn't speak to me. When we got home, I called a friend from the back deck. I noticed the neighbors were grilling across the lawn while I nervously smoked. My friend talked me off the ledge.

I realized I needed counseling and found a therapist. When the counselor asked about my past or present, about past trauma or trouble in my marriage, or anything else that might be causing anxiety or panic attacks, I revealed nothing. I was uncomfortable and ashamed. I could joke and talk about Beal with my friends, but for some reason I couldn't open up to the counselor. With the counselor, I would have to face the truth. I was being abused by my husband, and I had a lot of issues from my upbringing. I knew I needed help, but I wasn't ready to be honest about my situation. If I faced the cold hard truth, what was I going to do? How was I going to live?

"There's really nothing I can pinpoint," I told her. I wasn't ready to talk about Ted and his temper. I wasn't ready to face anything.

"Liar," I thought to myself. I would be satisfied if the counselor could help me get some sleep and find a way to deal with the panic.

I don't know if she believed my evasive answers; maybe she saw I wasn't ready to explore my past or my present. She gave me some mental tools to use when I had an episode as well as a prescription for insomnia. The episodes subsided. Problem solved. I had the ability to file horrible things away, and I believe many abused children possess that same ability. Problem is you can only stuff bad feelings away on a temporary basis before they start making their way back to the surface. Today I realize my marriage wasn't so different than what I had grown up with. With Ted, I had no voice and my feelings weren't validated, the same as growing up with Beal and Earl.

My summer rolled on. I poured myself into anything rather than face the truth about my marriage. I had done the very same thing growing up, always trying not to miss the kind of family nurturing I craved. I was comfortable with this type of life, evading the hard truths and finding band-aids for the things that really mattered.

Towards the end of summer, I was sitting at our country club, Big Spring, while Kennedy was swimming in the pool with her friends. I was chatting with some other mothers when my cell phone starting ringing. It was Ted.

"Libby! I'm making an offer on that house in Indian Hills today!"

"Ted, they want way too much money for that house, and it needs a lot of renovation!"

153

"I know you said, 'no' to the house when we toured it but, Libby, they dropped the price by $200,000 dollars and I can have it completely renovated before we move in!" I had serious reservations. I loved Indian Hills but was concerned about what it would take to do a complete overhaul. We had paid $300,000 for our house in Bridgepointe, and this was going to be in the neighborhood of $650,000, maybe more. "Libby, I know what I'm doing. It's an investment." I didn't want to leave a completely renovated home and start from scratch. The new house needed serious cosmetic changes, expensive changes. I was hoping for a house in that area, but one that required only minor changes. This was not that house. Ted continued to make his case, and eventually I was all in. If Ted said he could do it, then I believed he could. He made an offer the next day. It was accepted and we put our house on the market.

It seemed like bad timing to put a house on the market in Bridgepointe. A much-needed bridge was finally going to be built after thirty years of controversy regarding eminent domain and the neighborhood. In the paper, Bridgepointe was named as one of the neighborhoods that would be affected. Ted didn't seem worried at all. I don't remember how much time elapsed between planting the "for sale" sign and when we got the offer, but it seemed like only a few days. My girlfriend, Alex, from Biloxi was visiting. We were sitting on the back deck, catching up and drinking wine. Ted announced he was showing the house to Khalid, the guy he and Nathan had been flipping houses with downtown. I had no idea Khalid was interested in our home; nevertheless, he and a group of "his people" as Ted called them, came for a tour.

"His people" had nicknames like "Baba" and "Two Four." I don't remember the women's names, but there were two of them. The next day, Ted said Khalid was buying the house. I asked what he offered, and Ted replied, "He's paying the asking price." I couldn't believe there was no negotiating. I wasn't complaining, but it seemed odd with the bridge publicity and the fact no other homes were getting the asking price. I had an uneasy feeling.

I was glad to move closer to Kennedy's school, but sad leaving my neighbor. She had become a good friend, and Kennedy adored her daughter. Kennedy was an only child, and I felt bad taking her away from her friend. I always wanted her to have a sibling, so I'd gotten pregnant again when Kennedy was three. The hyperemesis gravidarum was even more violent than it had been with my first pregnancy. I became so ill that a central line was surgically inserted into my neck to supply food and fluids. I never got better and miscarried at ten weeks. I looked on the bright side and decided I was lucky to have Kennedy. Pregnancies showed me little mercy.

The day of the closing, I showed up at Chris Mooser's office with Kennedy and two of her little friends. Chris was a closing attorney Ted frequently used with whom we socialized with from time to time. He was laid back, so I knew he wouldn't mind the kids. They were certain to be well behaved since they were previously threatened and simultaneously guaranteed a swim later. I left the kids in the reception area and walked into the conference room. I was immediately confused, because Khalid wasn't present. Instead there was an older man who was already signing paperwork. When the paperwork was passed to me, I noticed his name, Alpheus Green, and he was the buyer. Ted never said a word before the closing, and until that moment, I had no idea Khalid wasn't the buyer. I left unsettled. It didn't make sense. I questioned Ted when he came home that night. He told me Alpheus Green was Khalid's uncle.

"Why didn't you say anything to me before the closing?"

"It was a last-minute thing, the financing had to be restructured. You don't need to be concerned." I accepted his answer, but it still seemed odd and, as I knew nothing about the mortgage business, I let it go. It seems I always let things go, and continued to do so, often to my own detriment. I always did what Ted told me to do and didn't ask too many questions until it was too late. To this day, I don't know if Alpheus Green was Khalid's uncle or not. I never laid eyes on him again.

Kennedy had been invited to a sleepover at her friend's house and they were going swimming. Since my afternoon would be free, I called my sister and we made plans to get pedicures. The next morning, I woke up groggy, grabbed a Diet Coke and a granola bar and headed to the back deck. The heat hit me as soon as I stepped outside. According to the weather bullies, it was going to hit 93 degrees with a chance of storms. The weather bullies always exaggerate. I think it improves their ratings.

Feeling cold, I welcomed the heat outside on the patio; the hotter, the better. Earl was the same way. If Earl's life had worked out the way he wanted, he would be living in Florida and taking in the beach air. Rocking back on my chair while the air warmed me, the caffeine woke me up. I heard the hum of lawn mowers in the background. That sound reminded me of Earl too. Earl was an early riser. Every Saturday he was mowing before my eyes opened. Earl was a hard worker. He had a Saturday morning cleaning routine that he NEVER deviated from. The funniest thing Earl did was prepare a bucket of Spic and Span before getting in the shower. He took the grey metal bucket filled with blue liquid along with a black chubby brush into the shower, cleaning himself and the shower at the same time. I never saw Beal lift a hand to the bathrooms – it was always Earl. He preferred it that way.

I sipped the last drop from the can and began to water the flowers. My flowers were parched, and I gave them a drink in case the bully report was wrong. One never knew. I loafed around my yard, still in my jambo's, until I finished the job. Walking upstairs to shower, I heard Ted speaking angrily to someone on his cell phone. By the time I reached the top of the staircase, the conversation was over. I walked into the bedroom and saw Ted in his white t-shirt and boxers leaning onto the vanity with his head down and his arms spread apart as if he was suddenly sick.

"What's wrong, Ted?"

"NOTHING!" he snapped.

"Nothing? You're sweating and glassy-eyed! Are you sick?"

"No, that black mother-fucker, Khalid, is fucking with me! Damn Nathan!"

"What? You're not making sense!" The next thing I remember Ted saying is, "I don't know what that mother-fucker will do. He might kill you and Kennedy!" My back muscles tightened, and my feet felt heavy. I had to process those words.

"What do you mean? What are you talking about? What's going on?" I didn't take a breath. I just kept ripping off questions. "What do you mean kill? Why would Khalid want to hurt me and Kennedy? Why? What's going on?" Every synapse in my confused brain was firing. I couldn't wrap my head around what Ted was saying.

"Say something!" I demanded even though I had not given him a chance to speak.

"Kahlid is mad about a deal Nathan and I did with him."

"That's it? That's it? Khalid is SO mad you think he's going to kill Kennedy and me?" I was crazy mad. "What kind of person is he? This is insane! Call the police!"

"Libby, no, he didn't say it, but I think he is capable."

Why? I never got the why. Ted kept rambling on about how he unknowingly got into business with a thug. He said he was never going to do business with Khalid again and blamed Nathan for the introduction. I was getting his thoughts in fragments. Nothing made sense other than I now understood Ted's failure to sleep through the night. No wonder he had trouble sleeping. Ted was afraid.

"Ted, if you think Khalid might kill us in retaliation for some deal gone bad, call the police!"

"I'm not calling the police I'm just popping off because he's a thug and he's mad."

"You're talking like this is normal! Ted, Khalid is moving into THIS house! Did you think he was dangerous then?"

"No, Libby! I didn't."

"Is the man who bought our house even Khalid's uncle? Is he dangerous?"

"Libby, stop it!"

"Stop it?" I shot back. "You tell me a man you do business with, and have for some time, may or may not kill Kennedy and me because of a deal gone bad and you want me to stop it? That man is going to be living in our house amongst our neighbors. I care about them!"

My thoughts were getting tangled. Repeated thoughts were tumbling straight out of my head to my lips. Ted couldn't or wouldn't answer the particulars. He got dressed and said he was going into the office. I was paralyzed, his words hitting me like waves.

CHAPTER 8

I weighed in my mind whether to go get Kennedy or leave her where she was. I elected to do the latter. I wasn't thinking clearly, but I didn't want her coming home before I had a better understanding of the situation. I knew the only people to get to the bottom of what was going on with Ted were his parents. I called them immediately but got no answer. Virginia! I forgot about my date with her, and by now she must be waiting. I wanted to be out of the house. A diversion might be good until Ted's parents called back. I was wrong. I rolled up to the nail salon and took a seat in the pedicure chair next to my sister. I stuck my feet in swirling water and tried to relax. Virginia was upbeat and laughing, and I was zoning in and out. Fear started to take over my mind. I suddenly burst out crying. The Vietnamese woman working on my feet looked horrified.

"You don't like it?"

"No, I like it."

Virginia was shocked as well. She whispered, "What's wrong?" My mind went blank after that. She tells me I never told her what was wrong until much later.

Caller ID identified the call as Ted's parents. I was a wreck when I answered. I thought how do I even begin to explain what Ted had told me? I lunged right in.

"Scottie, this is going to sound rather shocking but I'm frightened about a guy Ted is doing business with. I believe he is consorting with the wrong type of people."

"What do you mean, Libby?"

"I mean, Ted told me this morning that he is afraid of Khalid, the guy he and Nathan buy houses with downtown," my voice was shaking. "He said he thought Khalid might kill Kennedy and me over a deal gone bad. I questioned him over and over again, Scottie, but couldn't get a straight answer."

Crickets. Nothing. My eyes darted around my surroundings while I waited for a response.

"Libby, I want you to say exactly what you just said to me to Donald," she explained they were sitting by the pool in the backyard. The phone was handed off and Donald came on the line.

"Hello, Libby, what is going on?" I repeated EXACTLY what I had just told Scottie. He took in my words and casually said that he and Scottie needed to talk it over and would call me back. Their reaction, or should I say lack of reaction, baffled me. They were eerily calm about the whole thing. I felt like I was talking to strangers. Was the possibility of me and Kennedy being murdered not alarming enough? What the hell was going on? Where was the concern now? When we hung up, I was just as stunned as when Ted left the house. Kennedy came home later that day, so there was no more talk about what had happened. I settled down with her and watched the Disney Channel until we both fell asleep. After I got her off to school the next morning the phone rang. It was Ted's mother.

"Libby, Donald and I talked it over and we believe you are wrong. We don't think you should say what you told us to anyone else, your words could be used against Ted in court if there was a problem."

"I don't understand. Is there a problem and why are you bringing up court? I'm not following? Have you spoken with Ted?"

"Donald spoke with him and everything is under control, Teddy just got a little spooked, He explained that He is no longer in business with this 'Khalid.'"

"Spooked? He was panicked! Obviously, something is going on and it can't be good. I'm still not understanding your comment about court."

"Well, if Khalid is a bit unsavory, it doesn't look good that you say he was consorting with him."

"He *is* consorting with him. He buys houses with him."

"Donald feels assured that there will be no more problems. Teddy is not going to have any more business dealings with Khalid."

"I still feel uncomfortable."

"Honey, Donald has advised Ted, everything is going to be fine." It didn't feel fine, I felt like the underlying message was "shut your mouth and stand by your man." Unfortunately, I did shut up and I did stand by my man. Even though my man, furious I had called his parents, slapped me in the head and stomped on my big toe so hard that blood poured out from under the nail. I remember waking up the next day in Kennedy's bed with dried blood all over my foot. I did nothing and told no one.

Kennedy and I had been to Big Spring. We were both still in wet swimsuits. I was about to step into the shower when I heard knocking at the front door. I looked down the steps and saw it was a sheriff. Quickly, I grabbed a cover-up and walked downstairs. I was terrified that something had happened. I took a deep breath and opened the door.

"Ma'am, is this the residence of Edward House?"

"Yes, he's my husband."

"I have a summons for property violations on a house owned by your husband." He handed me paperwork and told me Ted needed to address the situation immediately. I had no idea what was going on. I read the paperwork and saw it pertained to broken windows and door locks. I wasn't getting it.

I accepted the paperwork from the sheriff and closed the door to find Kennedy standing behind me.

"Why is the policeman here?"

"On honey, it's nothing. Sometimes policemen make special deliveries, and they had one for your Dad."

Ted assured me moving to Indian Hills would be a smooth transition. It wasn't. Our house had many unforeseen problems and it kept us busy.

Ted was no longer in business with Khalid, so his temperament was on cool again, at least for a while. I knew I was living with an abusive man, but I wasn't doing anything about it. My ability to compartmentalize helped justify life with a violent husband. Denial is a dangerous place to live.

Indian Hills had originally been one of the largest horse farms in Kentucky, but was later developed into residential lots. Owned by the Veech family, they contracted Frederick L. Olmsted, designer of Cherokee Park in Louisville and Central Park in NY, to develop the golf course and subdivision. The golf course was named, Louisville Country Club, and was considered by many to be the most prestigious country club in Louisville. The Baptist Church I attended as a child sat across from the subdivision so I was already well acquainted with the area. Many church members resided on the generous lots of Indian Hills, so Beal was thrilled with the move. I believe she thought I had finally arrived. I never felt that way. I loved Indian Hills because it was beautiful, and who wouldn't want to live there? I didn't think of it as a way to climb the social ladder but Beal did. That was her game, not mine.

The first six months were peaceful. Well, as peaceful as my life ever got. I had everything a person could want but deep down I wanted more. I wanted what money doesn't buy, a loving husband. I tried to repress those feelings, but one frigid January evening they came bubbling to the surface. Ted and I went to a fraternity reunion party at the Louisville Slugger Museum. I'm really not sure why we were there since Ted's fraternity was not part of the reunion. Nevertheless, there we were. Walking into the vast museum I recognized many faces I saw regularly and many I hadn't seen since college. I was thirty-three now, and some faces were virtually unrecognizable while others hadn't changed. There were clusters of small groups with a band playing old favorites in the next room. Feeling rather sociable after drinks and dinner, it was fun telling old stories and catching up. By now everyone I talked with had children or a baby on the way. Wallets flipped open and pictures were shown as quickly as beer cans had been pop topped in the past.

I mingled through the crowd trying to get a peek at the band when Ted tapped me on the shoulder.

"Libby, there's an ice storm coming, and we need to leave before the roads get too bad." Agreeing, I went to get my coat while Ted retrieved the car. With coat in hand, I sat on an empty bench in the dimly lit entrance. Watching the sky spit ice on the sidewalk, it was coming down hard, I heard a familiar voice.

"Libby! Libby! Libby on the Label! Label! Label!" I looked up; it was Benny! My Benny from college! It had been twelve years since I had seen Benny. He had moved away to Louisiana and I never heard from him again. I couldn't believe it. An apparition was standing in front of me. He reached to give me a hug and I quickly stood to return it. I clutched the thick wool of his coat tighter than I should have and sat back down on the bench. I looked up at Benny while he asked the same series of "catch up" questions being asked and answered in the next room. He spoke smooth and easy, whereas, I stuttered.

"Libby, is your Dad still living?"

"Yes, he is." He paused for a moment and then said with a grin,

"How's Beeeal!" Laughing, I couldn't believe he made a joke about her after all the abuse she had heaped on him. It confirmed what a good soul he was.

"Beal's alive too!" then Benny started laughing. A woman walked up amidst our laughter and he introduced her as his wife. She was bubbly, with a mane of blonde ringlets. I introduced myself but she acted as if she already knew me. I supposed Benny had told her about our relationship. Ted's headlights appeared. "Well, my ride is here, it was great seeing you Benny!" I told his wife it was nice to meet her too and walked out through the entrance doors. It was surreal.

Barely speaking on the ride home, I never felt more distant from Ted. All the old memories of Benny flooded my mind and continued for a week until I repressed them again and went on with my real life...the life where I convinced myself I had everything I wanted.

Kennedy's spring break once again was upon us. We planned on making our yearly pilgrimage to Naples, Florida. I was especially excited this year. I became friends with another mom from Kennedy's school. Their family was also going. A week before the trip we realized we all were on the same flight. Even better!

The day of the trip we sat by the gate chattering about our upcoming plans. Preoccupied by conversation I thought nothing of an airport employee asking me to raise my feet so he could sweep. When the gate attendant called for us to board, I grabbed my carry-on bag and reached for the video camera I had stowed under my seat. Nothing! Nothing but air! I couldn't believe it was gone. My first thought wasn't of the camera itself, it was of the cassette inside, a precious, irreplaceable memory. I rushed to the ticket counter and told the agent what had happened. I knew it was an inside job, obviously a two-man job. One person distracts you while the other behind your seat swiftly swipes your personal property. She said there was no time to go to security so I had to call once we landed. Hopeful, but as expected, I was told no one turned in a video camera.

"Why can't you look at the security video? I believe they were airport employees."

"Well, ma'am that's not possible."

"Why not?" I queried.

"We won't have that."

"What? Everything is on video since 9/11?" The voice on the other end continued to tell me a video review was not possible. I was crushed because it was the only video I had of Earl, other than my wedding video. Earl read "T'was The Night Before Christmas" to the grandchildren. He was sitting in one of my oversized chairs by the fire and Traveler was lying by his side with the grandkids on the floor. It was a Norman Rockwell moment right off the cover of the Saturday Evening Post. Earl never read a storybook to me as a child so when I handed him Kennedy's book to read, I wasn't sure what he would do. Well, he opened the hardback book right up and began to read out loud in a way only Earl could.

"T'was the NAHT before Christmas when ALL through the HOUSE not a creature was sturrin', not EVEN a MOUSE!

The stockin's were hung BAH the chimney with CARE,

In hopes that St. Nicholas soon would be THERE!"

As he continued reading, I became that little girl wanting her daddy to read her a story, and that night he did. It was hard not to get emotional. It was the best Christmas Eve ever. I was going to have the video copied when the tape was full, but those gummy-handed thieves took Earl's and my memories along with the camera.

When we got to Naples, Ted's parents were warm and welcoming, in spite of our conversations regarding Ted's claim that Khalid might kill us. Over the years, I developed what I thought was a great relationship with them. I felt like I belonged to a real functioning family. I loved them and felt like they loved me as well. They were fabulous grandparents and active in each of their grandkids' lives. On each grandchild's tenth birthday, they got to choose wherever they wanted to go in the United States. Kennedy and her cousin chose San Diego. Since Kennedy was an only child, they went together.

It was always a treat for Kennedy to see her Gigi and Grandad. They were genuinely sad that I lost the video of Earl. Scottie and Donald liked Earl and he liked them, too, a lot. It wasn't about the money, either. Earl either liked you or he didn't, whether you had a dollar in your pocket or not.

I thought the worst was over when I lost the video. I was wrong. One afternoon my mother-in-law, Kennedy and I were shopping in downtown Old Naples. We were weaving our way in and out of the boutiques along the promenade when, out of nowhere, I started to lose my balance. I had a fleeting sensation of imbalance a couple times before the trip. The ENT doctor I went to see thought it might be due to allergies and told me not to worry. This was nothing like before. I rushed to the wall to stabilize myself, but the sensation only got worse. I panicked. When I returned to our condo, I asked Ted to take me to the emergency room. After hours of lying on a bench, because I couldn't sit in a chair anymore, I was finally called. According to the CT scan, I had no brain abnormalities and no ear infections. They gave me Valium and said to follow up with an Ear, Nose and Throat specialist. I felt like the diagnosis was "Hysterical Housewife."

For the rest of the vacation, I felt like I was on a rocking boat. This dizziness continued for months. Countless tests, scans, surgery to put in an ear tube and another procedure to remove it, physical therapy to regain my balance, and even Earl's old-time remedy of Sweet oil (used in his day to remove ear wax) were to no avail. It was an insane way to live and I thought I might go insane. Ted outwardly acted concerned but behind our closed doors, he was indifferent and cruel. Waking up day after day on "the boat" had reduced me to an emotional mess. I wanted to dock, but I was trapped at sea. One evening I called for him to come home from Big Spring. I was feeling so bad I simply wanted comfort. Enraged he yelled, "You fucking freak!" and hung up on me. I couldn't stop the tears running down my face. Wiping them away with my t-shirt, I called a friend. I needed a distraction fast.

Spending countless hours on the computer, I tried to self-diagnose. It was horrible trying to read. The words shook, making it hard to focus. I was convinced I had some rare disease that was being overlooked. Everything had been ruled out that reflected my symptoms. I wasn't giving up. I had a daughter. I was finally referred to Johns Hopkins. There was a doctor, Dr. Zee, who specialized in vertigo, dizziness and imbalance. I was ready to go. I would have gone that day. I would have booked a flight no matter what the cost, just to stop the rocking.

It took four months and some lobbying on the part of my oldest sister, Lottie, to get me moved up on the waiting list. Dr. Zee was a kind, gentle man. He performed the most unusual and sophisticated tests. I felt like I was in a planetarium during one of them. What I remember most about Dr. Zee is that he asked me, "Where is the Kentucky husband? Do you experience a lot of stress? Have you had an assault to your head?"

I had left my Kentucky husband out in the waiting room. I hadn't forgotten how Ted treated me, and I didn't want him back there with me. I guess it was my way of asserting control. "No, I'm not under stress and haven't had any kind of assault to my head." Liar. Dr. Zee continued with his battery of tests. He remarked on my hypermobility. "Your hypermobility most likely made you susceptible to spinal issues." I didn't think anything about his statement at the time, but later those words meant a lot. Ted and I returned after two days of testing. Dr. Zee would send his diagnosis and recommended treatment after he studied the results.

I was diagnosed with Vestibular Migraine, a migraine that often occurs without headaches, vomiting, light-sensitivity and so on. My sister, Virginia, suffered terribly from migraines and apparently Sweetie did too. Migraines affected my middle ear, which caused a rocking sensation. The medication Dr. Zee prescribed began to work within a month. I was no longer a captive passenger on a boat. I was free. I was finally free.

A month later I was in Kennedy's playroom. She had a slumber party over the weekend, and I was picking up the remains, Bratz dolls everywhere – the fashion-forward dolls with almond eyes and big glossy lips that were all the rage. Our cleaning ladies were coming. I heard the doorbell ring. Joyce and Donna always let themselves in, so I knew it must be someone else. I put the dolls in their purple Super Cruiser and went downstairs. Our postman was standing at the front door. "Mrs. House, I have a certified letter for you." Signing the green card, I wondered why I was getting a certified letter.

November 10, 2003

Elizabeth House
1 Indian Hills Trail
Louisville, KY 40207

Dear Ms. House,

I am writing to request your help in resolving a matter concerning your application for Anthem Individual Health coverage. The application includes questions about the medical history of the individual(s) applying for coverage.

Answers to these questions are evaluated along with any information obtained during the claims review process. Through this process, we learned that some medical information, regarding advice, diagnosis, care or treatment was not noted on your application. The undisclosed information in question includes but is not limited to unsteadiness and balance. For your reference, I have enclosed a copy of your application with the application sections highlighted for your convenience.

Please clarify why this/these condition(s) was/were not included on your application and forward that explanation to my attention by 11-30-03. Your written response is required for us to determine the future status of your contract with Anthem Blue Cross and Blue Shield. As explained in your policy, omitting important information from an application may result in cancellation of your coverage.

*** Important Notice***
If we do not receive a written response for our review
by 11-30-03, reformation or rescission of coverage will
be made retroactive to the original effect date.

I appreciate your help as we work to resolve this matter. If you have any questions, I will be glad to assist you

Sincerely,
Dana Jenkins

You're damn right I had questions! I hadn't seen the application before. I quickly flipped through the pages to find the signature. It was my name all right, but Ted's signature. Oh God! My fingers couldn't call Ted fast enough. It went straight to voicemail. Dammit! I decided to call Robert Wells, a good friend of ours who had sold Ted our insurance policies. When he answered, I apprised him of the situation. I told him Ted had signed with my name, but that I'd never been given an application. I wasn't aware of Anthem's protocol for signing up people, but I thought Robert should have spoken directly with me. He seemed as shocked as I was.

"Libby, I had no idea it wasn't your signature; I faxed the applications to Ted for you both to review."

"Robert, I haven't gotten hold of Ted yet, but I want your advice before I write back to Anthem. I'm going to explain Ted signed my name, but I'm not sure what else to include in the letter?"

"Libby, you CAN'T say Ted signed your name!"

"Why not? He DID sign my name and I have to tell the truth!"

"You can't! If you say Ted signed your name, then you will definitely lose your insurance. You have to say you omitted the information. I promise that's what you need to do."

"But I don't want to lie, Robert. I never saw the application and Ted signed my name."

"If you do that, I really believe you will lose your insurance."

"Robert, I'm going to try Ted again and I will call you tomorrow."

"Ok, Libby, call me tomorrow."

I continued to call Ted. I couldn't reach him. I decided he must be in a closing. I sat on the basement stairs for hours, paralyzed and panicked.

"What will I do without insurance? They are going to come after me for every claim they ever paid. I just got medicine to stop the rocking. How much is the medicine going to cost without insurance? Why didn't Ted allow me to see the application? Why would he sign my name?"

Ted's mother called me in the midst of my panic.

"Oh Libby, it's just like signing your wife's name on the back of a check. I've signed Donald's name many times."

"Scottie, I don't think this as simple as signing Donald's name on the back of a check. Anthem is threatening to cancel my coverage!"

"Don't worry, honey, it will all work out." I did not share her confidence.

I never heard back from Ted until he walked through the door. I pounced.

"Didn't you get my messages? What is going on?"

"Yes, Libby, I had meetings all day!"

"And you didn't think my message was important enough to warrant a call back? It doesn't matter now. Tell me why you signed my name on an insurance application I never saw? Why?"

He didn't answer me and went on to his home office. I was on his heels.

"Ted, according to Anthem, I would have been denied coverage if they knew about my ear issues and endometriosis! Why didn't you let me see the application?"

"I was in a hurry. I signed your name and must have checked the wrong boxes."

"You were in a HURRY? How long did you have the application? Being in a hurry is not an excuse! I had a right to fill out my own application! I might lose my health insurance. Ted!"

"There's nothing I can do about it now. What's done is done!"

He was right, there was nothing he could do about it, but the question remained.

"How do I answer Anthem's allegations that I omitted pertinent information?" I told Ted how Robert said I should respond. Ted said,

"I think you should do what Robert says."

"I don't. I think YOU need to write Anthem and tell them that I never saw the application and you signed it!" He stared blankly at me as if puzzled by what I had just said.

"You should do what Robert says to do." I was too angry to continue chasing my tail anymore. Later that night, I heard Ted trashing Robert to one of our other friends. "It's Robert's damn fault!" It was obvious that our other friend was in agreement. I couldn't understand why it was Robert's fault. At this point, it didn't matter whose fault it was, keeping my health insurance was the important thing.

I lay awake for hours worrying about my insurance. Ted slept like a baby. The next morning, I was back on the phone with Robert. He reiterated that I couldn't tell Anthem I had not seen nor signed the application.

"Libby, you will jeopardize your insurance if you say Ted signed it." I made the decision to accept responsibility for the omissions. I fearfully typed the letter with my fake explanation on November 13, 2003. Once I finished, I tossed my lie into the mailbox and held my breath. I didn't realize I would be holding it for two months. On January 9, 2004 Anthem rescinded my policy, citing the application contained incorrect and/or incomplete information. I was devastated. My conscience got the best of me, and I went to see Lawn Spalding, who is a well-known attorney in the healthcare field. I told him the truth. I told him I heeded the advice of our friend and insurance agent.

"I was scared. I've had some recent health issues and have a bad back." Mr. Spaulding didn't mince words.

"It's unfortunate Mr. Wells instructed you to claim you signed the application. He certainly was not looking out for your best interests; he was looking out for his. This is NOT a friend! This is a case of CYA (cover your ass), and that's all this is."

"Mr. Spalding, I believe he didn't know that Ted signed my name to the application."

"That's beside the point! He knew he never spoke with you and he knew you were vulnerable! I'm going to write Anthem on your behalf, but I doubt anything can be done. They would never have issued you an individual policy with your pre-existing conditions. Period."

I appreciated Mr. Spalding not admonishing me for doing such a stupid thing. Even if he thought it, he never said it. I left the office with little confidence I would regain my coverage. I tried not to think of Mr. Spalding's opinion of Robert. Ted and I had known him and his wife for years. They were great in my opinion. I was angry at Ted. None of this would have happened if he had shown me the application.

Mr. Spalding expounded on what I already knew. All my providers would be coming after me for every penny Anthem took back from them. They did. Letters arrived daily demanding thousands and thousands of dollars. If that wasn't bad enough, I had to go a year without insurance before I could apply to Kentucky Access, a program set up for Kentucky residents who have pre-existing conditions. Insurance premiums were astronomical. Basically, you're punished for having *any* health issues. The whole ordeal was terrible. I wondered if Ted knew all along that I would have never been covered and that's why he did what he did. It didn't matter anymore. What's done was done.

My friend and I counted down the months until I could re-apply. It was a horrible feeling not to be insured. I got a glimpse of what it must be like for families who cannot afford health insurance. You prayed you didn't get a serious illness or have some catastrophic accident. Ted began paying back the money, and rather quickly. I was grateful we were in a position to pay the medical bills. If there was a silver lining, that was it.

I saw Robert at a party not long after Anthem rescinded my policy. He apologized and thanked me for not suing him. I hadn't considered suing him. I just wanted to keep my health insurance. Twelve months later, I was approved for Kentucky Access' overpriced policy. Ironically, it was run by Anthem.

Ted came home one summer evening announcing he was taking me to one of our finest steak houses for dinner.

"Libby, you've been through a lot, so let's go have a nice dinner. I've arranged for your sister to watch Kennedy." In came Virginia. I was shocked by his words. Ted never talked to me like that. Ever. Quickly I did a Wonder Woman change and out we went. At dinner, he announced we were going to complete the renovation on our home. "Business has been good, Libby!" he said with a hearty laugh. It wasn't the endearing conversation I thought we were going to have, but business was booming for Ted so why not be happy about renovating? Right?

We returned from dinner and Ted showed me his ideas for the house. "It's a major renovation Libby, it will probably take six months or longer," Ted explained. It did. We spent countless hours on the details. We tore down a good portion of the back of the house and had a contractor build a TV room and a gorgeous kitchen. He also put in a beautiful patio. I enlisted a decorator we knew socially who was extremely talented and a dream to work with. Many different professionals helped on our project, but one in particular stood out. Her name was Linda and she designed our kitchen. I found out her husband, her high school sweetheart, was gravely ill. I could tell she carried a lot of sadness and pain. Even with her suffering, she designed a fabulous kitchen. Her husband died two months later.

Ted was flying higher than ever, for a while anyway. I was too. We took a second trip to Kennebunkport. Ted planned a family trip to Cabo San Lucas, but Kennedy had an accident and needed stitches so we switched our plans and went to Chicago where there would be no swimming (her stitches had to stay dry). Ted bought himself a new SUV and considered buying a boat. I vetoed the boat.

Ted bought two more houses near us to flip. He took a guy's trip to Taos, New Mexico, and in December I planned a girls' trip to Chicago. He regularly paid for everyone's dinner. One in particular cost $600, which made me feel uncomfortable. We were at Porcini's, an upscale Italian restaurant, with a party of ten, and when the check arrived, Ted put down his card and quickly whispered in the waiter's ear, "I got this." I thought it was an ostentatious display. Glad Ted was doing so well, I didn't think he needed to shake it around town. It didn't matter what I thought, Ted was going to shake whatever he wanted. I learned that a long time ago.

The remake of *The Alamo* was showing at "Tinseltown," Louisville's shiny new movie theater. I had never been to a movie with Earl. He talked about going to "the picture show" in his old life, life before Beal, but he never took us. I decided I was taking HIM. I had waited long enough! I was thirty-six and Earl was eighty-five.

"Hi Dad, it's Libby! I want to take you to the movies on Wednesday."

"A picture show, Libbah?"

"Yes, I want to take you to *The Alamo*." Earl loved Westerns.

"*The Alamo?*" I saw that movie back in 1960, Libbah!"

"Dad, it's a remake, a remake of the old movie."

"Well, that'll be fine! What time?"

I couldn't believe it! I had expected Earl to turn me down. I guess being told "no" all the times I wanted my parents to take me to the movies, meant Earl would say "no" this time too. It was Sunday, and like a child, I couldn't wait for Wednesday. Earl and I were going to a movie!

"Saddle up Dad, we're going to see *The Alamo!*" He laughed, "I hear ya, Libbah!"

Wednesday came and we saddled up. I was giddy. Earl had no idea what it meant for me to go to the movies with my Dad. We got to the ticket booth and Earl went for his wallet

"No, Dad! My treat!" He still carried a wallet filled with cash. He always had. Ted used to ask, "Earl, how much cash you got in that wallet?" Earl always replied, "It's my gettin' out of town fast money!" I bet he seriously thought about gettin' out of town fast many times.

"Two tickets to *The Alamo* please." The young man in the booth replied, "One senior?" Earl raised his eyebrow, "Who the hell is a senior?" The young man laughed. Earl walked through the lobby, paused and looked around wide-eyed. I could see the little boy inside the eighty-five year old man standing in front of me. Everything was lit up in bright neon colors. I watched his eyes take snap shots of every detail. It might have been decades since Earl was in a theater.

We walked across the black and white floor and bought refreshments. Earl didn't eat popcorn when I was growing up, but he talked about how much he loved it to the point it made him mad.

"Dad, why can't you eat popcorn?"

"It gets stuck in my bridge work."

"You have a bridge in your mouth?" He smiled.

"Libbah, I can't get it out of my teeth."

"It doesn't get stuck in my teeth."

"I just can't, Libbah!"

"Okay," still not really understanding. Earl had dentures now. I ordered a giant refillable tub and two soft drinks. As we walked towards the theater, he was looking at giant posters of old Hollywood stars. Most people just pass them by without a second thought, but not Earl. They were his contemporaries and he studied their faces like he was at an art exhibit, maybe taking a walk down memory lane with Olivia de Haviland or her sister Joan Fontaine.

We settled into our seats. "These seats are right comfortable, Libbah!" As the lights went down, Earl's face lit up. It was like watching

a child at the theater for the first time. Earl didn't just enjoy the movie –
he was IN the movie! He was shoulder to shoulder with Jim Bowie,
Davy Crockett and Sam Houston, shooting at the Soldados Mexicanos.

"GOD DAMN YOU, SANTA ANA! YOU SONOFABITCH!"
Earl roared. I lurched forward in surprise and started laughing so hard
Diet Coke came out my nose.

"DAMN YOU SANTA ANA!" I swear, if Earl had a bayonet, he
would have jumped into that screen and speared Santa Ana himself.
Other patrons were amused, too. I could hear them laughing. Earl's eyes
never left the screen, even when he put the empty popcorn tub in my
lap, "Here, Libbah, I believe I'll take me some more popcorn." I gladly
obliged.

When Davy Crockett was killed in the end, Earl shook his head.
"SON OF A BITCH!" and when Santa Ana was captured, he yelled,
"SHOOT HIM, SHOOT THAT SONOFABITCH DEAD!" We walked
out of the theater, and one of the patrons who had been in the theater
with us tapped me on the shoulder. "I've never been more entertained!
I don't know what was better, watching the movie or watching your
grandfather." I didn't correct him on the grandfather thing. I felt the
same way.

On the way out, I told Earl I needed to use the ladies' room. I
didn't, I was just overcome with emotion and didn't want him to see
me. I shut the door and let the tears roll down my face. I knew this
was probably the first and last time Earl and I would go to the "picture
show," and it was.

I don't know how long I was napping before I was awakened by
Ted's screaming on the phone outside my bedroom window. "JERRY,
WHAT THE FUCK DID YOU DO? (Pause). I DON'T GIVE A
GODDAMN! WHAT THE FUCK IS WRONG WITH YOU? ARE
YOU FUCKING STUPID? (Pause), I DON'T WANT TO HEAR IT!!
YOU FUCKING HEAR ME?" I bolted outside.

"Ted, stop it! What is going on? Who is Jerry?" I demanded. "You
woke me up from a dead sleep!" He shut his flip phone. "I don't fucking
care!"

"You don't care? Your daughter's inside!"

"Leave me the fuck alone!" I did. I went upstairs to check on Kennedy. I found her engrossed in a *Lizzie McGuire* episode. I crept back down the stairs. Ted was standing with his hands pressed up on the wall and his head hanging low. His face was blood red and I saw sweat beading on his neck. Jerry? Who was Jerry? The only Jerry I knew was our beloved handyman, and I knew he wasn't talking to him like that.

Kennedy and I watched *Lizzie McGuire* together for the rest of the night. I didn't want to talk to Ted anymore. I knew he would erupt.

Ted was sitting in his office the next morning. I hustled Kennedy out of the house and dropped her off at a friend's home.

"Ted, what's going on? Who is Jerry?"

"Libby, I got mad and popped off."

"You didn't pop off – you were verbally berating whoever Jerry is."

"Libby, don't worry about it! It's been handled!"

"What does that mean?" Ted didn't answer. Pushing for more information was an exercise in futility. I wouldn't find out who was on the other end of that call for two years. That night Ted came to bed with his laptop, and every night thereafter. He stayed up way into the night. Finally, I built a pillow wall blocking the glow. Mentally I was building a wall as well.

I was weary from never getting a straight answer; first Khalid, and now Jerry. I put my weariness aside and started asking Ted pointed questions about his business, many questions, but Ted shot them down as if his business didn't concern me. We were married, it concerned me.

I left the "Jerry" situation in the back of my mind with all the other unanswered questions, continuing to let life happen. Summer had soured and so did Ted. I'll never know what that conversation with Jerry entailed, but it changed Ted. Ted always had been quick-tempered, but now he was raging. The smallest things set him off. One time we were at the Antique Mall where I found a tray that I wanted for the kitchen. The tray was $35 dollars. I picked it up and was walking to the register when Ted shouts in a booming voice.

"Libby, what the hell is wrong with you? You think there's a fucking money tree growing in the back yard?"

A couple in the next booth look horrified. I was horrified. I quickly dropped the tray and left the building. Once in the privacy of our SUV, I shouted, "What is wrong with you, Ted?"

"Me?"

"What is wrong with *you*? He shouted back.

How dare you talk to me like that in public? Why did we even come here? We're spending over eighty thousand dollars on a renovation and you're worried about a $35 dollar tray? Those Viking appliances are over thirty thousand and you HAD to have them. I just wanted a tray!"

With that, he grabbed my sunglasses, crushed them in his fist, and threw them out the window. The side of my nose was stinging. I felt blood and tears running down my face. I stared out the window the entire ride home. I didn't want Ted to see my cry. I thought about leaving Ted. Instead, I called his mother and said he was having angry outbursts. Later in the week, she sent Ted a book on anger with a post-it-note on the chapter, *Sudden Anger*. It read, "Son, you might want to start with this chapter."

As the renovation was coming together, our marriage was falling apart. Honestly, it hadn't been a marriage for years, but I wouldn't admit that to myself, because admitting it required action, and I wasn't ready to act. I was fearful of the unknown. I resigned myself to living in misery rather than face change and all that change implied. I didn't have a career and I didn't have skills.

Late at night after Kennedy fell asleep, I went out back and smoked cigarettes. For hours, I watched the lightning bugs mingle with one another. There were so many that the bushes glistened, and it was easy to lose oneself in the moment. I looked forward to their light show. I didn't want to be inside with Ted. I couldn't figure out what was wrong. Suspecting financial problems, I left it alone. Confrontation with Ted never went well. Watching the lightning bugs perform another night, a friend called. We talked a lot about anything and everything, and then she dropped a bomb. She told me Ted was not on the up-and-up and there were questionable things going on at his office.

"Why would you say that Laura?"

"Cindy told me, Libby!" Cindy was Laura's friend.

"I don't believe it!"

"Believe what you want. She works there. She ought to know."

"What kinds of '*things*' Laura?"

"I don't have the details."

"Then why did you call?" The conversation was getting heated. "I'm going to ask Ted!"

"Don't say I told you, I don't want to be on his radar!" I ended the conversation and chained smoked for an hour. Khalid, Jerry, the metal tray incident, Ted's behavior, all these thoughts turned like a carousel in my mind.

That conversation changed everything. I started asking Ted questions without giving Laura up. He knew it was her, though. It wasn't hard putting two and two together.

"Why is that insecure bitch trying to start something? She's miserable! She's always miserable!"

"Ted, the question still stands – is there something going on at work that you need to tell me? Be honest. Please be honest!"

"Libby, there is nothing going on at work! I'm stressed, the renovation is over budget and I need to get deals closed!"

"Swear it!" Ted shut his eyes. Ted always shut his eyes when he didn't like what someone was saying, or when he was lying.

"I swear it!"

I came home from my girls' trip to Chicago in early December. It was so much fun I was still giddy. It was Christmas time, the renovation was complete, and I was ready to celebrate. I tuned out all the noise in my head and focused on the holidays. Kennedy was especially excited when I showed her an ornament I purchased for her on my trip. It was a wooden painted pickup truck with a Christmas tree in the back and a Bernese Mountain Dog driving.

"Traveler is driving Grandad's truck!"

Earl had traded in his Pontiac sedan for a red pickup years ago. Earl liked the ornament, too.

"Big Dog driving the Big truck!" Kennedy proudly centered it on our tree.

The Polar Express was playing at the theater. Kennedy couldn't wait to go. What she didn't know was that I bought tickets for a Polar Express train event in French Lick, Indiana. I surprised her and told her she was going on the Polar Express and could invite three friends. On the departure night, she and her friends showed up at the station wearing pajamas as instructed on the website. Ted and I produced the tickets and we boarded the train. It was just like the movie.

The conductor came around and punched their tickets, and a hostess served hot chocolate and cookies. It was a starry night, a fairy tale of a night. A recording of the book was read as the train wound through the hills of Southern Indiana. There was music and singing too. It was delightful. When the train reached its destination, we were at the North Pole! Everything was lit up in Christmas lights, and Santa was waving to everyone. The kids on the train barely contained themselves. Santa boarded and handed each child a beautiful bell, just like in the movie. It was a special memory.

Meeting some girlfriends to have Christmas cocktails, I showered and began the process of washing, drying, straightening and styling my thick, curly hair. People didn't believe me when I told them I have curly hair. I could get my hair poker straight if weather conditions cooperated. Humidity and rain? Forget it! Kennedy used to laugh, "Mommy, you have giant hair, you look like a lion." I did. My mane loved fall and winter. Anyone with hair like mine knew those were the best hair seasons. Once I finished the process, I put on a newly purchased shirt from a Lincoln Park boutique, some dark jeans, and my new holiday heels. I needed to get the chicken in the oven before Ted got home. I walked past the family room where Kennedy had made a palette for Traveler and her beside the Christmas tree. Apparently, they were watching Animal Planet. Traveler did seem engrossed. It was a sweet scene. I got the chicken in the oven and closed the door when the phone rang. It was Laura. I told her I had about ten minutes. She explained that there had been some blow-up between Cindy's friend and Ted.

"Libby, something is going on there!"

"Laura, I already spoke with Ted."

"Libby, I'm just concerned for you and Kennedy."

"What exactly happened?" Laura was vague.

"Laura, if you can't give me specifics, then don't call."

"Libby, I'm not trying to upset you."

"Okay, I have to go now – Ted just walked in."

"Okay, I'll call you tomorrow."

Laura's phone call sent me back to a place I desperately did not want to be. Doubt. Ted said, "Hello," to me and Kennedy and disappeared to change out of his work clothes. I told Kennedy to pick up her things for the night. She dragged the covers upstairs with Traveler trailing behind. Ted re-emerged more comfortably dressed. He grabbed a pitcher and filled it with water. "The peace lily in my office is pretty thirsty." I dove straight in.

"Ted, what is going on at work?"

"WHAT NOW, LIBBY?"

"I was told there's an issue at work with Cindy that turned ugly."

"That fucking bitch, Laura! Why doesn't she mind her own god damn business?" Realizing Kennedy was upstairs I instantly regretted bringing up the topic.

"Is that what you two talk about every day? Ted's double life?"

I smartly responded, "You said it! I didn't!" I waited a minute, looking at Ted who was staring into space. "Never mind I have to go," I said and turned to walk away when Ted took the water pitcher and poured it over my head. I was stunned. If there ever was a time, I wanted to slap somebody, that was IT! I didn't. I rushed back to the bedroom, changed my clothes and quickly attempted to dry my hair. Twenty minutes later, I put my still damp hair up in a bun and ran out the door. I was thankful Kennedy never came downstairs.

Of course, my night was ruined. It was surreal. My friends were chatting about the goings-on in their lives, while I pretended to enjoy myself. One of them was telling us what she was getting her husband for Christmas. Then she asked me.

"Libby, what are you giving Ted for Christmas?"

"A divorce! (What I was thinking?) A leather desk set for his new desk. Sexy, huh?"

They all laughed. I faked having a good time for two hours. That night, I slept in the guest bedroom. The next morning was my turn to drive carpool. Kennedy and I were out the door before Ted woke up. When I got home, he was still in bed. I literally got on my stomach and crawled like there was barbed wire I had to go under. I changed into my workout clothes in my walk-in closet and then crawled out of the room the same way. I didn't want to wake Ted. I wanted no interaction that morning.

The days filled with tension. Laura kept buzzing in my ear, and I kept buzzing in Ted's. "Keep it up, Libby! Keep it up!" I did. I kept it up, until I refused to go to Ted's family's Christmas party in protest for not getting answers. I was at a tipping point. I wouldn't be able to fake the holiday spirit at the party, so I stayed home. I had terrible guilt regarding Kennedy. I felt selfish. I felt confused. I felt ashamed for loving the husband who treated me so badly. It was the longest day. I sat in my pajamas and watched "It's a Wonderful Life," while I thought about what would happen when Ted got home.

"Maybe this will be a wake-up call? Maybe he will take me seriously? Maybe he will be sorry for everything he has put me through?"

The next day, Ted left me.

Kennedy's holiday program was two days later. I didn't get there early enough to get a seat, so I had to stand up by the gym wall. Ted didn't either and was standing on the opposite side. All of the children and parents who managed seats were in the middle. It was a moving program. Kennedy's class stole the show, singing, "Love Can Build A Bridge." I barely held it together while watching my daughter sing in her crimson velvet dress. The sea of people between Ted and me seemed symbolic. I kept my composure, but inside I was falling to pieces. It was a terribly sad day.

Christmas Eve I took Kennedy to Mass by myself. It was incredibly hard. I got there late and left right after communion to avoid having to make excuses for Ted's absence. The wounds were too fresh.

I was hosting Christmas Eve dinner. My sister, her family, Beal, Earl and Kennedy would eat the one and only family dinner ever in my newly remodeled home. After my family left, Ted came back to sleep so he could see Kennedy open her gifts Christmas morning. I was on autopilot, just trying to get through the day. He was gone again by nightfall. Kennedy fell asleep and I sat by the Christmas tree with Traveler and a bourbon. We were separated.

Bad news travels fast and mine was no different. It's amazing how many "concerned" friends you have when life starts to unravel. Truly, there were kind people who reached out, but there were also the "fishermen" who had no interest in me until they heard the news. A fisherman would cast a line upon seeing me and hope to reel in some juicy details.

"Hi, Libby! How are you?"

"I'm fine, how are you?"

"Oh, I'm good, I just wanted to say how sorry I am to hear about you and Ted. My friend's husband was cheating on her and it was devastating. Men can be such cads!" I wasn't biting.

"I'm sure that was devastating." I gave up nothing, and I saw the disappointment on her face.

I found myself more at peace as the weeks went by. There was no chaos; it was just quiet. I exhaled. Then there was Kennedy. I worried how she was affected. I thought it better for her that her parents were separated.

Kennedy went back and forth between Ted and me, and life was calm again. That is, until Ted revealed the truth one day, his truth. Kennedy was at school, and I was home alone when Ted came over. We were in the family room. Ted was sitting on a chair in the corner in front of some windows and I was on the sofa.

"I used poor judgment in a couple of investments, Libby, and lost a substantial amount of money." I was looking at the window treatments and thinking we had just spent a hundred and twenty thousand dollars remodeling our home. Things had changed, but I expected my life to stay somewhat the same. I wasn't open to any big surprises.

"All those times I asked you what was going on, you put me off. You let me worry. I begged you to explain things."

"Libby, I didn't want to let you down. I didn't want to let my parents down." Ted said we needed to put our house on the market, whether we were together or not, and so we did.

The weeks after Ted's admission were surreal. The house that we had just spent six months renovating was on the market. Showings were taking place. One potential buyer was someone I knew from Big Spring Country Club. The realtor brought him early and I hadn't left yet; I could tell he felt bad walking through my home. I soon learned that many acquaintances were coming through. It was humiliating, and the hits just kept coming.

Weeks later, Ted informed me that we had to file bankruptcy, complete liquidation. I didn't understand how it had come down to this. Then again, Ted was secretive regarding our finances, *that* door was always shut. It's not an excuse but that's the truth. Ted scheduled a meeting with a bankruptcy attorney. She laid out all the specifics of filing chapter 7. I was there, but my mind wandered. How did we go from picking out counter tops to picking out what items should be declared in the bankruptcy filing? After the advisement, we left in separate cars. I didn't want to talk. I wanted to think.

Time marched on while I staggered through the showings, Ted's vagueness, the fishermen, and worry about Kennedy. She was nine years old, and her whole world was falling apart. There was no way to shield her from the fallout other than to say everything was going to be okay. I wasn't so sure.

Two weeks later, things took a turn from bad to the unreal. It was a Thursday when Ted showed up.

"Libby, I need to speak with you about filing bankruptcy. "

"Okay."

"I think you should file bankruptcy, but not me."

"What?"

"It would…"

"Stop right there! You want me to ruin MY credit and yours remains blemish-free? Get out!" Ted tried to plead his case, but I was having none of it. All I could hear is, "Let's saddle Libby with all the burden!" A fire started within me, and NOTHING Ted said could put it out now. "I don't know what your angle is, Ted, but GO!" Ted was furious. He didn't move, he just stood there staring at me with cold vacant eyes. I felt uneasy. It seemed an eternity though it was just a couple of minutes. After Ted stormed out, I called the attorney I had been talking to since the separation.

He advised me to get my own bankruptcy attorney. I did. I called Ted the next day, because I needed money for groceries. "Get a J-O-B, bitch!!!" (He spelled it out.) Click. I called the attorney.

"You have to assume Ted plans on leaving you homeless."

"You mean the law doesn't require him to provide housing?"

"You can't bleed a turnip, but you can buy yourself some time. You have leverage. The house is solely in your name. Go out there now and pull the sign. Get that house off the market. Foreclosure takes time, but if you sell, you will have nowhere to go and from what it sounds like, Ted doesn't care."

I pulled the sign and called our realtor. The house was off the market. The next day, I was at my friend, Lindy's, house. We had walked in her neighborhood and I stuck around to chat for a while. During our chat, she suggested I check up on Ted at Houston's, his regular watering hole. I had never thought of stalking Ted, but I decided to heed her advice.

I enlisted my friend, Karen. She was a good friend who quickly got on board. I picked her up at her home and drove to Houston's. We spotted Ted's Lexus in the parking lot. Parking in the back corner, my black Land Cruiser was virtually invisible. Karen got out of the car and went on a reconnaissance mission. Running low to the ground in misting rain, she peered in the large glass window. Like a Navy Seal, she went undetected and saw Ted at the bar. For the next three hours, she ran back and forth from window to car with updates as to whether Ted was with another woman. It was now nine o'clock. Two hours later, Ted emerged with the young bartender in tow. I was left open-mouthed. Imagining it a possibility and seeing it as reality were two different things. It had a finality to it and felt like a hand was gripping my insides.

She couldn't have been more than five feet tall and with Ted at 6'4", they looked like the Jolly Green Giant and Sprout. Like a true gentleman, Ted opened the passenger door for Sprout and she hopped right into MY seat. They drove away with Karen and me on their trail. It was a short drive. We pulled into another restaurant. I waited to give them time enough to get settled. My heart raced and perspiration built up on my chest. I couldn't let the moment pass. Entering the double doors, we sat on a bench just inside the vestibule.

I didn't have to see Ted; you could hear him. Plastered, he was loudly telling people about the "for sale" sign. "MY FUCKING BITCH WIFE YANKED THE FOR SALE SIGN OUT OF THE FRONT YARD AND IS GOING TO STALL THE SALE OF MY HOUSE!!!"

His house, I thought?

On and on he went with Sprout by his side swallowing every word. Having had enough, I calmly walked in. I stood at the bar until he stopped ranting and took notice. I introduced myself to Sprout, "I'm Ted's wife." She immediately volunteered, "I'm married!" That was confusing, but I suppose she meant to say because she was married, she and Ted were just friends.

Ted started yelling, "SEE, SEE MY FUCKING BITCH WIFE FOLLOWED US. SHE'S A PSYCHO!" I turned and walked out. I was crying uncontrollably. I never found out if Ted was having an affair with Sprout, but that didn't matter. My marriage was over.

I spent the next day letting the previous night's events sink in. By evening I had calmed down enough to let Ted's father know I was filing for divorce, and why. If I could do it over again, I would never have made that call. Ted's behavior was disturbing, and it concerned me. I didn't want an outraged Ted showing up at the house. Ted's father said he wouldn't pass judgment, but made it clear he sided with his son.

I told him it wasn't about sides it was about Ted's rage. That fell on deaf ears.

Monday morning came and reluctantly I cracked my eyes open. Lying in bed looking at the ceiling, I was thinking my life was about to change forever. I couldn't imagine what lay ahead. Traveler jumped up on the side of my bed to remind me he had not had his breakfast. I got up and filled his bowl and mine. It was a beautiful day and I didn't feel like looking at empty chairs around the table, so I ate outside. The natural stone flooring of our newly created patio was gorgeous. I imagined the new owners were going to enjoy it and the rest of the house for that matter. It was hard to fathom, but everything was gone. Nothing made sense.

I showered and flipped through my clothes to find something suitable. Choosing a black dress, I thought, "It's a funeral after all." Driving downtown with my radio turned up, I tried to drown any thoughts if even for a minute. I walked into Mr. Turnbow's office and waited for him to make an appearance. It didn't take long. Explaining the divorce process to me, he started with his retainer and fee.

"I'm not cheap, but I'm good!"

Nodding, I knew his meter was running. He called Ted's attorney on speakerphone to let him know I was filing for divorce. Ted had spoken with an attorney, too, of course. As Mr. Turnbow waited for the receptionist to patch him through, I felt the back of my legs sticking to the leather chair. I didn't know if I was sweating from apprehension or if it was just hot. Either way, I kept picking them up in a marching fashion to release them.

"Mr. Fine, this is Bob Turnbow. I've got Elizabeth House in my office. She's here to file for divorce from your client, Ted House ......

"Oh, he is? Let me tell Elizabeth. Elizabeth, Mr. Fine has Ted in his office. He's stated Mr. House is there to file for divorce as well."

I knew exactly what had happened. I told Ted's father, who, of course, told Ted, and Ted had wanted to be first.

"Wow," I thought. "It's like a game." Mr. Turnbow had explained that it was $113 dollars to file. If it meant so much for Ted to be the petitioner, so be it. He could win. I needed to save every dime. "Mr. Turnbow, let Ted file, I don't care." He relayed my message to Mr. Fine and it was done. Spending the next hour answering questions to the best of my ability, my attorney said, "Mr. House is going to have to fill out a full disclosure of his assets." I told him I had no confidence that would happen.

"Ted's self-employed, and unfortunately, I was not involved in our finances."

"I see it every day, Elizabeth." That made me feel a bit better even though I didn't trust Ted, and I certainly didn't think he was going to willingly disclose anything financial. Our meeting concluded, Mr. Turnbow and I shook hands. He escorted me to the elevator.

"Thank you, Elizabeth, you'll hear from me by the end of the week."

"Thank you, Mr. Turnbow," and I stepped into the elevator. Maybe it's a cliché but the closing doors seemed symbolic. A chapter of my life was closing, and when the doors opened to the lobby, I felt empowered.

Arriving home, I changed out of my divorce dress. It was spring break, and all my friends were shipping out. Kennedy was leaving, too; Ted was taking her to Naples. Wandering around the house, not really sure what to do with myself, I finally decided to clean out my drawers. "Stay busy, Libby!" my friend would say. "It keeps you going!" Sitting on the floor, I started at the bottom.

Having barely started, Ted roared into the bedroom. I was still sitting Indian style when Ted looked down and spoke.

"LIBBY, THE MONSTER IN ME AND MY JEWISH ATTORNEY ARE GOING TO TEAR YOU APART!" There was no mistaking Ted's declaration of war.

"Did I hear you right? The monster in you and your Jewish attorney are going to tear me apart?" I had heard Ted right, I just wanted to echo his words to see if it registered how disturbing they were. It didn't.

"Why would you want to tear me apart? I don't know where this hateful contempt comes from, but it's sick. Think of your daughter! What do you want from me?" Ted didn't respond at first.

"You're a fucking bitch and that's why I'm divorcing YOU!" He held out some legal papers he had signed with his attorney. They floated down on my head and onto the folded t-shirts. Boasting like a child, he said, "I have to go! I'm going to Florida! Have fun with yourself!" I thought I knew every "Ted" but not this one This one was new. This one was unhinged.

Louisville was a ghost town, and it was a lonely week. Everyone I knew was gone. I missed Kennedy. Rambling through the house thinking of her, I went to her room and organized all her Bratz dolls. I vacuumed and lay on her bed. It tore me up not to be with her on spring break. Things would never be the same for Kennedy, but I hoped they might get better. I didn't belong with Ted anymore, and I hadn't for years. Our relationship wasn't good for Kennedy, and I blame myself for not leaving sooner. Ted and I fought incessantly after bedtime. She was supposed to be asleep, but I know now she could hear us, because she told me. I wished I had handled things in a more mature manner, but in the end, maybe it all would have come out the same. Whereas I had felt empowered when I left the attorney's office, financial dependence and fear eroded my self-confidence.

I tried to keep myself busy. I cleaned closets, watched movies, drank wine and made lists, lots of lists. The longest list was for my attorney, Mr. Turnbow. I had an insane number of questions. Where was I going to live and how? Was Ted responsible for Kennedy and me? Was he required by law to support us? Where was the money coming from if Ted was filing bankruptcy? That was my main worry, the bankruptcy. I had no idea what the next step would be. Everything was a mess, but I took solace in knowing that I had an attorney, Mr. Turnbow, who could sort through the muck. I had no way of knowing how deep it was.

Three weeks after Ted and Kennedy returned from spring break, negotiations commenced between our attorneys. Ted wanted the house back on the market, but my attorney insisted Ted provide Kennedy and me a place to live. Ted's declaration of war, "The monster in me and my Jewish attorney are going to tear you apart," was never far from my mind and caused great anxiety. I suppose I shouldn't have been surprised by all the meanness Ted showed, but I was.

Ted stopped making payments on everything but neglected to inform me. One morning, the phone woke me at 7:00 a.m. It was an overzealous collector calling on behalf of Discover Card.

"Mrs. House, the card is in the name of Elizabeth House, and the Social is...." That was my number.

"Sir, I don't have a Discover Card and haven't applied for one."

"Ma'am, your name is on the account!"

"Can you send me a copy of the application?"

"Well, you will have to call Discover Card. Will you be making a payment today?"

"I just told you I don't have a Discover Card," I insisted and hung up. Calling Discover Card immediately, they confirmed the application in my name had been approved on January 24, 2003. It had been done on-line with no signature required, and Ted had used the card to buy clothes and get cash advances, maybe up to eight thousand dollars. Hanging up, I called my attorney for advice. His appendix had burst, and he was in the hospital. I would have to wait.

Over the next month, I was bombarded by collectors, the phone screamed from sunrise to sundown. It was maddening. One day I received a phone call from our dental office. I loved our dentist, recently having had a lot of work done. The receptionist called about the bill. When I explained about the bankruptcy situation, the once warm and welcoming lady adopted an icy tone. "Bankruptcy! Well, if we're included you won't ever be welcome again in this office."

That was shocking. I felt ashamed. I didn't have much in my bank account, but I thought I could pay them installments. After hanging up I drove to the bank. To my dismay, our bank account had been frozen by the IRS. Ted hadn't paid taxes. His father paid them for him. I made a couple of installments to the dentist with some of the money Earl gave me for food, but was unable to keep up. It may not have been the smartest thing, since we were headed to bankruptcy, but the attempt made me feel better.

That same week, I got a visit from "Linda." The kitchen; designer. I recognized her Jeep in my driveway immediately. By now anyone showing up at my house wanted money; the painters, the lawn company, and presumably, "Linda." I couldn't face her. Her knocks on the door went unanswered. When they ceased, I exhaled. Creeping up to the window to ensure her Jeep was gone, my heart started racing when I realized it wasn't. She appeared at the side door and the knocking began again. I cowardly hid behind the kitchen island she had beautifully designed. Years later while writing this book, I called Chris's Custom Cabinets. Linda still worked there and she definitely remembered Ted and me. I explained the situation and told what I did and why. She graciously accepted my apology. We spent a while on the phone and before we hung up, she said "Make sure you plan for the unexpected when you marry." A little late for me but good advice nonetheless.

Deciding not to talk with anyone collecting debts, I finally disconnected all the phones to get a break. It got so bad that when I did plug a phone in, the call-waiting signal never stopped. I created a list of collectors from the voicemails, but not every collector stated on whose behalf they were calling. I scoured through the mail as well, searching for information.

About a month later, I met Spence. Inviting me to a birthday party with her and her husband, my friend, Karen, left a message a couple of days before the party asking if I minded if we brought Spence. He didn't want to go alone. "Of course not," I replied. When they came to pick me up, Spence was in the car.

The party was down by the Ohio River on a rooftop clubhouse. It was a classy affair, with an open bar and catered food. My weight had plummeted with all the drama swirling around me, so I made sure to load up on the heavy hors d'oeuvres. It was good to get out and have a chance to leave all the troubles behind. I enjoyed myself. Spence tried to engage me in conversation a few times. I was polite, but I wasn't interested. At the end of the night, I was happy to go home and for the first time since the separation, I had a good time in a social situation. I had not been single for a while.

After getting home early, around nine, Spence called. I didn't take the call, but I heard his message. He asked that since it was early, would I be interested in going to Gerstle's, a popular bar with live music in St. Matthew's. Suddenly, like glass shattering, I was back in my world filled with dark, foreboding clouds on the horizon. I quickly got ready for bed, got in my jambos, jumped into bed and pulled the covers up to my chin, just like I might have done when I was little.

A couple of weeks later, I was out with Karen and her husband again. We had dinner and stopped off at Saints, a local bar. As chance would have it, Spence was there, and we had a nice conversation. I apologized for not returning his call and explained that I had been married for a lot of years and wasn't ready to go out with anyone. He was nice about that, understanding. He was in the process of getting divorced as well, so maybe he was sensitive to what I was going through.

Going through my closet to decide which clothes to donate, I heard the side door shut. It was Ted. I tossed the clothes aside and headed to the door. "Libby, I'm here to get some clothes." He walked past me and headed for the bedroom. I didn't say a word. I went to the kitchen searching for a task to keep me busy. Seeing two lonely plates sitting on the counter, I ran them through the dishwasher. Then, I wiped down the counters. I couldn't find anything else to do, so why not confront Ted now and get it over with?

Back in our bedroom, Ted was pulling out plastic sheets filled with large coins. I knew Ted didn't collect coins. They probably had something to do with Sam, one of Ted's shady associates. They looked like old coins in mint condition. They seemed out of place in our house, and they weren't in the safe. I startled him and he quickly shoved them into a duffle bag along with some clothes.

"Ted, YOU opened a Discover card in my name! There's cash advances and charges to Territory Ahead. What the hell is that? Territory Ahead? What are you doing? Why is it in my name?" Ted turned to me with a look somewhere between annoyance and hatred.

"A collection agency is harassing me for payment on this card. You opened this card in MY name and charged thousands of dollars? That's identity theft! How could you do that to me?"

He kept packing clothes from his dresser. I repeated the question. Silence. "What YOU did, Ted, was illegal!" He stopped and glared at me. "Prove it, bitch!"

Mr. Turnbow was right. Ted wasn't going to admit to anything. He started shoving things into the bag now. When he could barely zip it up, he shut the dresser drawer and walked out. I followed to the door.

"Ted, I would never do this to you." He turned around without hesitation, "Why don't you just die!" and slammed the door in my face. Ted might have been happy if I had done just that. I was no longer a person to him, just an irritation.

Mr. Dickerson was very different than the bankruptcy attorney Ted and I met with together. Unlike the big law firm we visited, Mr. Dickerson had a modest office and was a one-man show. He was laid back and friendly. He spoke of one day retiring to Seattle where he would kick back and drink coffee all day. I suppose that was where he was from, but I don't recall.

Stacks of files cluttered Mr. Dickerson's office. After we talked for a bit, he reiterated what I already had learned from the other attorney. The difference was now I was on my own. I told him about the endless calls every day. He instructed me to get the names of every creditor I knew of so I could submit a list.

"It's going to get worse before it gets better. Once you file, it's against the law for them to contact you." Sarcastically I said to myself, "Well, there's the silver lining!" His fee was eight hundred seventy-five dollars. I didn't have a hundred dollars. Earl wrote a check. Mr. Dickerson explained the consequences of filing Chapter 7.

"Your credit will be ruined for a decade."

He talked about what had to be filled out and explained that when everything was complete, I would go to bankruptcy court and stand before a judge. "Like a criminal awaiting sentencing," I said. Half smiling, he continued to advise me. When we were done, he shook my hand, just as Mr. Turnbow had, and sent me on my way. This time I felt a lot less empowered.

I returned home, plugged the phone back in and made sure my list of creditors was complete. The voicemail was full. My cell phone was blowing up now. I don't know how they got my number, but they were bill collectors after all and they were crafty.

Every day I was more and more overwhelmed, and my friends knew it. After I gleaned all I could from the voicemails, I went outside in the backyard. It was late afternoon and I was drained. We never got to furnish the patio, so I lay on top of the stone wall and Traveler lay beside me. The spring sun felt good, and I was almost lulled into a nap when Traveler started barking. He had a deep bark that scared people who didn't know him, so I tried to get him to stop but he wasn't having it and started barking faster. Something was wrong. Before I got down, I felt a shadow over me.

"Ma'am?"

"Oh my god!" I flinched. It was two sheriffs. Traveler was in full bark mode now.

"No! Traveler, lay down." He did but with protest, letting out a few more barks.

"Ma'am, we tried the doorbell but got no answer, so we came around back. We didn't mean to startle you."

"I don't usually lie on my wall," I explained. I didn't know what to say and I knew they weren't interested.

"Are you Mrs. House?"

"Yes, I am."

"Is Mr. Edward House here?"

"No, we are in the middle of a divorce. He doesn't live here anymore." Saying it out loud sounded strange.

"Do you have his address?" I gave it to them. Asking them what it concerned, they politely said the matter concerned Mr. House. They thanked me and apologized for startling me. Peeking around the house as they pulled out of the driveway, I was flashing back to the day the Sheriff came to our home in Bridgepointe. What was going on now?

I didn't want to deal with Ted. I didn't want to deal with anything. Divorce, selling the house, bankruptcy and now a Sheriff's visit, I just wanted away from it all.

I didn't want Kennedy to know about the sheriffs. I'm sure things were stressful enough. Grateful she was at a friend's, I worried the news would get to her. We lived in the first house on the main artery in Indian Hills. Everything was on display. A sheriff's car sitting in the driveway certainly was grapevine material.

The sheriff's visit did raise eyebrows. Running into a neighbor at the Rite-Aid up the street, she asked me if everything was ok. She was sincere. Telling her everything was fine, and not offering more, I acted as if I was receiving a call and left the store.

"Thank you for your concern, I'll see ya later!" I'm sure she was skeptical. I didn't even know myself what was going on, but I knew it wasn't good. I could feel it. The number of collectors calling me intensified, and my cell was ringing as much as the home phone.

A few days later, after the sheriff incident, I was on the phone with my friend Karen. She told me Spence still wanted to go out with me. "It will be fun! The four of us will go, Libster!" I said, "yes," wanting a reprieve from life. She called me later to say that she and her husband would pick me up to go to Spence's for drinks and then on to dinner. Spence lived in a charming Cape Cod. I was impressed how tidy it was for a bachelor, plus he was a great host, very attentive. We all chatted and sipped cocktails until a decision was made for dinner. Feeling human for the first time in a long time, I tied up my cares and worries in a box for the night and just enjoyed myself. Spence was the perfect gentleman. I hadn't been with one of those in a while. He made me feel relaxed and comfortable. Karen was right. It was fun. I was glad I went. It was a nice diversion.

Forgetting to unplug the phone, it screamed at me the next morning. The angry voice was from Huntington Bank. My car was in arrears, and the man demanded the missing payments. Explaining that he needed to speak with my husband, who had leased the car, the man quickly shot back,

"You are Elizabeth House, aren't you?"

"Yes, I am."

"Well, may I remind you when you are the guarantor on a lease, YOU are responsible when the other party defaults on the payments!"

"Sir, I never signed a lease for the SUV." This was a surprise.

"Ma'am, your name is on the paperwork, so if you don't want the vehicle repossessed, you need to make arrangements for payment!"

"I didn't sign any paperwork!" He didn't believe me, so it seemed futile to plead my case. "I'll have to look into the matter, thank you," and I hung up. I was seething. I knew that man was right. I knew my name was on the paperwork, and I knew it was forged. Ted leased all our cars through Alpha Leasing and was tight with Bill Ward, a dealer at the company. Calling, I asked to speak with him, but after a long pause, the receptionist said he was unavailable. I requested a copy of the lease and said I would be by later that afternoon. She asked if I needed it for any particular reason. I replied, "Yes, I need a copy for my records."

I arrived later that afternoon and confirmed what I already knew. Ted had scrawled my name above the guarantor's line. I asked to see Bill Ward, but again he was unavailable. I left a message with the receptionist to have him call or I would call back tomorrow. This time I told the receptionist what I wanted and why, mentioning Bill had approved a lease that had a forged signature on it.

I didn't make it home before Bill Ward called. I didn't mince words. I wanted to know Alpha Leasing's protocol.

"Bill, Huntington Bank is hounding me for payment and threatening to repossess the vehicle. They say I'm the guarantor on the lease. I didn't sign a lease; Ted forged my name!" I could tell he was uncomfortable.

"Do both parties have to sign the paperwork before you drive a car off the lot, Bill?"

"Libby, let's just keep this light."

"That's not an answer Bill. Ted forged my name on the lease, and I want to know if he had to sign the paperwork in your presence?" Bill danced around the question.

I said, "Obviously, you are not going to answer, but no answer is an answer in itself." I hung up.

Inviting me to play tennis one afternoon, Spence offered yet another reprieve from my burning house. I had taken lessons as a beginner the previous summer, so he was on notice there would be more fetching of balls than play. The next week, he invited me to a movie. I went. I started looking forward to the next invitation for all the wrong reasons. I had no business going on dates. I should have stayed focused on the matters at hand, but each time another dark secret came to light, the farther I wanted to run. Unfortunately, I was running in the wrong direction.

It didn't take Ted long to figure out I was seeing Spence. If I thought Ted had been ruthless before, I hadn't seen anything yet. He'd been on vacation down in Naples. He ostensibly called about Kennedy but quickly changed the subject.

"Libby, I hear you're dating some LCC (Louisville County Club), faggot!"

"Ted, my personal life is no longer your business."

"I hear his family owns Falls City Beer. He looks like a turtle and has a goiter on his back. He over-achieved and so have you!" Ridiculous conversation. I hung up on him. I was stunned.

Ted's statements gave more insight into the person I had been married to for so many years. For Ted, it was all about the appearance of a person. Ted was extremely handsome, but he had become ugly on the inside. I questioned if he ever loved me for me, or just for the way I looked.

I was surprised by Ted's vitriol. This was the same guy who left ME! He wanted to tear me apart (with the help of his attorney), and most disturbing, he wished me dead. Why did he care who I was seeing as if I was seeing anyone, anyway? I considered that maybe Ted thought I was trying to make him jealous, or maybe, he was jealous, or maybe he felt slighted or insulted, or maybe some of all these things. I felt I was a possession and now that I was desirable to someone else, his ego was damaged. Maybe that was it. Regardless, he was motivated to harass and belittle me at every opportunity.

There were the days I wished I had pursued counseling. Had I gone I might have seen the pitfalls of getting into a relationship too soon. I might have been wary of the probability of repeating the dynamics of one relationship in the next, or quite possibly becoming involved with someone who shares some personality flaws with the first partner. At any rate, I was somewhere between naïve and selfish. I regret I didn't notice that the pursuit of my own equanimity in these matters could have repercussions in Kennedy's life. Counseling might have made me more self-aware. Spence was showing me kindness, which I had grown unaccustomed to, and it was intoxicating.

Ted showed up at the house one afternoon. I was in the backyard picking weeds. Our house had sold and the new lady-to-be of the manor was angry that weeds were taking over the flowerbeds and lawn. Ted had long since abandoned yard work, and the guys who mowed no longer came. They hadn't been paid in months.

I stood up bracing for impact. Ted was a loose cannon now. I didn't know what to expect. He walked towards me.

"Libby, I left some legal paperwork on the chair in the guest bedroom."

"What kind of paperwork and when were you here? I don't understand. Why didn't you call me? Why would you leave paperwork in the back bedroom and not in the kitchen? I would never see it in the guest room."

"Libby, that's where I left it, does it matter? I want to go over it with you. Will you go get it?" I raised both hands in confusion. I wasn't in the mood to try and figure out illogical Ted. I went to fetch the mystery paperwork. It didn't make sense. Mr. Turnbow would have called concerning any legal matters.

There was no paperwork that I could see. I searched around, under and behind the chair. No paperwork. Nothing. I walked back down the long hall to tell Ted the mystery paperwork had mysteriously disappeared. When I opened the back door, Ted had mysteriously disappeared as well. I walked around to the driveway and my SUV was gone; in it its place sat an old white mini-van with gold hubcaps.

All my belongings from the car were strewn across the front lawn. He had made the whole "paperwork in the guest bedroom" story up. It was a ploy to give him time to empty out my car. I was horrified. I picked up everything, while making sure I made no contact with the passersby. Ted was showing a much darker side of himself. I wondered if he had lost sight of the fact that I was the mother of his child and that she, too, would be riding around in this van.

"Libby, how ya like your new *whigger mobile?*" Ted was calling from a party at Big Spring. It felt like I could smell the liquor on his breath.

"We're up here at the club, laughing how I got ya the gold package." He was so proud of himself.

"That's what you're doing, Ted? Telling your friends how you tricked me and threw my stuff out on the lawn? How you left your daughter and me the *whigger mobile* to drive around town? Disgusting term Ted! I'm glad you and your friends, who used to be my friends, too, find this all so amusing. Don't call again, understand?" Click!

CHAPTER 9

I kept Earl in the dark regarding what really was going on between Ted and me, other than that Ted had lost all our money and we were getting divorced. I shielded Earl from the truth. He was old and I knew if he got wind of Ted's abusive behavior, he would have felt frustrated and helpless. A young Earl would have confronted Ted.

Earl couldn't drive any longer. He now negotiated his whereabouts with a four-prong cane. The younger Earl was the type of man who would get in his car, find Ted and have a "conversation." I can only imagine how that might have gone. It didn't matter how much Earl loved Ted, and Earl did love Ted, what mattered was Ted's abusive behavior and that would cancel out any love Earl felt for him.

When I was a sophomore in high school, I wanted to get a long sleeve Panama Jack t-shirt. It was Christmas vacation and we were in Florida, so I asked Earl if he would take me to a shop on the A1A to get one.

"Libbah, who is Panama Jack?" Earl asked.

"I don't know," I replied.

"Well if you don't know, why do you want him on your shirt?"

"Dad, it's the style and it's cool!" Honestly, all I knew about Panama Jack was that he wore a pith helmet, a monocle and a safari jacket. I also knew I *had* to have him on my long sleeve tee.

"Please Dad, I really want one."

"Alright, Libbah, let's get on it now so we have time to get ready for dinner."

I was super excited. We drove down the scenic A1A, passing all the shops and hotels looking out on the Atlantic. A bright sunny day, tall palm trees swaying in the sea breeze, I could smell salt in the air.

We parked across the street and Earl handed me twenty dollars.

"Libbah, go get your shirt and do it in a hurry, ya hear?

"Thanks, Dad," and I disappeared into the shop.

I sifted through the inventory searching for the perfect shirt. They had some spectacular OP (Ocean Pacific) bathing suits. I wanted one of those, too, but I wouldn't press my luck. I found a pink Panama Jack shirt with his name written down the arm, and I was thrilled. They even air-brushed my name on it!

'This shirt looks great with my tan!' I thought. I paid and started back to the car. Waiting for a break in the traffic, a man, probably in his thirties, approached me. He had dark hair, wore a sleeveless muscle t-shirt and tattered old jeans. His eyes couldn't be seen behind mirrored sunglasses.

"Hey, baby, what's your name?" I was uncomfortable, so I didn't respond. "Baby, why don't you come around the corner and I'll show you what a real man can do!"

I ran across the road and dove into Earl's Bonneville. Sensing something was wrong he asked me, "What's the problem Libbah?" With some embarrassment I told Earl what the man had said. Earl put on the brakes and backed into his parking space, asking me to point out the man. He was leaning up against the side of a building.

"What are you going to do, Dad?"

"Libbah, you stay here and keep the doors locked, we're going to have a 'conversation!'"

Earl was in his sixties and I was afraid for him. I needn't be. I slid over to the driver's seat to get a better view and watched as Earl walked directly towards the man and clamped his giant hand around the man's neck. I don't know what Earl said, but I'm guessing it wasn't a cordial conversation; the man looked terrified. After a quick exchange, Earl knocked the man's head against the brick wall a couple times for good measure. I was shocked. He came back across A1A and got in the car and we drove away.

"Libbah, he was a bad man!" That's it. That's all Earl said. I knew Earl was not one to mess around with in his younger days – I had heard the stories – but now I knew he still had it. I tuned in the radio and rolled down my window like Earl and enjoyed a peaceful drive back to our hotel. I didn't know which was cooler, my new long-sleeved tee or that my dad taught the "bad man" a lesson.

Bankruptcy, divorce, Kennedy; all were problematic. The more I felt burned, the more I turned to Spence. The minute I came through the back gate to Spence's, I felt like I was in a different world. Some nights when Kennedy was with Ted, we sat out on his patio and talked, listened to music, and had drinks. Spence was fun and we had the silliest conversations. He was carefree and enjoyed life to the fullest. I didn't know anyone as carefree as he was. As we grew closer, Ted grew angrier. He started calling at all hours of the night, over and over and over. I didn't answer. He came and went as he pleased, so it wasn't uncommon for him to eavesdrop on my phone conversations. When caught, he would mock me, "Spence is sooooo nice! Spence really listens to what I have to say!" Ted made up a rumor that I was engaged. A fisherman congratulated me, and I set her straight. I wasn't engaged. This went on for months. If Ted found out I was going out with Spence, he sometimes dropped Kennedy off at the house and left her on her own. She was ten. She would call and I would come home. Never angry about leaving where I was, I was angry Ted used her as a pawn. I started to ignore Ted, rather than fight back. That made matters worse.

Late one summer night I was sitting on the back steps, talking on the phone with Spence. Kennedy was in Indiana visiting Ted's parents. In mid conversation, I saw a figure step out from behind a large oak tree. Paralyzed with fear, I saw it was Ted. Spence asked over the phone,

"What's going on Libby?"

I told him. I also told Ted he needed to leave, but sometimes there was no reasoning with him. He lunged at me and tried to grab the phone. I resisted and he wrestled me to the ground, cutting my hand. Spence heard the commotion and called the police. Indian Hills has their own force, so two officers were at the house in minutes. After assessing the situation, one officer took me to the guest bedroom.

"Ma'am, you can press charges."

"Oh no, it's not a big cut, I just want him to leave."

"Are you sure, Ma'am?"

"Yes, I'm sure." They made Ted leave, but it didn't stop anything. It only fueled an already burning temper.

When our house sold, I was relieved. The showings stopped and I could finally breathe. By then, my friend Lindy and I had found a condo that would take Traveler. Although very tiny for the three of us, Traveler, Kennedy and me, it was only two minutes from our old house, so I wasn't moving Kennedy across town. Rumors swirled about the condo. People thought it was purchased for me. One guy I knew remarked,

"Libby, at least you got a condo in a great area. It will only go up in value!"

"No, it's not mine. I have to be out in two years."

"What?" I got a look of disbelief. "You've been married all these years and it's not yours? What are you supposed to do after two years?"

"I don't know. Ted didn't buy it, his parents did. It's theirs."

"What about the money you'll get from the house?"

"There won't be any money, it was mortgaged to the hilt."

"What? Where did all the money go? What about Belterra? What about Ted's mortgage company?"

"I don't know. I didn't handle our finances. Ted is bankrupt and I have to file bankruptcy, too." This guy was a banker, so he knew what I was facing.

"Libby! Your credit will be ruined for years. How does Ted think you are going to live two years from now?"

"He doesn't seem to care."

"Libby, you all have a daughter."

"I know, but he says he can't give what he doesn't have. My lawyer says I'm lucky to get the two years. He told me I could be homeless."

"That's pathetic. I have zero respect for Ted." The sooner I moved the better. I hated there was so much upheaval for Kennedy, but there was nothing I could do. I wanted to get out of the house. It was no longer a home.

I questioned Mr. Turnbow, my divorce attorney, regarding alimony, and he said Ted showed no income or property, so there would be none. The next question was regarding child support for Kennedy. According to the Agreed Order, Ted was to pay three hundred dollars per week. Also, according to the order, Ted and I shared custody. Kennedy spent Monday and Thursday nights with me, and Tuesday and Wednesday nights with Ted and alternating weekends with each parent. I thought this was better for Kennedy, because every other weekend I would have her Thursday night through Monday night. Kennedy needed stability and structure in her life, and I felt Ted's lifestyle was not particularly stable or structured. There were some other things of interest in the order. Ted would pay for Kennedy's health insurance and my insurance for two years. Ted agreed to pay for Kennedy's tuition and related school expenses at the de Paul School. I would have the use of a condo owned by Ted's parents for two years. If I married, I'd lose the healthcare benefit and the use of the condo.

Ted paid the child support for a year and then stopped paying. Ted had a key and came and went as he pleased, going through my drawers and belongings, pretty much to let me know that he could still trespass in my life. On the disclosure statement, Ted showed no income, and the equity in the properties he showed was applied to debts. The question in my mind, then and now, is how was Ted able to fulfill the financial responsibilities of the order with no income or assets, but had nothing for alimony? I had a sixth sense about the way Ted operated, and everything about the order rubbed me the wrong way. Ted continued to live in the manner and lifestyle to which he was accustomed, most likely with financial support from his family, whereas according to the order, in two years I could be on the street.

That all felt terribly wrong and left me feeling frustrated, belittled and emphatically angry.

I moved out of the house in stages. Ted provided no money for moving, so friends helped out, even storing furniture I couldn't fit into the condo. Another friend found some guys who moved the heaviest items for next to nothing. The day they arrived it was ninety-five degrees. Everyone was in a bad mood; hot, humid Kentucky air has a way of doing that to a person. I was mentally exhausted and wanted the house ordeal over. Ted decided that wasn't going to happen. In the basement, I was measuring the washer and dryer. I wanted to see if they would fit through the basement door.

"Libby! What are you doing?" Ted roared. "I'm measuring the washer and dryer?"

"Why?"

"I'm having them moved today."

"No, you're not!"

"Ted, how do you expect me to do laundry?"

"That's your fucking problem!"

"Ted, I don't have money to buy a washer and dryer!"

"Bitch, like I said before: Get a J-O-B!"

"That's nice Ted! You're filing bankruptcy, can't give me money, but you keep up with the Country Club payments! Let me tell you this, too; I *know* you drained Kennedy's savings account! That was hers and you didn't put in one red cent! Every dime came from my family! I never gave a second thought to you being the custodian on her account because I trusted YOU!"

Ted shut his eyes. He always shut his eyes when he was lying or not liking what I said. I walked up the stairs and continued to focus on moving.

"You're NOT taking the washer and dryer!" He shouted. I ignored him and kept moving. I had piled quite a few boxes outside. I wanted the movers to get in and get out. When the truck pulled in the driveway, I was outside and ready to direct them. "Hi, I'm Libby House! Would y'all like a bottle of water?" They gladly accepted.

"I've got a washer and dryer in the basement. I think they're going to be the most challenging."

I went into the garage to get a couple of bottled waters, and when I returned, the police were in the driveway. I looked towards our side door and Ted was blocking the entrance. Ted walked towards the police and started explaining that I was removing items from the house before we had a formal divorce agreement. This was true. I never even thought about having a conversation with Ted about the washer and dryer. He lived in *The Commodore*, a luxury condominium community that had its own laundry center. He didn't need them. He just wanted to make my life miserable. It was working. Once the police got involved, the movers bailed. They told me they were sorry, but didn't want to get involved in a domestic dispute. I didn't blame them. Ted got his way. Two days later, he let me have the washer and dryer.

It seemed I had a double life; the one where I was divorcing Ted, and the one I spent on Spence's patio. Spence's home had previously been owned by a landscape artist, so the back yard was beautifully designed. It had clever lighting that was sunk in the ground and shone upwards. There were benches set in decorative concrete amid perennials, day lilies, hydrangea, black-eyed susans, lilies, aster, catmint and ornamental grasses. Spence also always had candles lit everywhere. It was an idyll, a harbor, a haven that I sought refuge in. It was seductive and it was easy to escape there and leave my other world of divorce and bankruptcy behind.

Spence and I were becoming extremely close. It was easy to perceive the nice things Spence did as negating the wicked things that came from Ted. I was willing to grab the hand of someone to pull me out of the chaos, or so I thought. Regardless, that was the story I was scripting.

Spence was pouring some wine, when I got a call from a friend. She didn't get two words out before I heard call-waiting. I told my friend to hold on and clicked over without thinking. It was the man from Huntington Bank looking to repossess my SUV. I told him about the "whigger mobile" and what had happened to the SUV, but he didn't believe me.

"Ms. House, it is illegal to hide a car!"

"Mr. Huntington Bank Man," I took a tone with him, "I don't have the car. My husband tricked me and took it! You are welcome to come see the mini-van he replaced it with!"

"Ms. House, since we are unable to contact Mr. House, it is your responsibility as the guarantor!"

"I'm NOT the guarantor! I have a copy of the lease. My husband forged my name!"

"We go by what's on the paperwork, Ms. House!"

"Well, why don't you go by *MR. HOUSE'S* condominium? It has a parking garage, where it's more likely you will *FIND* the vehicle!" I told him I was hanging up and not to call me anymore, and I did. He called every day, twice a day for a week before finally stopping. I never knew what happened to my SUV. I don't know if it was repossessed or if Ted surrendered it voluntarily. Either way, it was gone and so was Mr. Huntington Bank Man, one less person harassing me.

Camp Piomingo was about thirty minutes away. I signed Kennedy up for the equestrian program, with money Earl gave me. This was her first time at an overnight camp. She was excited. I was hoping it also might offer relief from the earthquake in her life. I still had loose ends to tie up at the house and didn't want her to witness any more drama. Ted and I both went to get her settled. I did it for Kennedy's sake. Once I returned home, I surveyed the house, checking drawers and tidying up for the new owners. I turned on the countertop radio and got to work. It was strange to think this was the last time I would be cleaning the house. I started to vacuum.

I vacuumed the whole house with the exception of the kitchen. I unplugged the cord and dragged the vacuum behind me. I was shocked to find Ted sitting at the kitchen table.

"Libby, I need to talk to you."

"What could you possibly want to 'talk' to me about?"

"Libby, I love you! I don't want a divorce." My body felt heavy.

"I've called my attorney and called the divorce off!"

"You've called the divorce off?"

"I never wanted a divorce; I called your bluff and now you're calling mine!"

"Are you trying to tell me this was all a game? For what, to teach me a lesson? Everything you've done and said, and now you've simply decided, without notifying me, that you've called your attorney and called the divorce off! I wasn't trying to call your bluff! You treated me so badly and you were with another woman! I've had enough!"

"Libby, I never cheated on you!"

"I don't care, I saw enough!"

"Libby, just give me a chance to show how much I love you! I don't want to tear our family apart!"

"Oh, I've seen how you show your love!"

"Libby, I'm a new man!"

"Ted, I don't trust you. I don't want to talk about this anymore!"

Ted was getting desperate.

"Libby, I do love you!" and with that he started towards me with out-stretched arms. I walked around the table still pulling the vacuum. He followed me until I had made a complete circle.

"Ted, this is ridiculous! You can't just walk in here and expect me to forget everything and run into your arms! And what about Kennedy? What about the damage that's been done to her?"

"I know, Libby, I want to fix this, I want another chance!"

"Ted you have to go, or I will!"

"Libby, if you stay with me, my parents are going to buy us a house."

"Your parents are going to buy us a house? And what? Everything's wiped away, clean slate?"

"Libby, they want to help us!"

"I don't want to talk about this anymore. Do I have to leave or are you?"

"I'll go Libby, but I wrote this letter for you to read. It better expresses my feelings. I'm going to stick it up in the cabinet."

I didn't say anything, and he left. I couldn't wrap my head around him saying, "I called your bluff and now you're calling mine." To him it was like a game. I grabbed a cigarette to calm my nerves and a leftover beer from the fridge and went outside. I would have preferred bourbon, but I'd already packed up all the booze. I stared at the lightning bugs.

"What a mess!" I thought. "God only knows what Ted is up to next."

I never considered going back to Ted. The trust was gone and I had stayed in the abusive relationship far too long. It was two weeks before I read Ted's letter and he knew it, too, because he came by the house to find it unopened a week later. When I did read it, I didn't feel anything. I felt Spence's interest in me was the reason for Ted's change of heart. I thought Ted just wanted his possession back because another guy had taken an interest. Ted told me countless times how worthless I was, and I couldn't help but remember that with every line I read.

"If I do go down, I'm taking you with me!" Ted yelled out the window as he plowed through our side yard in his SUV. My car was parked behind his so rather than wait for me to move, he was going cross-country. Peeling off down the road, he yelled, "You're a co-conspirator, Libby!" Standing in the driveway, my worst fears that had been shadowy forms took shape. Ted was talking about mortgage fraud and that somehow, I was to be implicated.

My hands trembled and sweat was running down my back. We lived in a fishbowl. No. 1 Indian Hills Trail was the first house on the main artery of the neighborhood. Once you stepped outside, you were on display. Under most circumstances, I wouldn't have trailed Ted outside. Making a spectacle of myself in front of passersby was something I normally would never do. I cared what my neighbors thought.

Today was different. I had just learned that Ted had committed fraud and was in serious trouble with the FBI. Today he had come over unexpectedly. We were in the middle of an ugly divorce. He frantically searched the house for something though he didn't tell me what.

"Ted, what have you done? Answer me!" He looked anywhere but at me as he continued going through the drawers of his desk.

"STOP! I want to know the truth You owe ME the truth!" He snatched some paperwork from his desk, looked at me and coldly said, "I don't owe you anything, bitch!"

I was no longer ignoring rumblings about Ted and his nefarious acts; he had dragged me in! I stood outside in my powder blue pajamas in disbelief. In the past, I had seen much of Ted's anger, but nothing like this. His searing gaze, his eyes aflame, and the words, "If I go down, I'm taking you with me!" meant that I was implicated. He said those words with such conviction. I didn't know what he had done, but I believed he would try to take me down with him.

I called Spence, who immediately called Kendall, a lawyer acquaintance. Kendall worked with a well-known criminal defense attorney, Sean Pierce, who was privy to the case. I recognized Sean as a member of Big Spring, but we didn't know each other socially. Two days later, Sean called Karen and instructed her to have me call him from her home. I did just that. He told me I needed to cooperate with the FBI or I could be prosecuted. The hair on the back of my neck stood up as he was speaking. He went on to say we would be meeting with the FBI in a few days and gave me the time and his office address. Just like that, it was confirmed that my husband was under investigation. I talked with Karen a bit and then left for my favorite spot to think when I was worried about being disturbed at home.

I drove down to the Ohio River. There's a path through some rugged terrain to a log where I sat for hours. I watched the moving water, the clouds ambling across the sky, and thought about all that had happened. How did I get involved, and how had I been so blind to the events that were engulfing me now? I couldn't understand how Ted, with so many advantages and so much family and business support, became involved in criminal activity. Why? Nothing made sense. It seemed surreal, but there was no denying it. What was going to happen to Kennedy and me? How would we make it?

The day arrived to speak with the FBI. That was a black day, full of emotion. I was sad and consumed by rage at the same time. Ted, the man I married who promised to love me, didn't care about me at all. Why did he want me to suffer for his sins? All the lies, the complete disregard for our family and, most disturbing, his willingness, if not pleasure, in implicating me as part of his schemes, started to make sense. All those questions he answered with vagueness, the 3:00 am awakenings, Khalid, sheriff visits, and screaming at whoever Jerry was, fit a pattern of his behavior as the net closed. I had no idea how everything fit together, but now things were coming into focus.

One thing I did know was Ted hadn't broken ties with Khalid. I recently had gone through months of cell phone bills that showed Ted and Khalid were in constant communication. Another lie. "Unsavory Khalid," who might kill us, so said Ted, was really his partner in mortgage fraud, along with Nathan Frisbie, his business partner, and Jerry Crenshaw, the mystery man Ted raged at outside my bedroom window.

I met Sean at his downtown office. I felt beads of sweat forming on my chest. Anxiety had plagued me for months, but today it felt as if I might be wrestled to the ground. Sean took me to lunch before going to the U.S. Attorney's office. We walked to a close restaurant busy with the lunch crowd. We sat in a booth amongst suits and ties, women in business attire, the clanging of plates, clinking glasses, tables being bussed and orders served. Everywhere patrons laughing, talking, eating and drinking, and I imagined returning to normal jobs and lives after lunch. My afternoon was anything but normal. I was going to speak with the FBI. All the sounds and sights were magnified. My senses intensified, and it was impossible to ignore what was going on around me. I tried to focus on what Sean was saying and made my best effort to stay composed. My dark dress absorbed beads of sweat that continued to form as we talked. Sean was kind and tried to put me at ease. It was futile. I was terrified.

On the drive to the U.S. Attorney's office, Sean explained his decision to become a criminal defense attorney. Ironically, he had been an assistant U.S. Attorney and gained national attention for his role in prosecuting Mel Ignatow, the man from Louisville who brutally raped and murdered his girlfriend with the help of an old girlfriend. The story went national and was featured on the *American Justice* TV show.

My mind wandered again as Sean told me about the transition from prosecuting on behalf of the government to representing for the defense. I thought about the statement, "Life can turn on a dime," which I knew to be true from past experiences, but never to this magnitude. Ted had betrayed me in so many ways, but this cut me to my core. His words, "If I go down, I'm taking you with me!" and calling me a co-conspirator as he cackled and drove off played over and over in my mind. The more it played, the angrier I became.

I walked through the thick glass door Sean held open, felt as though I was walking into the abyss. To my right were two policemen standing by a metal detector. I pulled off my sunglasses and handed over a small purse. As the policemen ran the metal detector over my body, I stared at a portrait of President Bush hanging in front of me.

I thought, "If they pat me down, my secretly sweating body will be revealed." Sean was calm and collected and looked it, too, in a blue and white seersucker suit. We were a study in contrasts. "Ma'am, you can collect your belongings."

I followed Sean through a bank of doors into the main lobby. The air conditioning blowing from above, normally unwelcome, was a relief. My body temperature must be in the fever range, I thought. We were met by an agent who shook hands with Sean and introduced himself as Rick Spears. I was surprised how much he fit my image of an FBI agent: tall and fit with a serious looking face. He led us into a conference room where two other agents were already seated at a long table. I asked if I could use the ladies' room as if I might be told "No." Once the bathroom door closed behind me, I went straight to the mirror.

"Libby, get it together! Don't break down, stay composed!" I ran cold water over my wrists to cool off. After recess, my third-grade teacher had once told me that running water over your wrists cools the whole body and, for some reason, I remembered.

I wish I could remember the conversation with Agent Spears after I returned, but I can't. I was on autopilot getting through the moment. I only remember snippets. Embarrassingly, I remember I had the letter Ted wrote me begging to stay together. I thought the part where he acknowledged I knew nothing of his business practices could be important in proving my innocence. I felt like an idiot handing over a love letter, but I was scared. We had a daughter, and the thought of being accused of participating in a crime made me sick to my stomach. Agent Spears said it appeared that nothing I knew was earth shattering and dismissed me by saying, "Mrs. House, we believe the only thing you are guilty of is trusting your husband." I was guilty.

The day finally arrived for the new owners to take possession of our home. Even though I had moved out, the closing was yet another reminder of what had been lost, not just the house but all those memories; the unraveling of our marriage, the bankruptcies, and Kennedy's loss of a mother and father living together. I arrived wishing I could be there by proxy. I didn't want to make small talk. I wanted to sign the papers and get out.

The new owner was aware of our situation but was hardly gracious. My realtor had told me that she, a realtor herself, was unhappy the weeds had taken over the flowerbeds, and pointed out the property was supposed to be in the same condition as when she and her husband bought the house. She had suggested to my realtor that I recruit family members to pull them. I had a suggestion of my own concerning where to put the weeds after they were pulled, but I kept that to myself. Her first offer wanted inclusion of the lighting fixtures. I declined. She was smart and knew her business; some of the fixtures were quality, expensive and added value to the house. Her next offer wanted inclusion of the furnishings, much of which had belonged to my grandparents. I declined again.

I knew the buyers were right, that the house and grounds were to be kept up through the closing. But things were just not sitting that well with me. Now the complaint concerning the weeds felt like insult added to injury. I came to the closing angry, hardly in the mood to engage in small talk. Ted was his usual charming self and chatty, while I responded with one-word answers.

I should have let it roll right off my back. It was humiliating to sit at the closing while the buyers assumed the liens and unpaid taxes on the house.

"Well, at least the kitchen designer from Chris's Custom Cabinets got paid," I thought. When the endless signing of paperwork concluded,

CHAPTER 9

a check for the proceeds from the house was presented, three thousand, three hundred sixty-five collars, after they had paid almost a million. I walked out of the closing with the same feeling I had when I stood before the bankruptcy judge, totally depleted. The house had been in my name, so the check was made out to me. Ted followed me out and I endorsed the check in the parking lot. Ted had put the house in my name only, so if he got sued (imagine that) they wouldn't be able to attach the house. Technically, it was my money. I assumed we were going to split the thirty-three hundred sixty-five dollars and thirty-nine cents, but Ted snatched the check and sprinted as fast as he could to the next parking lot as if I might give chase. He jumped in his car and sped off. I presumed to cash the check, I got in the van that Ted had carefully selected for me. I never saw a dime of that money.

CHAPTER 10

Traveler and I drove in a caravan to Waynesburg for Christmas dinner. Kennedy was spending Christmas in Naples with Ted and his family. That was the hardest part of the divorce, having to split time with Kennedy, especially over the holidays. Ted fought hard to have a week on/week off schedule, but I wouldn't have it. I didn't want to go a whole week without Kennedy. For Ted, it was about the money. I didn't trust Ted, either. Kennedy had gotten the flu while she was with him earlier in the year. Calling constantly to check on her, I found out he had left her home alone. A friend of mine knew Kennedy was very sick, and when she saw Ted at around eleven o'clock at Brendon's, a neighborhood Irish pub, she called me. Seeing her, Ted raced back to the house he was renting. I was already en route. Ted claimed he was not at the bar even after I told him my friend saw him. He lied without hesitation, but then again, he always had. Kennedy was ten.

We followed my sister and her family down Highway 127 towards the tiny place where so many unhappy memories lay buried. I didn't like going, but I did it out of obligation. We no longer were going to the old farmhouse, but to what used to be my Aunt Flossy's home. My grandparents, Sweetie and Paul, had moved into her house after she died. My Uncle Eugene moved into theirs. By then Paul had added indoor plumbing.

Aunt Flossy's house also had a bathroom. When Beal and Sweetie took my sister and me to her house when we were little, I used her bathroom over and over in hopes that if I went enough, I wouldn't have to use the dreaded outhouse. That never worked.

I pulled into the driveway with Traveler hanging his big head out the back window. We entered through an unheated side porch where Sweetie kept her confections. She made the most wonderful candy. I can still taste her assortment on an antique metal tray: white chocolate with walnuts, peanut brittle, all kinds of fudge and my favorite, chocolates with a vanilla cream filling. She topped each of them off with a pecan. I liked Sweetie's sweets. I liked all of Sweetie's cooking. Too bad Sweetie didn't like me.

Sweetie gave me a half hug and wished me a Merry Christmas while Traveler received a hearty pat. Sweetie loved animals. Chico, the chihuahua I aggravated as a child, had long since died. Sweetie now doted on a cat which only ate vegetable soup. Heading straight to the living room, I sat next to Earl. We were crammed in pretty good. There wasn't nearly the room that Sweetie had in her old house, but this one had central heating and air in addition to the indoor commode. The old farmhouse had a giant coal stove for heat and no air conditioning, which is why they moved into Aunt Flossy's after she died. I remember waiting for Paul to pour coal in, so I could stand in front of the heating vent. I loved his metal coal bucket for some reason. Its shape reminded me of Beal's gravy boat.

Sweetie and Aunt Flossy had a giant loom and they wove all kinds of things: beautiful wedding quilts, covers for Kleenex boxes and the colorful afghans that hugged both chairs in the living room and the two in what we called "The Two Man Room." We called it "The Two Man Room" because there was only room for two chairs. It was actually a tiny foyer converted into a TV room. There were two cloth-covered recliners and a TV that sat on an old metal food tray. Before Paul died, he and my Uncle sat in "The Two Man Room" watching old reruns of

The Dukes of Hazard, only coming out for dinner and gifts. I felt like an intruder just like I had when I was young.

This particular year, there was a guest. It was my uncle's mother-in-law. Marrying a woman also named Beal, I quickly named my uncle's new bride "Other Beal." I didn't like Other Beal. Other Beal came every Christmas equipped with a video camera. She was always telling my sister and me, "Git! Git out of the way," because we were blocking her view. Other Beal was all about Sweetie. Videotaping Sweetie, talking like Sweetie, trying to cook like Sweetie and finally dying her light hair black just like Sweetie's. I got that made-for-TV movie feeling around her. I imagined one day we would show up for Christmas, Sweetie would be gone, and Other Beal would act as if nothing was wrong. Later we'd find Sweetie stuffed into a bin in the cellar.

Other Beal introduced her mother-in-law, and I just couldn't believe it! She was elegant with stylish snow-white hair and her purple suit with scallop trim looked like something straight out of the Jackie Kennedy era. All she needed was a matching pillbox hat. Other Beal certainly didn't inherit her mother's taste in apparel. She favored loud prints and theme sweaters.

"Everybody, supper's ready," real Beal announced. Although I wanted the coveted seat next to Earl, I got sandwiched between Other Beal and her mother. Everyone wanted that seat next to Earl. Earl was funny and entertaining. Beal morphed into her country girl persona, talking little girl talk, "Mother, Daddy..." in a high-pitched tone.

Last Christmas, Other Beal told me, "Libby, I had my daughter at fifteen and it was really neat. We grew up together like sisters."

"Yes, I'm sure that was neat," I responded, not sure where this conversation was going. This time she told me she made Sweetie's dressing to go with the turkey. Sweetie was older now and surely needing a helping hand, so I was hoping Sweetie had supervised the preparation because her dressing was my favorite part of the meal. Beal offered to say the prayer, and I shot my sister, Virginia a look across the table. She glared at me but quickly looked away, so she wouldn't start laughing. Beal loved to hear herself talk and saying the prayer was like being on stage. Once that mic was in her hand, she had a captive audience.

The joking all started one Thanksgiving when we were teenagers. Beal started a prayer with, "Let's all think back to the first Thanksgiving. Let's think about the harvest. Let's think about the Pilgrims," and she went on and on until one of my smart-aleck nieces said, "Let's think about wrapping it up and eating!" I got so tickled I started laughing and it soon became contagious, so most of us were shaking trying to compose ourselves. Beal was *not* amused. Every Thanksgiving Day prayer after that she ignited the same reaction, so much so we were reprimanded even before the prayer began. This Christmas was no different, except we were in Waynesburg where humor was not appreciated.

Beal wrapped it up and everyone began filling their plates. I was ready for some dressing, it being my absolute favorite. Loading up my fork with a generous bite, I dug in, dug in with gusto… It was awful, just awful! Secretly spitting the hard, greasy lump into my napkin, dammit, I was mad! I looked forward to Sweetie's dressing. Virginia had a similar reaction. I stared at her while she took her first bite, and she looked at me horrified, opening her mouth like a kid who wants to play the "Do you want some seafood?" game. I retreated to the bathroom to compose myself. I sat on the commode and took my shoe off so I could feel the wavy peaks in the carpet I remembered from my childhood. Returning to my seat, I noticed Traveler circling the table looking for handouts. Earl gave "Big Dog" a bite of country ham. I thanked him on Traveler's behalf.

"Libbah, I don't think Big Dog is satisfied," he said laughingly. "He keeps raking his paw across my hand!"

"He knows who's gonna give him the goods!" I replied. That's how the conversation shifted to dogs. Beal started a non-compelling story about her dog, Rosie, when Other Beal's mother suddenly blurted out, "Shot me a dog once! I was sitting on my front porch in my La-Z-Boy with my dog, Shadow, and my neighbor's dog kept worrying mine all the time. One night I just pulled out my pistol and shot that dog dead." She paused, looking around the table for approval.

"Called Jackie the next day to get the carcass." I had so many questions. Why did she have a La-Z-Boy on the front porch? Who was this Jackie? And why was Other Beal's mother packing?

She took a sip of sweet tea and went back to eating in her sweet purple suit. Stunned, I asked if the neighbor's dog was attacking her dog.

"No, he was just worrying mine!" In Waynesburg "worrying" meant bothering. I was accused of "worrying" a lot in Waynesburg. I'm glad I wasn't a dog. Virginia and I locked eyes, and I couldn't take it. I started shaking in my seat, trying to control my laughter. Virginia was doing the same, her elbows flapping like wings. I egged her on, making a gun out of my thumb and index finger. Real Beal was giving me "the eye," and I know Earl wanted to laugh but instead just hung his head. It was too much. I finally got up and went into the kitchen, turned the water on and let out a big hee haw laugh.

When I returned, I paid close attention to Traveler for the rest of the day. I didn't want him "worrying" anybody; I wasn't taking chances. Traveler never made it down to Waynesburg again.

Spence and I kept dating despite the constant drama. I came to rely on his emotional support and the lifelines he threw when the crisis of the week occurred. Whether it was moving the groceries to his refrigerator when the power was shut off, rescuing me when the van broke down, or the various other debacles that presented themselves, Spence was there. It was all too easy to convince myself I was in love. In reality, I was infatuated with Spence, but I couldn't see that. All I could see was a man eager to rescue me when trouble came knocking.

I married Spence a year and half after meeting him. Unhealed and traumatized, I convinced myself a relationship with Spence was going to make up for everything I didn't get from Ted, even though all indications pointed otherwise. I wasn't yet divorced from Ted emotionally. You can't build a relationship on hurts from the past. I hadn't learned that yet, and I was to learn that marriage to Spence was not the answer.

We had obstacles from the start. Spence had given his first wife primary custody of their children, and the day after their divorce was final, she married and informed him she was moving six hours away. He was crushed.

Meanwhile, Ted's situation with the investigators hung in the balance and weighed heavily on my mind. Naively I thought the situation would be resolved one way or the other not long after my interview with the FBI. I was wrong. It dragged on for two years, during which time Ted taunted me, "Libby, we all know you spoke with the FBI!" I knew he was trying to intimidate me with the "we." I didn't know if he did know I had spoken with the FBI or was trying to squeeze it out of me. Either way I didn't crack. It was disturbing that Ted still only cared about himself and had no remorse for attempting to terrorize me. It would take years for me to accept that there would be no epiphany. What's worse, his anger seemed to ignite spontaneously. One time, Ted became so enraged he tried to keep me in a closet and threatened to have Khalid rape me while he watched, or in Ted's words, "I'll get that big black motherfucker to rape you while I watch!" It was sickening.

Rarely did a day go by without me wondering when it would all be over. I worried how Kennedy was being affected. Mired in the Ted situation and never fully present in my marriage, the veneer was wearing off quickly. One morning I woke up and things felt different. It was as if someone had stolen my rose-colored glasses and life was suddenly in focus. I wasn't happy. I was depressed and angry. Everything I had suppressed caught up with me and was spilling over into my marriage with Spence. Ted's hate campaign wore on me as well. We had a daughter we were raising together while riding a co-parent roller coaster.

Ted found it amusing to taunt me. He would say, "The money's gone and Libby's gone!" I reminded him that it was he who left me. In Ted's mind, when I wouldn't come back, he said it was because of the money. He couldn't accept that he might have something to do with it. When I complained about not receiving child support he would say,

"The money's gone and Libby's gone!"

"Ted, you're legally bound for child support!"

"The money's gone and Libby's gone, and EVERYONE knows it!"

I responded, which was a huge mistake. "Ted, how could you write that letter to me and behave so hatefully?"

"I never meant a word of it, Libby!" he shot back.

I remembered when not long after he wrote the letter, he told Lindy, "I know Libby isn't coming back, so I'm going to put down my sword and give her peace." That never happened. He honed the blade instead. Weeks turned into months and still no child support. I finally took Ted to court when he owed me almost five thousand dollars. I was angry watching him party about town while telling me he had no money.

Around that time, I was in Jack's, a cozy eatery where locals gather for drinks and dinner. I had come with Spence and some friends, not realizing that Ted was already there with his girlfriend and some other people. Some I knew, some I didn't. I steered clear of Ted. He was furious I was taking him to court. We stayed for a couple of drinks before deciding to leave and call it a night. Ted was standing with his girlfriend and a group of people at the bar, which I had to pass to exit the restaurant. On my way through the threshold I heard a voice yelling at me, "SEE YA LATER, SATAN!" It was his girlfriend! I was stunned. I turned around and she, Ted, and a few of their posse were laughing wildly. It felt like one of those scenes in a movie where laughter is set into slow motion. Knowing his girlfriend from college, and as a member of Big Spring Country Club, I had thought she was a nice person. I was wrong. It was surprising behavior from a forty-year old woman. I had no idea what motivated her other than showing off for Ted and his court. Although she attempted to embarrass me, all she managed was to embarrass herself. I decided that her taking Ted's position on the child support issue must stem from the fact that she had no children herself.

Ted and I continued to battle over child support. He wanted to pay me $600 a month, down from $1,200, because now he was getting Kennedy every other week. He wanted me to forgive the arrears as well. He said he didn't have the money.

"Ted, I don't trust you!"

"Well, the monster in me is dead!" Those were his exact words.

I refused. We ended up in court, and he was found not to be in contempt. I was shocked. What was contempt anyway? It didn't end there. Based on what he presented as income, child support was reduced from $1,200 per month to $149.00 per month. He was ordered to pay the arrears, which outraged him, but he gloated over his $149.00 "win" as he saw it. A win for Ted and a loss for Kennedy is how I saw it. He blamed it on me. "Libby, you took me to court and the money could have gone to you instead of my attorney!" That was his logic. Even after he paid off the arrears, he never paid a dollar more than the $149.00. I never received the $600 he vowed to pay, despite the court's order.

Kennedy was in the seventh grade. Her needs only increased in high school, but that didn't bother Ted. A few months later he showed up in a new Jeep Cherokee with blacked out windows and all the bells and whistles. It was confusing how he now had money for a new car but showed income low enough in court to reduce child support to $149.00. I made a comment. He just dropped the check out the window and pulled out. He must have liked seeing me pick it up off the ground, because that became a habit when he didn't like what I was saying.

A week later, Spence and I were out of town for our first anniversary. When I got on the treadmill, I felt a jolt inside my body. I instantly recognized the feeling as the same I had a decade before when I fell to my knees trying to pick Kennedy up from her crib. The pain was tremendous. My neurosurgeon delivered the news, "Your discs above and below your fusion have worn out." He went on to tell me that if he had to guess my age based on the MRI, he would think he was looking at someone in her seventies. I was thirty-eight. I did everything imaginable to control the pain, but I couldn't get over the hump. Any relief I got from medication, epidural injections or physical therapy was short-lived. The pain always returned. It got to the point where I started wearing a Tens Unit, a small device that used electric current to stimulate nerves and reduce pain. It was a cumbersome device attached to wires, but it helped and I was grateful. Trying to keep the smile on my face and soldier on, I was now suffering emotionally and physically. I was in a marriage that was crumbling and so was my back, but the marriage part was my fault. I realized that I wasn't in love. What I'd had with Spence was infatuation, but with no money and a failing back, I felt desperate and hung on. I wish I hadn't.

On July 7, the grand jury indicted Ted on five counts of mortgage fraud. It wasn't a surprise to me, but I was surprised by Ted's reaction. He called to deliver the news. "Libby, you may or may not know that I have been indicted, but I *will* be found innocent in a court of law!" he dramatically stated, like he had watched one too many episodes of *Law and Order*. All that was missing was the theme music. That was bizarre, but there's more.

"I'M TEFLON TED AND THE CHARGES DON'T STICK!"

"You're who?"

"I'M TEFLON TED, LIBBY!"

"What?" It took a moment to register. "Like the Teflon Don?"

"You are correct!" Ted was referring to John Gotti, the powerful and dangerous crime boss from New York. He was given the nickname "The Teflon Don" after three high profile trials in the 1980s resulted in acquittal.

"Um, Ted, I'm not sure how to respond to the comparison. He's a Mafia boss who murdered innocent people, and the charges *did* eventually stick. He's in prison. Call me when you're ready to talk seriously. You, Ted, not the non-stick pan."

The thing was, though, Ted really was serious. Big setbacks didn't faze Ted – they always made him bolder. His arrogance and above-the-law attitude in the face of an indictment was unsettling. His comments haunted me the rest of the day.

The news was all over the internet. I immediately got calls from friends. It was humiliating. Further, I worried for Kennedy with good reason. One of the mothers from her school got wind of Ted's indictment and shared the news with her daughter. Of course, the news spread like wildfire and there was no way to contain it. Maybe I was naïve, but I wasn't expecting people to be judgmental. I got my first taste of unwanted notoriety at a nail salon. I was sitting talking to Bao, the Vietnamese owner of the salon and the nicest of people. We were chit chatting when a girl recognized me, "Hi Libby!" I was in mid conversation with her when a woman sitting to the far right from me blurts out in an accusatory voice,

"Are you Libby House?"

"Yes, I was," I replied.

"From No. 1 Indian Hills Trail?" her voice rising towards the end of the question.

"Yes, that was my address." I suddenly felt hot. "Why do you know my address?" I asked in a tight tone that alerted the fisherman. Her voice, now wobbly, said,

"Oh, well, my friend lives in the neighborhood and remembers your house going on the market."

"Is that right?" Bullshit! No one frames a question that way to a perfect stranger. I excused myself and went to the bathroom because I didn't trust myself not to say what I really wanted to; that she was cruel and wanted to publicly humiliate me. I didn't take the bait, but I wanted to. I wanted to yell, "Yes! I'm the former Mrs. House, Louisville's most notorious divorcée!" but I didn't because I had manners. I came back to my seat. She never spit out another word. I'm sure she had plenty to say after I left.

That was to be my first taste of what it was like being caught in the fray. People I knew socially who used to stop and chat in the grocery store suddenly looked away and kept moving down the aisle. At a basketball game, I was in earshot of a gaggle of women talking about me.

"She's the one whose husband committed fraud. I wonder what she knew?"

I could feel judgmental eyes staring at me. While Ted was tried in federal court, I was being tried in the court of public opinion. In their minds, I was either complicit or stupid. Ted had taken so much from me, but having my credibility and honesty questioned sent me spiraling. You never get that back. It's always a looming question.

Earl was getting on in age and could no longer drive. He was resigned to staying home. He hated it! As long as I could remember, Earl had a separate life away from the house. He went to work, and then he went to the reservoir with the Brown Bottle Club, a group of tipplers who weren't allowed to drink at home. I believe his parallel life kept him going. Beal took a job at a school office when I was a senior in high school and remained there for the next twenty years. Too bad she hadn't taken that job when I was growing up. I would have enjoyed some after-school peace.

Beal loved being away from home as much as Earl did. The truth is that they loved being away from each other. To me their marriage existed only on paper. Growing up, I never witnessed a loving, caring moment between them. I imagined whatever they might have had was now obsolete. Earl had grown weak and was susceptible to falling. This being the state of affairs, I and my sisters, brother-in-law and various friends took Earl out as much as our schedules permitted. It was never enough though. Earl called and called, wanting to escape.

"Libbah, it's me!" I would hear on my voice mail. "Libbah, it's me," sometimes ten or more times a day. It was sad. I took him out until my back got so bad, it wasn't safe for either of us.

One of the last outings I took Earl out on was to vote. He was ready two hours before it was time to pick him up, and he called to let me know.

"Libbah, I'm ready!"

"Dad, I'm not supposed to pick you up for two hours."

"Libbah, I know that but I'm giving you an update!"

"Dad, I'll be there on time!"

"See that you do, Libbah! ya hear?"

"I hear!" He was ready all right, sitting on the front porch in his jacket and signature fedora. My whole life he had worn a fedora and had one for every season.

We made the short trip to the polls.

"Dad, you ready to vote?"

"What the hell kinda question is that, Libbah? of course I'm ready to vote, I'm here aren't I?" I wanted to laugh, but Earl was serious. I followed him inside. The poll worker gave him his ballot and showed him to a table where he could sit comfortably.

"Libbah, you read the candidates to me and mark off what I tell you to!"

"Okay Dad. First, we have a US Senator. Would you like to re-elect Mitch McConnell?"

"Hell no, I'm not voting for that bastard! He's a crook!" I shook my head and looked at the floor "We are so getting thrown out of here," I said to myself. There was no stopping Earl now.

"I don't know how the hell he's been in Washington this long! Lining his pockets is his only accomplishment! Mark down that other guy, Mitch McConnell, hell, he gets elected, we'll be in the poorhouse!" I was having déjà vu. It was like we were at the movies again watching *The Alamo*. He was now yelling to everyone in the polling station. Earl had a comment for every candidate, which he shared with the public at large.

After the ballot was complete, Earl walked it over for submission. "Thank you, Sir!" the poll worker said to Earl. "Yes, Sir!" Earl responded.

The poll worker was an older gentleman, not as old as Earl but at least in his seventies. Our eyes met, and he winked at me in obvious acknowledgment of Earl's biographical critiques. Earl placed his fedora back on his head and off we went. I was glad he hadn't asked me to take him to a town hall meeting. I can only imagine candidates fielding his questions.

Earl's physical health became unstable as the months passed. It was no longer a matter of "if" he would fall. It was a matter of "when." My sister and I worried that Beal had made no provisions for him while she was out of the house. Her habit of hoarding made the house a complete disaster for Earl's getting around. I offered countless times to help organize things, but Beal exploded, "Libby! Don't you dare touch a thing in *this* house!" It was sad how neat Earl had kept it when we were growing up, but now it was a dangerous maze where getting from one part of the room to the next was like negotiating an obstacle course. Beal told everyone Earl had a motorized wheelchair, but failed to reveal it was unusable because the house had been transformed into a storage locker. When I brought this to her attention, she snapped at me, "Libby! He won't use it!"

"Mom, he can't use it!"

"I don't want to hear another word Libby!" I always had another word and it always got me in trouble.

"Mom! That's not true! You won't move anything, and that's why he can't use it!"

"Libby, march yourself right out of this house! NOW!"

"Mom, then at least get him a medical-alert bracelet!"

"He won't wear it!"

"You're being ridiculous – of course he'll wear it! You're gone all day and some evenings. He's eighty-nine years old, he's got a fused spine, and he's already fallen many times. You need to make provisions!" Then I marched myself out the door.

Beal never made provisions for Earl. The motorized wheelchair never moved – it became another place for her to store junk, which she refused to part with. It sits in the same place today piled high with old magazines.

Earl did eventually fall in his bedroom. He couldn't reach the cordless phone, so he dragged himself through the house to the kitchen. They still had an old phone attached to the wall with a long cord. Earl waited for someone to call so he could pull the cord and get help. I happened to be the one who called…four hours later.

"Libbah, I'm down!" Spence and I immediately rushed over, and Spence got him off the floor. I called Beal over and over and over. She'd turned her phone off, so I left a million messages. When she got home, I was waiting.

"You turned your phone off and Dad has been lying on the floor for four hours!"

"He has NOT! I've only been gone for three and a half hours, Libby!"

"What! Dad has been on the hard kitchen floor and you want to split hairs over how long it's been!"

"Well, YOU said it's been four hours and it hasn't"

"Dad said it's been four hours and he's wearing a watch!"

"Libby, leave! I don't want to hear your mouth anymore!"

"You're cruel! Dad is a hostage!"

"Get out! Get out of this house this minute!"

I left, my blood boiling. I don't know why I was surprised. This was the same woman who drove away from Earl in the restaurant parking lot after his knee replacement surgery. Nevertheless, I was.

Sometime after Earl fell, a neighbor stopped me on my way in to see Earl. She politely asked if there was anything that could be done about the "clutter."

"Libby, isn't there anything that can be done so your Dad can have a safe walking path?" I told her "no," there was nothing we could do. There was no reasoning with Beal and no way to explain that the Beal behind closed doors was different than the one she knew. That door always stayed shut.

Four months had passed since Teflon Ted had declared "the charges don't stick!" but they did. He pleaded guilty on November 28, 2007. I wasn't surprised. I was told the guidelines for his sentencing required a minimum of eighteen months to eight-and-half years. He got the eighteen months, with two years' probation, and had to repay $2.7 million in restitution. To my mind, there was something unfair in that the financial institutions that Ted had defrauded would be recompensed, but I was ruined.

Ted made sure he let me know that his backers and family had filled the courtroom and cheered the verdict. I imagined Ted standing with his hands clasped above his head, smiling, acknowledging the crowd just like a conquering hero. I suspected the risk of receiving the maximum sentence at trial was a motivator for Ted to accept a plea. I also expected contrition on Ted's part, but he remained the same. I thought a conversation would be appropriate on how going to prison might affect Kennedy. I didn't expect –

"Libby, my friends think I should appear on Oprah after I get out." He was excited.

"For what? You haven't even been to prison yet." His remark confounded me. Ted was already scripting his future and, of course, it all revolved around Ted.

In Ted's mind he was special, unlike his co-conspirators who were also sentenced to prison. I questioned him on why he was different from the others. He immediately hung up. Some days it was hard to imagine I had ever married him.

Earl continued to decline, but still managed to sit on the porch for long periods of time. I would find him there with his worn-out face and haggard body. I often wondered what he thought about. I knew if I asked, he wouldn't tell me,

"Just watching the air, Libbah," he replied with a grin, so I imagined he thought of jumping trains, working with his Daddy at Jersey Milk Co., the fun he had with his Phi Si fraternity brothers, playing football for Purdue, the moment he proudly pinned a General's star on his son's uniform, or other memories he revisited from his distant past. Oddly, in my mind, I never saw Earl reminiscing about our family. I loved Earl and I knew he loved me, but I believe if he had to do it all over again with Beal he wouldn't.

One of those days Earl was sitting outside on an unusually warm February day when he called me. "Libbah, Ted came and dropped off The Poodle (Earl's nickname for Kennedy), and he didn't even get out of the car! Not a word!" He was too yellow to face me!" Ted hadn't seen Earl since he left me. Ted couldn't look the old man in the eye, the man who had loved him like a son and would have done anything for him. I knew it hurt Earl and that hurt me. Ted was a coward. Suddenly I was overcome with emotion. Repressed memories of the past floated through my mind, memories of the good times Ted and I shared with Earl. I was angry at the invading thoughts. I wanted to reprimand my disobedient self for letting them in.

Finishing up at work, I got a call Earl had taken another fall. I arrived to find Beal screaming over him, "Earl, quit moving! Earl! Earl! Don't move!" He lay on the kitchen floor, his shirtsleeve soaked with blood where the skin had been torn. Beal was still yelling at him even though he wasn't moving.

"Mom! Stop it! He knows! Quit yelling!" I said.

"Libby! He is going to make it worse!"

"He's not moving! Please stop screaming!" The more I told her to stop the more she ratcheted up her voice, so I stopped asking. My eardrums were blistered from her piercing screeches, "Earl, Earl." Arriving, my brother-in-law got Earl to his recliner in the family room. The blood had soaked through his shirt and his left arm was completely red. Earl was disoriented and not making sense. I called 911. It seemed like they arrived only moments after I hung up.

Time was standing still. Earl was in the recliner with his bloody arm, ensconced in the middle of Beal's clutter. There was an old cradle that had been in Beal's family for generations that had been made into a table with a wooden top. It was now covered with stacks of old Disney videos. Then there was a sofa against the adjoining wall with piles of newspapers, like old guests who wouldn't leave. There was a school desk with an iron frame and a hole for the inkwell that was filled with dated *National Geographics*, and there were two tall lamps with circular lampshades that kept guard on either side of Earl's recliner. They had trays burdened with copies of *Reader's Digest*. And in the corner, there was a dusty cardboard box filled with dirty laundry. The room was wrapped in old wallpaper with a pineapple motif. Moving the lamps, the paramedics commenced working on Earl.

They started by removing his shirt revealing an arm that looked like it had been skinned with a knife. His skin was like tissue paper that had given way when he fell. Standing in the back of the room, angry with Beal, my heart was torn by Earl's condition. Beal, not one to pass on an opportunity to command attention, hovered, trying to make conversation until the paramedics asked her to step back. The Lyndon Fire Department had responded to the call, so Beal talked about her days working at the Lyndon Vocational School.

"I worked at Lyndon and Mr. Harriman and I really loved working together. He once was in a movie as a character and was murdered. Mr. Harriman was the funniest man. Everyone loved him. Joanne and I were just absolutely devastated when the school closed, and we had to take jobs elsewhere." All of this was transpiring while the paramedics checked Earl's vitals and made sure he was stable. They pretty much ignored her, but she droned on and on until one of them finally spoke up, saying that he went to Lyndon when it was an elementary school. Beal became giddy, a connection had been made, a chance to commandeer the conversation!

"What year?" she asked. It was obvious the fireman was put off by her timing and wanted to focus on Earl.

"Ma'am, it was elementary school, so I don't remember exactly." She asked his age. "I'm forty-three," he replied. I wanted to duct tape her mouth. Again, he responded, clearly agitated, and changed the subject to the matter at hand. My Dad!

"Ma'am, do you have a list of Mr. Henry's medications?"

"Well, yes, the pill bottles are in the cabinet... It's Libby! It's Libby, It's Libby," pointing to me with both hands, her mouth pasted half open with a doll-like smile. "Don't you remember, Libby? You all went to school together!" I had been lost in my own thoughts and when I came to, I was horrified she had singled me out. I met eyes with the fireman and embarrassingly acknowledged my mother was off topic.

"That's it! That's it!" I thought. I'D HAD IT!

"Mom! That wasn't me!" my voice rising "He's five years older than me. I didn't go to Lyndon elementary, that was Virginia! And why are we having this conversation? Focus on Dad!" Glaring, Beal gritted her teeth, but I ignored her, turning my attention to Earl and the paramedics. They finished up, and Earl was taken to the hospital. No one knew then but he would never return.

Earl spent the next week at the hospital and once he improved, was transferred to a nursing home. On Valentine's Day, Spence and I went to visit. I had spent the morning delivering flowers and gifts for Rose and Miller, a floral company, with my friend Lindy, whose husband's family were the Millers. It was a beautiful day, cold and crisp – the bare trees etched against the blue sky. The sun shone brightly, putting me in a sunny mood. I was excited to bring Earl his gifts that afternoon.

I brought one of those giant-sized cards no one usually buys, balloons, chocolate and some flowers, the works!

"Hi Dad!"

"Aye!" Earl had a bright room with a big picture window and a view. I had gotten him a good TV, and there were flowers and balloons already.

"How are you today?"

"I'm above ground, Libbah!" Spence and I both laughed.

"I brought you some goodies, Dad! Why don't you start with your card?"

I'd rather start with the chocolate!" I handpicked the chocolates at Muth's, a Louisville chocolate company that has been around for almost a century, just like Earl. I told him that, too, and he frowned. I showed him the giant card.

"Libbah, that's not a card – it's a billboard!"

"I wanted to make a statement!"

"That you did, Libbah!" I opened the card and showed him where Kennedy signed.

"Libbah, you tell the Poodle I sure do appreciate it!"

"She's coming to see you the day after tomorrow." Earl smiled.

"What do you say, Spence?" Earl reached out for a handshake. Spence reciprocated.

We sat and talked for a while, and as the shadows grew longer, we stumbled on the topic of Waynesburg. Out of nowhere, Earl looked at Spence and asked him, already knowing the answer,

"Spence, have you ever been to Waynesburg?" asking like it was a popular destination spot.

"No, Mr. Henry, I haven't."

"WELL, DON'T GO!" Earl resounded. Spence had heard some of my Waynesburg stories and let out a deep laugh. Spence asked.

"What if I do go?" Earl grinned.

"They keep you there!" Earl was in rare form. About that time, a nurse came in to take Earl's vitals.

"Now, you're not here to measure me for a coffin, are you?" Earl asked.

"No! Mr. Henry, I'm here to keep you alive!"

"Alright then, you can proceed," and he gave her a wink. On the way out, she whispered, "I like your Dad, he's one of my favorites." That wasn't a surprise, wherever Earl was, he made friends. His quick wit and charm went a long way with people.

I often visited Earl and sometimes found him in physical therapy. He had made fast friends with the therapists who loved him and his wisecracking ways. His beloved Cats were well into the season and he watched them on TV. When I came to visit about a month later with Kennedy and Traveler, Earl was dressed in a cardigan and in a chipper mood. The Cats were playing that night in the NCAA tournament.

"Hi, Dad!"

"Howdy! There's the Poodle and hey, there's Big Dog!" The nursing home allowed me to bring Traveler to see Earl. Sitting outside their rooms, patients in wheelchairs were thrilled when they saw him. Most of them reached out as we walked by. Kennedy stopped with Traveler so each could pat him. It made me happy and sad at the same time. He was probably the highlight of their day.

Kennedy brought Traveler over so Earl could give him a pat.

"Poodle, whatcha know!" That was Earl's way of asking for an update on your life. Moose, my grandmother, used the same expression.

"Nothing."

"Nothing? Aren't they teaching you anything in school?" With a big smile, she responded,

"Yes, Grandad, they teach me something!" The conversation quickly turned to basketball.

"Libbah, make sure they turned the TV to the right channel!"

"It's the right channel, Dad."

"Be sure! My nurse is a Cardinal Fan!" and Earl gave his signature wink.

"I'm sure, Dad! Guess who I talked to today? The Damn Boy!"

"The Damn Boy, Libbah? What is The Damn Boy doing these days?"

"Dad, he lives in Iowa and works for John Deere."

233

"Hell, has he wrecked one of their tractors yet?" I started laughing, "No, Dad, he hasn't."

"I thought he might put his talents to good use!"

"Dad!" He then looked at me squarely in the eye with one eyebrow raised and said, "You and that Damn Boy caused me a lot of problems, but you know, Libbah, I liked that Damn Boy."

"I know you did, Dad!" smiling widely.

Kennedy, Big Dog and I watched the game while Earl cursed the referees. Glancing at Earl as he watched, I realized his wrapping may have changed over the years, but the gem inside shone brightly as ever. When it was over, we kissed him goodbye and told him we would be back tomorrow. That was the last conversation I ever had with Earl. Later that night he went into septic shock from a urinary tract infection and lapsed into a coma.

The next day when the physical therapist came to collect Earl, there was something seriously wrong. Earl was taken to Baptist East Hospital by ambulance. Beal called me and I called Virginia. The three of us met at the hospital and sat together with Earl behind a green curtain. The room smelled of alcohol. Earl's body was jerking and shaking, and he made strange noises. If he was conscious at all, I imagine he was in great pain.

Virginia hadn't been speaking to Beal for some time. Beal had been purposefully withholding information from Virginia and me pertinent to Earl's care. Again, it was about control – she had something we wanted. When pressed for answers, Beal shrieked, "Quit badgering me! I've got too much on my mind," and, Beal, at her most evasive, "I can't think about that now! I'll think about it tomorrow!" The Scarlet O'Hara bit went straight through me, and Virginia ceased communication altogether. Frankly, she didn't give a damn. Virginia would glean information elsewhere. Beal became wise to Virginia going around her. She retaliated and made threats, "I'll make sure you never see your father again!"

Now Beal, Virginia and I were face-to-face for the first time in months. Always ready for a fight and always convinced she was right, Beal wouldn't leave Virginia alone, not even in this, Earl's darkest hour.

She started taunting Virginia by spitting out what *everybody* and *they* thought about Virginia from the time she was a little girl to the present. In her singsong voice she said, "Virginia, YOU were always jealous of Libby, and *EVERYBODY* talked about it! *EVERYBODY!*" Beal managed a cruel smile as Virginia's face turned red. I watched in disbelief. It wasn't true; no one thought that.

Beal kept it up and then went for the jugular, "Your father talked about it, too! He talked about it ALL the time!" This was a new low even for Beal. I couldn't take it anymore. I felt like I was in a pressure cooker and the lid was about to blow. "THAT'S NOT TRUE! DAD NEVER SAID ANYTHING THAT LIKE! What's wrong with you?" She smirked at me and defensively shot back, "Nothing's wrong with ME!"

Relieved when the nurse came back, we needed an interruption, or supervision or maybe an intervention. As we left, we worried that Earl would never regain consciousness. I set the record straight for Virginia. I didn't think she believed anything Beal said, but it was painful to watch, and I didn't want Beal getting in Virginia's head. That was always Beal's intention, to meddle, instigate and foment distrust and hatred. Finding out later that Virginia had a long conversation with Earl at the nursing home made me feel better. She told me they had an honest talk about her childhood. It gave Virginia some peace. Relieved that she had this conversation to carry in her heart, I knew that was one thing Beal couldn't take away from her.

Earl didn't regain consciousness and died five days later. I felt numb. He was gone. Suddenly, the world was ordinary. I begged Ted not to attend Earl's visitation. After everything he had done, and his avoiding Earl, I couldn't believe he would have the audacity to show up.

"Ted, please don't come! Please be respectful."

"My mother says I have to do what I feel is right."

"What you feel is right? That's an interesting choice of words. When have you ever been concerned with doing what's right? Isn't it always about what's right for you? What about my feelings? I'm asking you again not to come." Ted pushed my feelings aside like he always did to make room for his own.

"I have to do what I feel is right, Libby!"

Ted did show up. Working the room like a politician for over an hour, Ted's voice carried, and the entire time I heard him over more hushed tones. Enraged, listening to him I felt like he was stealing one more thing from me. To avoid a scene, I disappeared into a private area. When I returned, Ted had finally concluded his "meet and greet." He was gone, and relief walked through the door. It was "The Damn Boy." He was wearing a white shirt and dark pants. I saw him paying his respects standing alone beside Earl's casket amongst a cascade of white lilies and gardenias. It's the one vivid memory I have from that day. We laughed and told the same stories we had been telling for years. "Damn Boy wrecked MY car; bettah have a license!" I told him what Earl had said in the nursing home, that he liked the "Damn Boy," and that made me feel better. I told the Damn Boy, "Earl just had to keep on his game face," and the Damn Boy smiled. He had been forgiven.

When the last visitors had departed and Beal was nowhere in sight, my sister, my brother-in-law, Ryan, and I secretly placed some parting gifts in Earl's casket. Ryan and Virginia brought Earl's favorite bourbon and I brought my favorite shamrock pendant I had kept for years. Earl liked it. Our half-brother, Larry, had placed his silver star on Earl. Wanting nothing more than to be an officer in the military, Earl had attended a military academy. Unfortunately, flat feet and poor eyesight kept him from achieving his dream. He later was recruited to play football for Purdue, but his son, Larry, fulfilled the dream, climbing the ranks to make three star Major General in the Air Force. I remember when Ronald Reagan nominated Larry. Earl beamed with pride and proudly pinned the third star on his uniform.

Our parting gifts were far less impressive than Larry's, but Earl would have appreciated them all the same. Well, maybe not just the same but he would have appreciated them. He now had honor, some luck and a drink for the journey to heaven. Earl had definitely done his penitence on earth, and we were sure the gates stood wide open for him.

Walking with the rest of my family behind Earl's casket on the day of the funeral, I caught a glimpse of Ted sitting in the back of the church.

I thought, "has he no shame?" As soon as I passed, I quickly put him out of my mind. I wasn't going to let him rob me of my last moments with my Dad. I listened as family and friends eulogized Earl. They all talked about his bigger-than-life personality.

"When Earl was around, he swallowed up all the space in the room," one of his acquaintances said, and that was the truth.

One of the stories was about a teenage me. I sank low in my pew as Earl's colleague spoke about one of my misadventures. I sank even lower as he told the story with flare. I heard Earl's voice coming through the mouthpiece of his friend. He was reaching out from the grave and giving me a public shaming. I suppose I deserved that. Somewhere between laughter, sadness and regret, tears welled up. God, I loved my Dad.

Earl's burial didn't go without incident. As the pallbearers pulled his casket out of the hearse, one of them lost his grip. The casket tilted slamming the bourbon bottle on the inside of the casket, making a loud clunking noise. My sister, brother-in-law and I looked down at the ground, we knew better than to look at one another. Apparently, it caught the attention of one of our cousins who quizzed Virginia later. Thank God Beal was oblivious – she would have opened that casket right up then and there and poured the bourbon out on the ground. Earl got the last laugh and took his bourbon with him.

That incident was a befitting end. Today Earl rests near a hundred-year-old tree at Cave Hill Cemetery in Louisville, Kentucky. I am a regular there.

My marriage was crumbling as fast as my back. The future terrified me. The possibility of two more spinal fusions, no money of my own and Ted going to prison was almost more than I could bear. As best I could, I kept patching holes in the sinking ship and, in the process, I was losing my mind.

Lines of communication were kept open with Ted for Kennedy's sake. It was uncomfortable at best. Ted had no respect for me, and I was the enemy. This was new territory and, having no guidance, I was winging it. Ted and I fought constantly. My friend, Lindy, implored me to have conversation with Ted only if it concerned Kennedy. "If Ted gets off topic and insults you, hang up or delete the text! DO NOT RESPOND!" I responded. That was a mistake. All I gained were feelings of despair and helplessness. Had I an understanding of Ted's personality deficits, I might have fared better. It wasn't in Ted's make-up to be conciliatory or contrite. You were either on Team Ted and stroked his ego, or you were an adversary that fueled his need to prove himself. I was belittled, cut off and insulted when I allowed him the opportunity. I might better have followed Lindy's advice.

The only thing Ted and I agreed on was Kennedy's education. We both thought she should go to Assumption, a Catholic high school for girls. She liked the school and it was a good fit. Ted explained that tuition, books, uniforms and anything else Kennedy might need would be paid for by his parents. Ted's mother was a huge advocate for education. She had paid for Kennedy to attend the de Paul School, an exceptional school for children with dyslexia, although Ted claimed he had paid it until she told me otherwise.

Kennedy, like me, was dyslexic. Assumption had a wonderful program for people with this learning difference. I cared very much about Kennedy not falling through the cracks like I had. Ted's parents had no obligation to pay, but they were doing this for their granddaughter, and I was grateful. I was planning to personally convey this to them at a meeting to discuss provisions for Kennedy while Ted was in prison. Ted took Kennedy and registered her for the 2009-2010 school year. I was relieved Kennedy was attending Assumption. In my mind, Ted had finally done something right. I wasn't treated any better, but it wasn't about me. The barbs he flung still found their mark.

Coming over one day to drop off some items for Kennedy, he arrived in his tricked-out jeep. Walking out to the car to collect them, I thought it would be a quick exchange. I had been crying before he came. I cried over what he had done to our family and I cried for him, that he was going to prison. As he handed me a bag and boasted, "My girlfriend is going to make the payments on my new Jeep and help rehab my credit." I paused not understanding. I guess he needed to get in one last dig. Funny thing, she didn't keep making the payments. I was called relentlessly when she defaulted. I have no idea how he found me, but the collector I spoke with said I was listed as next of kin. I explained I was Ted's ex-wife and had been for almost three years. He said I was currently listed on the paperwork. He wanted to know about Ted's whereabouts. I told him. Prison. He kept calling until I asked for the paperwork. I never received anything, and I wasn't contacted again.

Ted was leaning out the driver's side window, his eyes hidden behind sunglasses. Sunlight was glinting off the hood of the shiny Jeep.

"I'm not following, Ted, why are you telling me this?"

"She has more to offer than you ever did, but you know, Libby, you were always good for a laugh." Ted wasn't making any sense.

"It's tragic you still feel a need to put me down." I twisted a loose strand of hair between my fingers and looked Ted straight in the eye. "You're a convicted felon who still thinks he's above the law. That speaks volumes." I walked away wondering how I was going to sit through the meeting with Ted and his parents. I shouldn't have wondered. There was no meeting, and that was the last time I saw Ted House before he was incarcerated.

Spence and I had drifted so far apart, we were on different continents. Our marriage was over. Truly it had never been much of a marriage. He was a port in a storm that I regretted. It pained me that Kennedy was paying for my poor choices. Spence stopped paying the rent on the apartment we were living in. He wasn't working and could no longer afford house payments. He was living in his mother's basement. Two months later, eviction notices were posted on the door. I was unable to afford the rent with my part-time job. My back pain was also worsening every day. I needed back surgery. Ted was in prison, and I hadn't received the small pittance he called "child support."

I was spiraling. Desperate, I called Ted's mother. I explained to her about the meeting that never was. She claimed she knew of no such meeting. I explained my plight and asked how child support and school tuition were going to be paid. I told her since Ted was in prison, I should receive three hundred dollars a month, since we were no longer sharing custody. It was then that the person I called my mother-in-law and loved for well over a decade was not who I thought she was. She heartlessly responded, "One hundred forty-nine dollars is what the courts say, Libby!" I was in disbelief. It didn't stop there.

"Donald and I aren't paying for Kennedy's tuition."

"I don't understand. Ted assured me tuition was being paid. He registered her for Assumption last month."

"Donald and I can't pay for tuition. We don't have the money." Ted's parents were under no obligation to pay, but they were extremely wealthy people. I wasn't buying. She continued, "If Donald and I lived in Louisville, we would take Kennedy." She said this as if I would forfeit Kennedy to her. I didn't think her repertoire included preying on someone, a daughter-in-law no less, when they were in a greatly weakened state. I was wrong. She knew her son had put me through an unimaginable hell, but I guess since I didn't "stand by my man," I was to be shown no mercy. I wonder if it ever occurred to her she was showing her granddaughter no mercy as well. All the warm feelings I had towards Scottie turned cold. I never thought of her the same way again. I quickly got off the phone. I was so thrown off by Scottie's callousness. I didn't get through my list of pertinent questions. I would regroup and call back tomorrow. I needed to call the school anyway before I called Scottie back.

The next day I called the school office. I introduced myself to the voice on the other end of the phone, giving my daughter's name. I explained that her father had registered her, but I had some questions. She asked me to hold for a moment. I could hear her fingers hitting the keyboard. The voice came back and said I needed to be transferred to the business office. I didn't understand, but I said, "Ok" and didn't question her. Another voice came on and introduced herself as the business manager.

"Ms. House, your daughter is not registered at Assumption."

"I'm sorry? Her father registered her in March."

"Her father is Edward House?"

"Yes," I was getting impatient.

"Mr. House wrote two checks that were returned to Assumption High School. I wrote him two letters and made calls but there was no response." Feeling my heart racing, I asked, "Were there ever any arrangements made for tuition?"

"No," she replied.

"Could I please come in and get copies of the letters you sent to my ex-husband?"

"Certainly." This was no time to fall apart. I explained that my ex-husband was in prison, the words sounding foreign as they rolled off my tongue for the first time, and that I was unaware of the returned checks. I asked what I could do. Could I apply for financial aid? She said the financial aid window had been closed; all aid had been awarded.

"Please, please would you speak to the principal? My daughter has been through so much, she needs this program." Figuratively, I was standing in front of her with my hat in hand. She agreed to pass on my request. "Thank you! Thank you so much!"

I hung up and sat paralyzed. Ted had written cold checks and entered prison, leaving me, and more importantly his daughter, in the lurch! He actually had taken Kennedy and let her register for classes! How could he do this? Why do this? It's not like he wasn't going to be exposed. It was more of the same, Ted getting through the moment and leaving me to clean up the mess. I immediately called Scottie.

"Scottie, it's Libby." I didn't give her a chance to respond. I lunged right in. "I have just learned Kennedy is *not* registered at Assumption. He took her through registration, had her register for classes and secured her spot with cold checks!" she paused and quickly minimized the situation.

"Teddy's intentions were good. He meant well."

"What? His intentions were good? Scottie, Kennedy is not registered for school and school starts in three weeks! He knowingly wrote bad checks and left his daughter in a precarious situation! I have no idea if they are going to let me apply for financial aid. The business manager informed me all financial aid has been awarded!"

"Libby, Teddy just wanted to do the right thing."

"Well, the right thing was *not* to pretend to register his daughter for school before going to prison." At that moment, I realized how absurd it was that I was talking about "doing the right thing" with Ted just starting a prison sentence. I switched gears.

"Scottie, Kennedy needs that program. I know you all are under no obligation, but I don't want her to fall through the cracks like I did. She thinks she's going to school there. I don't want her to have to acclimate to a school where her needs can't be met and where she doesn't know anyone. Scottie, we are being evicted, and I don't think I can afford to rent in the same area," which meant she wouldn't be able to attend the good public school in our neighborhood.

"Just use your current address if you have to."

"Scottie, I can't lie. I can get in legal trouble, and Kennedy would be removed from the school."

"Libby, it's my understanding that Assumption has a high prevalence of drugs." I guess she thought that comment would magically dissuade me. Where was she getting her information anyway? I ignored the comment.

"Kennedy has been through enough. Could you and Donald please help?" She didn't budge.

As it turned out, Assumption did allow me to apply for financial aid, and the headmaster at The de Paul School lobbied on Kennedy's behalf. I was and am eternally grateful for his help. In the end, Kennedy received a sizable amount of financial aid. The rest I scraped together from a special donor who wished that I never reveal his name. He felt horrible about the situation but didn't want Kennedy to ever feel uncomfortable if she knew who helped her.

The clock was ticking before Kennedy and I were going to be evicted. Spence had rented the apartment in his name only, which was a blessing in disguise for me. He stopped paying the rent with six months left to go. By law, the notices had to come to the apartment. The apartment community had finally sought a judgment against Spence for non-payment and posted it on the door. Had I signed a lease there would have been one against me as well. My credit was already littered with bankruptcy, foreclosure and a federal lien from Ted's actions. I didn't need another monkey on my failing back. With Kennedy's school situation stabilized, I set out to find an apartment. I soon realized I couldn't afford anything in areas I was familiar with, and I began searching outside my bubble. One by one, my applications were denied. I couldn't pass a credit check. Eleven applications were denied in all. It was astonishing how kind and eager leasing agents were when I applied, and how cold they were when I got "the call." Apart from severe anxiety of having nowhere to go, I was suffering from incredible back pain and unable to get relief. I was terrified. I hid away from Kennedy in my closet and cried every day. I didn't want her to see me crumbling, but she knew. I was failing.

There was no way we were going to survive on my part-time job. I had to work two weeks just to afford health insurance. With my pre-existing condition, I either had to pay Kentucky's high-risk premium or go without, and going without was not an option. I got a second job at a jewelry store, full well knowing I was in no condition to work two jobs. I didn't care. As predicted, I didn't last long. While lifting the trash out of the garbage can one day, my back went into spasm. The pain I felt was so intense I vomited. Unable to stand up straight, I looked like a human question mark for the next week. I was lucky I had someone to fill in for me at my other job.

I made another appointment with one of the surgeons who had done my fusion back in 1997. The other one had moved to Miami. I had seen him before and thought he was going to perform a much-needed surgery. I was stunned when he said he wouldn't do it, because he didn't think I would be able to sit or stand longer than fifteen minutes. This was in stark contrast to the neurosurgeon he sent me to who, because of severe degeneration was prepared to perform a fusion above and below my current fusion. It made no sense, and I told him so. "I'm in so much pain. My daughter and I are about to be evicted. Ted is in prison (he remembered Ted well, because Ted almost passed out when he explained what a spinal fusion would entail). I need help. I need to be able to work."

I felt tears well up in my eyes. Getting up, he walked towards the door saying, "I'm not abandoning you," and then he was gone. I felt abandoned.

My primary physician quickly called on my behalf and made an appointment with another spinal surgeon. The appointment was just as quickly cancelled when the office learned of my history. He made many calls with the same result.

"Libby, it's all about liability; you're young with a complicated back. No one wants to get sued." I was livid.

"Then why did they take an oath to help people? I need help!"

"I know you do, and it's unfair and wrong!" I appreciated his candor. I left without knowing what my next move would be. I was losing all awareness of what was going on around me. I was trying to get through each day. Kennedy had a babysitting job, which was a relief, at least. I was constantly on the phone in the mornings, calling doctors and apartment communities…and crying. After a ritual of calls and crying, I went to a part-time job in the afternoon. I had never been so grateful to have a job where I got to drive around. The car was a moving sanctuary where I could shut the world out for a while. When it broke down, I was thrown into further distress. I decided I needed to see the counselor I had seen in the past. I called Beal for a ride, not telling her where I was really going. I told her I needed to go to the grocery. The counselor's office was across the street. It was a bad decision. Beal offered no words of encouragement, nor showed empathy for my situation. I didn't expect much. She did help drive Kennedy to places when I couldn't. I appreciated her help, but Beal never accepted my gratitude. She never had.

I wasn't in a position to be picky. Taking the help I could get, I had her drop me off in front of the local fruit market and waited until she was no longer in view. Setting out on foot across the parking lot towards my counselor's office, a former neighbor from Indian Hills passed by. I imagined how nice it must be to have your life intact; that world seemed so distant. Self-pity was sinking in. I walked faster. I got across the street into the parking lot and suddenly I saw Beal pull in. She must have followed me. I COULDN'T BELIEVE IT! Hiding behind a bush, I ran into the first office condo I could get to. I had no way of knowing the set up inside. Thank god it had a little walk-in area with a closed door behind it. My eyes darted around the parking lot through the door window. Beal drove her white car up and down the aisles. I swear if that car had a fin on top, she could have been a great white shark patrolling her hunting grounds. I stood there and thought how ridiculous this was. I considered giving myself up and inviting her to join me. "Why don't you come with me? We'll let the counselor dig in!" Beal gave up the hunt, and I slipped into the counselor's office. The counselor knew a lot of my history, but when I explained the incident and Beal in more detail she said,

"She sounds like a flaming borderline!"

"What's a borderline?"

"It's a personality disorder." She gave me literature to read later and listened while I told her I was on the verge of a breakdown. She helped me devise some mental strategies. I felt better, not great, but better. The one thing she said that lingered in my mind was that she had started her career in the prison system, and in her experience, people like Ted don't change. "They either come out the same or worse." I had to put that thought out of my mind. I couldn't think of Ted coming out a shinier penny. I strategized my exit. I went around back and took a side street, cut across a lawn and made it safely back to the grocery. I bought a sack full of groceries, stuck my Beal literature inside and walked out to her car like nothing was awry. I knew I was caught, but I was staying mute, hoping Beal might, too. Wishful thinking. I might as well have been back in college when I snuck out of the house.

"Libby, I *know* you didn't stay at the grocery! What were you doing across the street?"

"What were you doing following me?"

"Ah ha! I knew you weren't telling the truth."

"You want to know where I've been? I went to see a counselor!"

Her eyes grew big.

"Did you tell that counselor all the things you've done? How bad you were in first grade and what a horrible teenager you were?"

"Yes, that's exactly what I told her, not the challenges of the present situation but what a bad six-year-old I was! How do thoughts like that tumble off your tongue?" I was in for it now. I should have never engaged.

"I want to meet this counselor and tell her all about YOU!"

"Well, that's not what counseling is about. It's not about trying to sway the counselor to your side."

Beal fired back, "You're just afraid she will find out about, YOU!"

"Okay, I'll bite. I'll set up a time next week, and you can go with me! What works for you?" Beal ratcheted up her voice.

"Libby, I don't know what's good for me. I will have to look at my calendar. I want a list of days and times I can choose from."

"You get your hair done and go to church each week, you're pretty wide open." We had pulled into the apartment community now. She gritted her teeth.

"You know, Libby, you don't deserve any respect. Look at your life! Why couldn't you stay married to Ted?" I didn't respond. I was overwhelmed with emotion. I crouched down with my head in my hands and began to sob on the sidewalk. I was beaten down. Beal looked at me through her car window like my emotions were alien. She did nothing, said nothing and drove away.

I became well acquainted with sounds of the night, a car or two traveling down an otherwise busy road, barking dogs, an occasional siren and a train horn off in the distance. I could always rely on the train. The night sounds kept me company on sleepless nights, and I was having a lot of those. When I woke up from nights when I did sleep, worry pounced on me.

"Get help! Get an apartment!" Those were my first thoughts. Worry had taken a toll on my appearance. The pale reflection in the mirror revealed a weary woman with eyes at half-mast. Darkness had ensconced itself beneath them, and I barely recognized myself anymore.

Searching on Kennedy's mini laptop for the best spine doctors in nearby states, I was determined to find someone who could help me. If no one could help in Louisville, I would find someone elsewhere who could. I made countless calls, but it always came down to money. I was told that out-of-network doctor's visits, tests and surgery would run in the thousands, even with insurance. How would I pay? I had no idea. I kept at it. I visited the Cleveland Clinic, where the doctor said my case was too complicated to be of interest to him. He made a joke about trying voodoo. I didn't laugh but would have tried it if voodoo provided proven results. I kept searching, and then I stumbled upon Dr. Fabien Bitan, the Director of Spine Surgery services at Lenox Hill Hospital in New York City. He was one of the country's top spinal surgeons.

Dr. Bitan is a highly recognized surgeon from France. He has pioneered the use of artificial disc implants and has received New York Metro's Best Doctor's Award, the Castle Connolly Best Doctor's Award, New York Super Doctors, Top New York Physicians' Award and the Patient's Choice Best Doctor Award.

I called immediately and a pleasant-sounding voice answered the phone. Introducing myself, I explained my situation. She put me straight through to Dr. Bitan's assistant, "Luz." Luz listened patiently as I told her in an anxiety-ridden voice all the particulars concerning my back, everything. She instructed me to gather up all current scans, reports and x-rays and send them to their office. She said Dr. Bitan would study them and call back. I was elated. The thought of getting pain relief seemed within reach. It was the first time anyone had asked for my medical history and hadn't jumped right into payment options. Packing up my medical library, I mailed it with hope to New York.

The apartment community was decent, but a bit run down. The buildings sat right up against the railroad tracks. It caught my attention, because I saw two police cruisers parked side-by-side in front of one of the buildings. I wanted to feel safe. I thought it wouldn't be horrible if Kennedy and I lived nearby. I parked my car, walked past the cracked tennis courts with weeds sprouting out of them and into the leasing office. The leasing agent was a younger girl, probably in her late twenties. She showed me a tiny two-bedroom apartment. Mirrored bedroom closet doors gave an illusion the rooms were bigger than they were. It was clean and there were two bathrooms. Good! Kennedy could have her own bathroom for high school. Getting straight to the point, I told the leasing agent about my horrible credit.

"I need this apartment." I was no longer above begging.

She smiled and kindly told me I would most likely need a co-signer. She added, "A lot of people have bad credit." I would have to ask Beal. I knew she would co-sign for Kennedy's sake. She did, and I was grateful. I took home the paperwork and felt like I finally had a chance to secure an apartment. I returned the paperwork the next day, complete with a co-signer. It wasn't enough. The manager did not approve me. I explained why I had horrible credit, hoping she would have empathy. She didn't.

She asked why my credit was so poor if I wasn't guilty of a crime. It was an ignorant question. I explained, trying to keep my demeanor pleasant even though she had used an accusatory tone of voice. Going through all the details was humiliating.

"Why will you not approve me, when I have a co-signer with perfect credit?"

"Well, I just don't understand how your credit is so bad if you weren't involved?" she asked narrowing her eyes. I wanted to say sarcastically, "You don't?" You don't understand how two people can be married and how one of them makes horrible choices that unfairly affects the other? Is that too abstract for you?"

If there was ever a time I wanted to shake someone, this was it, but I didn't. I took that damn high road. "I can provide proof I was never involved. Will that do?" I wasn't backing down. I had already satisfied the co-signer requirement, and that should be enough. What was happening felt seriously wrong. We needed that apartment!

The manager replied, "I will have to review what you provide and make a decision from there." I nodded my head in answer, because I didn't trust my mouth.

"Ted, Ted did this to me!" I shouted in my head. "He may be in prison, but he doesn't worry about a roof over his head!" I was coming to grips with the full weight of having my credit ruined. In Kentucky, it was a ten-year sentence. I knew that when Ted got out of prison, he wouldn't have to worry about a place to live. His parents would see to that. Being bitter wasn't going to help. I had to fight that feeling right away. I had to be better, which wasn't easy. Calling my attorney, Sean Pierce, I apprised him of the situation. He was incredibly kind, and when he said, "I'll take care of this Libby – what's the address?" tears rolled down my cheeks. I thanked him profusely. Someone cared and I was approved.

Sean's letter:

Dear Ms. Holbrook,

I represented Ms. Henry (Libby), last year in a federal criminal case involving her ex-husband, Ted House. Ms. Henry (Libby), was never a target or subject of the government's investigation and was always seen by the federal authorities as a victim of her ex-husband.

I can tell you that I have had the opportunity to review the evidence in that case, and there is no doubt that Ms. Henry (Libby) was a victim. I am hopeful you will not hold her ex-husband's criminal activity against her. I have always found her to be an honest and honorable person, and I believe she would make a good tenant for you.

Please call me if you have any questions or comments about her application. I hope you have a nice holiday.

Sincerely,
Sean Pierce

CHAPTER 11

I answered the phone. A voice with a strong French accent was on the other end. He introduced himself as Dr. Fabien Bitan, I couldn't believe he was calling himself.

I braced myself. Having grown accustomed to rejection, I was much surprised when Dr. Bitan confidently said he could and would help. Tears came to my eyes, just as they had when my attorney had helped secure an apartment. I was finally batting a thousand. Dr. Bitan discussed what he was going to do for me. He agreed with the findings that the disc above my fusion was severely degenerated and the one below was also bad, but not as severe. Had it been the reverse, things would have been better, because the disc above, which receives the less invasive part of the procedure, would have less degeneration. In my case, the less degenerated disc was being fused and the more degenerated disc was reserved for the less invasive surgery. If the procedures had been reversed, and the more degenerated disc was fused, my lower body movement would be even more restricted.

I waited for the out-of-pocket price tag; things always cost more in New York. There was none. Zero. He would take whatever my out-of-network insurance paid, and if they didn't, his work would be pro bono.

The benevolent "Super Doctor" from Manhattan was going to help ME! My faith in humanity was restored.

The sun was blistering, the kind of brutal ninety-eight degree August heat that makes people agitated. I loved my part-time job except on days like this, when I was covered in sweat just from getting in and out of the car. The pain patches on my back slowly peeled off my sweating body. Relieved the day was over, I got out of my car and headed to my apartment.

"Hello Libby!" It was like a bullet to the back. I turned around to face the familiar voice and barely recognized the figure in front of me. Ted was thin and extremely muscular. I was shocked he was already violating the halfway house rules and, therefore, his parole. I shouldn't have been; this was Ted for whom the rules don't apply.

He wanted to see Kennedy. I was beyond angry and had been for the past week. When Ted entered prison, I received an email from the BOP (Bureau of Prisons) with a request from Ted to communicate through email. I agreed for Kennedy's sake. What followed was an email from Ted stating he was not to receive anything negative.

"Unbelievable!" I thought. I agreed to communicate, but he was giving conversation guidelines? It felt staged. I ignored the guidelines and kept him informed about Kennedy throughout his incarceration. There were no problems, until he was released. Ted informed Kennedy that his girlfriend would be present at their first meeting. Kennedy asked to see her Dad alone. She tried to express her feelings but was shut down immediately. Consequently, she decided she would wait to see her Dad until his girlfriend wasn't present. Furious, Ted emailed her before his release:

"You are rude! Please do not start to act like your Mother, it will cause you great problems in life and especially with ME! Do you understand? I am sorry that I have not been there (at home) for you this past 14 months; it's been hard on both of us! However, I have done everything I can do considering the circumstances, and all that I am asking is that you be a lady (nice and courteous) to Regina. Again, you may not like her, but she is my friend, and she has done nothing to you but nice things. So, remember that when you start saying something or doing something you might REGRET!!!"

Kennedy called me, in tears about the email and other nasty ones Ted had sent. Kennedy was with Ted's mother up in Indiana at the time and asked if I could come and get her, so she wasn't forced to see her Dad with his girlfriend present. I told her to think about it for a while, because I thought not seeing her Dad before he moved to the halfway house might be more hurtful. The decision was hers, and Kennedy decided she would see her Dad, but was still unhappy his girlfriend would be there too. She sent Ted an email that she had changed her mind. Ted then sent his daughter another email:

"I'm sorry you are upset, but you made the decision! Gigi (Kennedy called her grandmother Gigi) will take you to your mother. I will see you later in the week. Enjoy living w/your mother and thanks (sarcastic) for wishing me a Happy Father's Day!"

Ted held Kennedy to her original decision. Cruel and unhealthy thoughts lingered in my mind. Beyond not putting his daughter first and thinking only of himself, I'm fascinated that Ted sent negative content via email to Kennedy from prison, but according to the BOP, he wasn't allowed to receive any or so he said. To me it's a calculated effort on his part to blacken me, as he knew all emails are reviewed. Nothing new there.

"Hello Ted, what are you doing here? You're violating the halfway house rules by being here, but you know that!"

"I'm here to see my daughter!"

"You mess with your daughter's emotions, refuse to see her because she wanted to see you alone, and now you show up here without permission? Ted, *you're* supposed to be the adult!"

He stood there and stared at me. I glared back. I knew he wasn't thinking I was ogling, but what he did next might make one think differently. He proudly pulled up his shirt, exposing six-pack abs.

"Libby, this is what eighteen months in prison will give you: Shredded abs!" I was at a loss, in a surreal oblivion where the world no longer made sense.

"Was I really married to this person? He is the father of my child? Surely there's been a mistake?"

I came back down to earth to find him texting. Looking up at me and back down at his phone, he laughed. Clearly, I'm in some parallel universe. The texting continued and I felt like I was intruding.

"Ted!" and I raised both hands in the air, "what are you doing?" He cackled and told me his job assignment while at the halfway house was Moby Dick, a fast food seafood restaurant known for its "Whale of a Sandwich." The comedy continued, and I imagined Ted in a paper hat serving the "First Mate Meal," Moby Dick's most popular seller. "A tiny bit of justice," I thought. "Wouldn't it be nice to have Ted serve me the First Mate Meal?"

"When do you start?"

"Libby, I'm not working at Moby Dick!"

"You're not?"

"Hell, no!" He informed me he would be working for a friend.

"I'll be collecting minimum wage and enjoying the putting green on top of the building!" Of course, the rules don't apply, what was I thinking? Just as I was about to comment on the perks of the new job, exchanging stripes at the federal club for pinstripes at the roof club, Kennedy came out of the apartment and told me they were going to lunch. I knew Ted was breaking the law, and, in hindsight, I don't know if I made the right decision by letting her go. I thought if I call his parole officer and he goes back to prison, Kennedy will hate me. I didn't want to add to her pain or cause her more confusion. Right or wrong, I didn't make the call.

I arrived in New York City. My appointment was at the end of the day, so I visited Central Park to take in the beauty and, of course, people watch. Is there a better place to people watch than New York? Not having been to Central Park since my modeling days, I wandered around the sailboat basin just north of 72nd Street. Kids and adults were wishing for a bit of a breeze to power their boats across the pond. Boats and captains came in all sizes and shapes. There was a portly fellow with a polo shirt and white ducks who had a long varnished pole he used to nudge his fancy schooner off into the briny blue. What appeared to be brothers with clipped blond bangs had matching boats, miniature racers in red and green with spinnakers, who excitedly cheered as the main sails caught the breeze and the boats tipped precipitously before taking off through the chop, rifled by the breeze.

I bought an ice cream from a vendor and smiled at Alice among the toadstools with the Mad Hatter and the dormouse. Kids climbed and slid over the polished bronze, and in the shade sat a brother Grimm with a bronze book open on his lap.

Dr. Bitan's office was full. At one point, there was standing room only. I checked in and was greeted by a cheery woman. Remarking on my accent, she looked up at me, her eyes raised above reading glasses. Remarking on her accent as well, we shared a laugh. She handed me some paperwork, and luckily, I found a vacant chair. The walls were covered with awards Dr. Bitan had received as well as autographed pictures of NFL players. I was in good hands. It wasn't long before I was face to face with the renowned French doctor. Dr. Bitan was friendly and kind, immediately putting me at ease. Going over my medical history with a fine-toothed comb, he detailed the two surgeries I faced four days apart, his approach, recovery time and the outcome he hoped for me. There were no guarantees, but as he spoke, I imagined all the things I was going to do pain free.

Two days later I had the less invasive back surgery on the most diseased disc to try and preserve motion. Four days later, I had a spinal fusion on the other one. It was not an easy recovery, but months later I was completely pain free. Unfortunately, it only lasted a month. The disc Dr. Bitan hoped to preserve gave way and I required another spinal fusion followed by three succeeding surgeries. Dr. Bitan didn't perform these surgeries. He had a friend and colleague in Louisville, a doctor my research never led me to. Dr. Majd become the captain of my ship.

It was a hard four years. I had back surgery every year Kennedy was in high school, and it was miserable for her as well. It was a dark time. I wasn't the mother I wanted to be as surgery and pain ruled, while Ted capitalized on the situation. He stopped paying the $149 dollars per month in child support entirely. I took him to court, and he was ordered to pay. Recoveries were long and arduous. Setbacks were common and I had many. When setbacks inconvenienced Ted, he accused me of playing "the back card," meaning I was faking. He was living with a friend after he graduated from the halfway house, and for some reason he said it was inappropriate for Kennedy to stay over. That meant he had to drive fifteen minutes to pick up Kennedy and fifteen minutes back, which became a source of anger for Ted. He complained that I lived too far away. He never stopped complaining about me.

There were days the pain was so fierce I started vomiting, which only made it worse. My body was wracked, and I was screaming in the wilderness. My mind wandered to dark places. Selfishly, I didn't want to wake up another day. I remember Kennedy coming to hug and kiss me before she left for school. Trying to return her affection lit up every nerve ending in my body. When I heard the door slam shut and she was gone, I sobbed for hours and cursed God for my suffering. I was weak and I made deals with God all the time. If I could get out of the pain, I would be a better person, a better friend and most importantly a better mother. Maybe I should have been dealing with the Devil.

One Christmas Eve, a woman I met gave me a tiny silver box blessed by a priest. Instructed to write a prayer to God and put the prayer in the box, the following year I was to take out the prayer to see if it had been answered. Every year I look at my prayer, "God, please let me be relieved of chronic back pain." It hasn't been answered in the way I hoped, but I have decided God has a plan for me and I should keep the faith. It isn't easy but I try. I still carry the box with me.

Ted's lack of empathy was hard enough, but Beal's was downright cruel. When I could no longer work, I sold my soul and went to Beal for financial help. I was desperate. She helped me, but the emotional cost was overbearing. She, too, had no empathy.

"Libby! I don't want to hear about your back! My back hurts! Quit complaining!"

A family member I loved and always confided in was a source of comfort for me. Beal, being spiteful, told me the family member had called and didn't want to be burdened by me and my back problems anymore. Heavily medicated and ruled by emotions, I recoiled into a dark world for a week, staying up at night watching car headlights pass my window and wishing I was going somewhere, too. I was never grateful enough to satisfy Beal, no matter how many times I said "thank you." She took pleasure in my plight.

"Look at you! Look how your life turned out! You should be ashamed!"

"No, Mom, I shouldn't. You're ashamed of me, because I am poor now! There's no benefit for you! Dad would have never treated me this way!"

"Oh Libby!" He didn't even want you! When he found out I was pregnant with you, he didn't speak to me for two weeks!"

I believe that. I believe Earl didn't see the damaged part of my mother until after they were married. I believe he didn't want to have more children with Beal. It wasn't about me. It was about her. Tears welled up in my eyes as she continued, saying Earl wouldn't have helped me in my time of need. Crying in front of Beal made me feel weak and preyed upon. Her cold dead eyes registered no reaction to my helplessness. Quickly putting on oversized sunglasses, I sensed Earl hadn't the fortitude to leave her. When I was little, but old enough to understand, I secretly wished he would divorce Beal and take Virginia and me away with him.

I loved my Dad. These were dark times, but I still had golden memories. Like the time he took me to the Shaun Cassidy concert.

It was late March of 1978 and I was soon to turn ten years old. Embarking on double digits was a big deal in my world. No longer a child, I was going to be a preteen. I had two loves in those days, Champs Rollerdrome and Shaun Cassidy. My record player had practically worn out his self-titled solo album, *Shaun Cassidy*. I danced and danced around my room singing his hit single, "Da Doo Ron Ron."

I met him on a Monday and my heart stood still

Da doo ron-ron-ron, da doo ron-ron

Somebody told me that his name was Bill

Da doo ron-ron-ron, da doo ron-ron
Yeah, my heart stood still
Yes, his name was Bill
And when he walked me home
Da doo ron-ron-ron, da doo ron-ron

I had the album cover proudly propped up on my dresser. Shaun had dreamy brown eyes and his hair was kissed by the California sun. The cover photo featured him wearing a white painter's cap pulled to the side over perfectly feathered hair. I wore mine the same way at the skating rink.

I didn't dare remove the cellophane from the cover. I couldn't risk a facial injury. The most wonderful thing in the world was, aside from not only being my favorite singer and future husband, Shaun was one of those crime-solving "Hardy Boys." I NEVER missed an episode but was most unhappy when the boys teamed up with Nancy Drew. I liked Nancy, but when the article in Tiger Beat magazine suggested that romance might be brewing between the two, I was concerned. Shaun was off limits!

He was coming to play a concert at Rupp Arena in two weeks, and I'd been begging my parents to take me. Told several times that I couldn't go, I was deeply disappointed. My consolation prize would have to be an evening tribute skate at Champs.

Stumbling into the kitchen, still groggy, I sat down next to Earl. He was doing good work on his breakfast. He piled a couple of biscuits on my plate and a generous slice of cantaloupe.

"Where's the bacon, Dad?"

"Your mother hasn't fried it yet." I frowned. "Libbah, why don't you finish stirring up the orange juice?" I walked over to the counter and stared down the throat of the orange juice decanter.

"Dad, the concentrate is still frozen hard! It's not mushy! Can I wait until it thaws?"

"Get to it, Libbah!" I got to it. I stirred furiously until the frozen orange tube disappeared into the water. Two matching juice glasses were already by the decanter. Steadily I poured the juice into the squatty glasses and sat one beside Earl's plate and one beside mine. Almost completely under my plate was a nameless envelope.

"What's this Dad?" holding it up for inspection.

"Look inside, Libbah!" I unsealed the envelope and slid out two tickets! TWO BEAUTIFUL light blue tickets with Shaun Cassidy's name in raised glitter. I couldn't believe it. I WAS GOING TO THE SHAUN CASSIDY CONCERT!

"Dad, who's taking me to the concert?"

"I am, Libbah! Happy Birthdah!" he declared.

"Thank you, Dad! Can I call my friend Lisa? I want to tell her I'm going!"

"Finish your breakfast and then you can have at it." I scarfed down my food and ran to the phone. I was spending the night with Lisa but couldn't wait to spread my good news. Lisa was almost twelve, my more mature friend. I felt cooler being around her. We rode bikes up to the Magic Market that was close to her neighborhood. That stop-and-go market was the epicenter for preteens to hang out, buy candy and trade the latest Charlie's Angels cards. The only thing I didn't like about spending the night with Lisa was how she required me to speak to her Siamese cat, Carl.

"Don't talk in a baby voice to Carl!" she insisted. I felt weird not being able to say, "Hi kitty, kitty," in the voice I used for conversation with animals. I had to speak to Carl using the same voice I used to speak with people. I guess Carl was too mature for baby talk. I kept my conversations with him brief.

Dialing Lisa's number, I could barely wait for her to answer. When she did, I apprised her of my new status, "concert goer." She shared my excitement because she, too, was going. We didn't talk long as Earl would be dropping me off at her house around lunchtime. We could pick up our girl chat later.

Concert day finally arrived. I was prepared. My flared jeans with rainbow stitching were neatly laid out on my other twin bed with a yellow short-sleeve top. The outfit had been there for days. I took great care prepping myself for Shaun. I started my prep early because Earl wanted to get a head start on the traffic. My thick dark hair wasn't easy to feather, but I gave it my best effort. I pumped the water-filled curling iron, giving each curl a steam until I had completely traveled around my head. When Earl announced, "Libbah, it's time to hit the road!" I was ready!

I splashed a more than generous amount of Love's Baby Soft on my neck, grabbed my satin baseball jacket and jumped in the car.

Earl and I were more than on time for the concert. We were both hungry, so Earl made an executive decision to have lunch at one of his favorite places; aka, "The Chili King." When Earl lived in Lexington, Brooking was one of his closest friends and their friendship had been maintained even though Earl now lived in Louisville.

G.E. "ED" Brooking opened the restaurant in 1938, near the UK campus. It became famous for chili, which Brooking began serving in 1945. Kentucky basketball coach, Adolph Rupp, called it the best chili in Lexington and frequented the restaurant so much he had his own booth. Lexington legend has it if you were sitting in Coach Rupp's booth, he joined you, unless he had others with him. Then you moved.

Earl opened the old glass door and Brooking's booming voice immediately greeted him, "EARL HENRY, JR!" Earl walked over to Brooking while I trailed behind and gave him a hearty handshake.

"How the hell are you, Brooking?"

"Better now!" he replied. We took our seats at the counter. Of course, Earl ordered the chili and a generous Bourbon. I had a hotdog and a generous 7UP. Quietly eating while Brooking and Earl covered everything from sports to people from my Dad's day in Lexington, their conversation soon became white noise as I fantasized about Shaun. I was confident he was in his dressing room by now.

"Well Sir, we bettah wrap it up! Can't have Libbah missing that Cassidy boy's concert!" Brooking laughed and gave Earl a glance as if to say, "You're taking one for the team!" Brooking turned to me and said, "Enjoy yourself, little lady!" "I will, Mr. Brooking!" with a giant smile on my face. Earl reached for his wallet. Brooking slapped the counter. "Your money's no good here, Earl Jr!" Earl gave him another handshake and a pat on the shoulder.

"I'll be seeing you, Brooking!"

People were streaming into Rupp arena. Earl and I passed through the turnstile after the man tore the stubs off the tickets. I was relieved he tore on the perforated line. Shaun's name in glitter was still intact. Quickly, Earl ushered me to our seats. I could hardly stand it!

"Dad, can you hardly stand it?"

"Hardly, Libbah!" Girls were already screaming. I wanted to scream, too, but Earl's face had a grimace on it, so I didn't. When the lights went down, the volume of the crowd went up. Not able to contain it anymore, I shrieked in excitement! Multi-colored lights flashed all over the stage, and a fog started to rise. There was a covered giant ring standing upright on the stage. It reminded me of the rings tigers jump through at the circus, without the fire, of course. I just knew Shaun was behind that ring. The screams were getting louder as anticipation built. Soon everyone (excluding Earl) was chanting Shaun's name. He burst through the ring, most likely covered in paper, in a shimmering number that Earl later described as a mermaid suit. He was as glittery as the concert tickets. My mouth hung open for the first few moments. "Shaun and I are under the same roof," I had to let that sink in. Once I was over the shock, I joined Shaun singing, "That's Rock and Roll." I belted out every note in my husky voice:

C'mon everybody get down get with it
C'mon everybody get down get with it
C'mon everybody get down, that's rock and roll

Every song was a duet in my mind, (except "Morning Girl," Shaun sang that one just for me), and the rest of the crowd were just back-up singers. I was on my feet for most of the concert. I don't remember what Earl was doing. My eyes hadn't left the stage since Shaun graced it. Thinking back now, I'm sure Earl was glad he'd had a Bourbon or two with Brooking. He was sixty after all.

"Da Doo Ron Ron" caused me and my backup singers to practically drown out Shaun's voice. When Shaun made his final exit after several encores, and after the fog lifted, I didn't want to move just in case he returned again. Earl wanted to move. We walked down towards a railing overlooking the floor seats where a girl much older than me, a real teenager for sure, was wailing and screaming for Shaun. She was lying on the concrete in a three-piece lavender pantsuit with her arm outstretched. She just screamed and screamed towards the empty stage, people stepping over her exiting the arena.

"Dad, what's she doing?" Earl looked at me and then down at the distressed girl.

"What the hell is wrong with you? You need to get up off the damn dirty floor and act right!" She looked up at him with black tears running down her face and then went right back to screaming.

"C'mon, Libbah, she's on that Angel Dust."

He didn't explain to me what Angel Dust was, it sounded pretty but it had to be bad, so we just kept on walking. I relived the concert in my head on the ride home until I fell asleep. It was the pinnacle of my life up until then. I'm sure it was the pinnacle of Earl's, too.

Beal continued to shame me for needing help. She told anyone who would listen. Anyone.

"I pay bills for LIBBY and she isn't grateful."

Beal never asked me how I was feeling unless there was an audience. If I tried to give her an update, she became irritated.

"Libby! Get on with it. What do you want?"

When I got to where I could drive a little, she demanded I bring her the bills, which was fine, but sometimes the doors to the inside of the house were locked. I began leaving bills on top of the dog food in the utility room. I felt like a dog. One of the times she was there, she chastised me for not bringing the whole bill so she could scrutinize it and decide if there was any wrongdoing. I never understood what "wrongdoing" she was looking for and I told her. Beal became so enraged, she told me to get out and threw my keys into the front yard. Eight inches of snow covered the ground. Before I could leave, the doorbell rang. It was the mailman holding my keys.

"Do these belong to anyone? I found them in the yard."

"Yes, they are mine." I thought sarcastically, God sometimes gives us these little gifts. Beal interrupted before I could say another word. In a honeyed voice, she tried to give her explanation on why they were there. The mailman wasn't interested. He had a route to complete. Slamming the door, Beal said he was the worst mailman ever.

"He doesn't deliver my junk mail," and immediately called the Post Office to report a crime.

Today Beal remains unchanged. We have never had a meaningful conversation, and I accept we never will. Conversation with Beal is mostly confusing, upsetting and downright disturbing. Beal tells me how an upscale restaurant, *The Village Anchor*, crossed a line and she called them to "TELL THEM ABOUT IT!" I asked how? The Village Anchor sends out emails to patrons who wish to know about daily features. It's voluntary. Beal volunteered her email address as I did when I took her there for lunch years ago. I ask how did they cross a line? "Libby! THEY sent me an email with the menu for Mother's Day and MY MOTHER'S DEAD!" She claims the restaurant was insensitive and should know her Mother is dead. How does one respond to that logic? So I don't. I can only imagine the reaction of the person who fielded the call. Beal continues to tell me my father never loved me and wouldn't speak to her for two weeks when she revealed she was pregnant. It's an automatic response to any positive remark I make about my father.

I've tried to have a cordial relationship, but it always ends poorly. Beal leaves messages on my voicemail accusing me of committing various crimes in her house. It's like listening to a *Greatest Hits Collection!* There is no "Hello;" Beal plunges right in. "Libby! Did you take some of my hangers? After all, because THEY'VE been moved around, the ones that were on top were not on top!" CLICK. I was in her house looking for some old pictures for a class reunion, and I moved some hangers. "Libby! Did you take that bill? Did you take my cable bill? Let me know!" CLICK! I have no idea why anyone would *want* to steal someone else's bill? "Libby! I want to ask you a question? I had eight books of quarters in my closet and when I cleaned my closet the other day, there's only four. Did you take four of those things of quarters when you were here? When I was in Mississippi? Because you were up in that closet then, I'd just like to know, or do I need to call the PO-LEECE and report 'em missing?" CLICK! The "books" of quarters Beal is referring to is her collection of U.S. State series quarter maps on extra thick foldable boards with recessed coin slots for each state. No "real" valuables were stolen, only the collectors' maps buried deep in her closet. I did not commit ANY of the aforementioned crimes. I will go to my grave professing my innocence. All cases remain cold.

Unresolved rage is seared into my mother's very core. Anger has run through her veins as long as I can remember. I believe it's strongly rooted in her childhood. I wanted to love her, but she couldn't beat the odds and love me unconditionally. I'm conflicted. I guess in my mother's case, she couldn't give what she didn't get. I don't think she got a lot. I have no concrete explanation for her behavior other than what counselors have offered: a personality disorder. I find my mother in several of them, Borderline, Histrionic and Narcissistic, but I'll never truly know. My research suggests a link between personality disorders and childhood trauma. I subscribe to that theory, as I don't believe my mother just sprouted out of the ground damaged. It's easier to believe that than to believe her cruelty was for sport, though sometimes her actions appear designed to be cruel. Beal tossed aside a Christmas wreath I had placed at Earl's gravestone upside down on the ground, so she could have the prime spot. It's hard not to think of this as a deliberately spiteful, willful act. When confronted, Beal doesn't attempt to deny her actions, she smiles a cryptic smile, licks her lips and declares, "I GET FIRST CHOICE!"

She was and remains the minefield I tried to safely navigate as a child, purposely set off as a rebellious teenager, and try to understand as an adult.

Sweetie passed away in 2012. I didn't feel contempt like I felt towards Paul when he died, but I didn't feel a sense of loss, either. I had faced rejection over and over with Sweetie, so I was sad but sad for a relationship we never had. Out of self-preservation, I stopped trying to gain her affections and built a wall around myself. She became a distant relative I only saw at the obligatory Christmas dinner every two years, or at a few reunions, at Beal's request. Sweetie eventually moved to Mississippi to live with Aunt Faye and I never saw her alive again.

On a typical day in January, cold and overcast, I drove back to Waynesburg. A feeling of intrusiveness overcame me the minute we crossed the town line. Earl and I had shared a bond of being "outsiders," but this time Earl wasn't there, probably sharing a nip with the Big Man in the sky. I was on my own. When I was a young adult, I told Earl how I felt about the way Sweetie treated me.

"Libbah, Margie and B never treated me the same way they treated your Uncle Quentin, (Uncle Quentin was my Aunt Faye's husband), but that's okay."

I know Earl was being funny when he whispered, "Libbah, these aren't your people." But there was a truth to his jesting. That was a revelation to me. I had always felt like I was the only one.

Sweetie and Paul didn't approve of their daughter, Beal, marrying a newly divorced man twenty years her senior and two years older than they were, something I wouldn't know for years. Earl never would show me his license when I was young, and his age recorded on my birth certificate made him a younger man. The same error is on my sister's as well. Born an aunt of four older children was confusing enough. It was a blessing I didn't find out Earl was older than my grandparents until I was an adult. I miss Earl's whispers today. He always made me feel it was okay to be on the "Island of the Misfits."

I walked into the small funeral home I used to play above as a child when my uncle's girlfriend lived there. Her family had owned the funeral home, and my Uncle Eugene and his girlfriend lived in the apartment above the parlor with her children. I liked playing with her daughter, Angel. One day Beal told me I was never allowed to play with Angel again because her mother had pulled a gun on my Uncle Eugene. That was pretty heavy stuff for a child, but I guess that kind of thing wasn't so uncommon in Waynesburg. Maybe he was "worrying" her.

The strangers' eyes made me feel like I was Clarice in the *Silence of the Lambs* funeral home scene, when she is left alone with the scrutinizing sheriffs. I didn't recognize anyone other than Beal's siblings. Aunt Faye's clan was all huddled together in several pews, talking amongst themselves. I admired how they seemed to operate as a cohesive family; that was foreign to me. I saw my Uncle Eugene sitting with my newly found cousin whose existence had been kept a secret. It was hard not to stare at her. She shared the same coloring as Sweetie, dark, almost black hair, and fair skin. Beal sat next to me and chatted up her cousins. She had a hundred and twenty first cousins or so she said. Her dad was the youngest of thirteen and her mom was one of twelve. I couldn't name one of the cousins. I'm sure I had met some as a child, but again, there were no relationships and any memories I had faded into obscurity. I did my best to engage in conversation with a few of them, but recoiled when a woman blurted out in a condemning voice, "I was going to name MY daughter 'Elizabeth,' but Beal had her baby first and took the name!" (I was named after Sweetie's mother, which is ironic since I completely identify with Earl's side of the family.) I thought facetiously, "How dare Beal commit such an egregious act!" Waynesburg is the only place I felt an urge to defend my mother. That urge was always a surprise to me.

The service started. I heard the wind pushing a rusty swing outside, a familiar sound from my past. I listened to a woman I had never laid eyes on speak about Sweetie's character and the love her children had for her. Fair enough, but how did Sweetie love her children? Beal was the least favored and she defends her mother's overt favoritism. In my mind, I hear Beal saying in her childish voice, "Aunt Faye was the favorite!" The same voice she used when I asked as a child,

"Why doesn't Sweetie like me as much as she likes Virginia?"

"Virginia is the favorite!" Beal believes that's the way it's supposed to be. My mother was treated that way and so was Sweetie when she was growing up. Years later, I learned a story that must have been a painful time for Sweetie. The favorite was thrown off a small Ferris wheel at the county fair and broke her arm. Sweetie's mother went to pieces telling her, "If something every happened to your sister, I couldn't go on living!" That must have wounded Sweetie deeply, and when she grew up, she repeated the pattern. I believe Sweetie's blatant favoritism coupled with Paul's abuse molded Beal into who she is today. There's a saying, "Abuse is a horse riding through the generations with a different person in the saddle." That seemed to be true for Beal's family

Conflicting emotions spun in my mind as the strange woman eulogizing Sweetie became a faraway voice I no longer understood. Old memories came flooding back. Tears welled up in my eyes less in sorrow but more for the little girl who tried so hard to be loved. I felt transparent. The organ music jolted me back to the present. Wide-eyed, glancing around at relatives I didn't know, I couldn't have been more relieved when the service ended. I wanted out! Sweetie's funeral forced me to face painful memories I had buried. Layers of humor and sarcasm had been stripped away and left me feeling exposed.

The congregation made the short pilgrimage down the country road I had traveled so many times to a small cemetery where Paul was buried. Gravediggers had left a six-foot hole, exposing Paul's coffin. Peering down, I quickly stepped back, afraid I might fall in. I don't remember any of the final words said over Sweetie's coffin. I only remember the brown patches of grass that spotted the ground, a gray sky and a few birds that had forgotten to fly south that winter. Aunt Faye invited everyone to eat after the burial, but I couldn't pretend any longer. I left and never returned to Waynesburg. I wonder about Sweetie and Paul's eternal life together.

CHAPTER 12

I never thought to conduct a deed search on myself as the buyer or seller after learning of Ted's legal problems. Ted was convicted of the most elementary real estate fraud, buying distressed properties cheaply and selling them at a substantial profit, often within days, to a straw buyer and then defaulting on the loan and pocketing the profit.

Sometimes the same fraud was perpetrated several times with a single property, resulting in increased profits (and fees); with each sale and with the addition of straw buyers, Ted and Co. are distanced from the original sale.

It hadn't occurred to me that Ted might have used my name (or signature) for real estate scams. Ten years later I was calling up a woman in the mortgage business I believed could give a clearer picture on how Ted's scam worked. She also had known Ted and wasn't a fan. Suspecting him and his partner of wrongdoing long before the FBI got involved, she told me as much at a chance meeting over the holidays after Ted and I divorced. My quest to unravel the past had turned to action. I remember how kind she had been and the good advice she gave about building credit after bankruptcy, suggesting I get a credit card even if hardly used, and keeping payments current.

Honestly, I felt like an idiot calling a woman I had met only a few times, but I set that feeling aside and called anyway. Graciously, she remembered me when I introduced myself. Through our conversation I became acquainted with a new term, "straw buyer," commonly known as a "fake buyer." A straw buyer is "a real person with a real SS# who has real credit for whom the LO (loan officer) can create doctored up income verification (tax returns, W-2s, pay stubs), so that this person qualifies to buy the house, income-wise on paper." As she explained, my mind went immediately back to the closing on our new house in Prospect, Kentucky. I remember sitting in Chris Mooser's law office, shocked when Alphaeus Green was the buyer and not Khalid. Khalid was later convicted with Ted and the others.

My acquaintance told me there was nothing illegal about using straw buyers as they sometimes purchase properties when the real buyer cannot obtain financing for some reason, but in Ted's case, many were used to defraud lenders. "Libby, check online deed records; I wouldn't be surprised if you find yourself on deeds you didn't know about." It seemed as if she already knew, but then again, I felt like everybody knew what I didn't. Thanking her for the information, we hung up. I flew to the computer and sure enough, there was my name forged with individuals I had never met! Who was Kevin Hickman? Who was Kamal Stoddard? According to one deed, on February 4, 2002, Kevin Hickman bought a house located at 1637 Dumesnil Avenue, Louisville, Kentucky 40210, from Willie Mae Hobbs for the sum of 35,000 dollars (KY deed 202978). On the same day my signature was forged on a deed purchasing the same property for 70,000 dollars. Two days later, on February 6, 2002, Ted and I sold the same property to Kamal Stoddard for the same sum of 70,000 dollars (202988), and by the end of the year, the loan is in default. Kevin Hickman's signature appears often, which suggests he's a straw buyer, and, interestingly, his signature is often notarized by notary Bridgett S. Yochum. The attorney who prepared the deeds, is often David P. Haick, twenty-eight times to be exact. The aforementioned notary, Bridgett S. Yochum, appears on several of the documents where David P. Haick also appears.

Kevin Hickman, along with Nathan Frisbee, Jerry Crenshaw, Kamal and Khalid, are interesting characters in the cast of characters orchestrated by Ted. Kevin is nineteen and according to the deeds, Kevin and I collaborated together on the Dumesnil Avenue house which was sold twice in one day and then again two days later. Kevin, the nineteen-year old was busy in the real estate business. He appears on thirty-two deeds between November 8, 2001 and March 29, 2002, and sometimes the same house is sold twice on the same day.

I soon discovered another deed where I legitimately signed my name with Ted on March 5, 2003, but on April 23, 2003, my name is forged; I recognize his handiwork. He didn't even bother to sign my legal name on two of the deeds. My legal name is "Elizabeth House," and he signed "Libby House."

"IF I GO DOWN, I'M TAKING YOU WITH ME!"

Ted's cackling and calling me a co-conspirator in the yard all those years ago made sense now that it was placed in a proper context, and I re-lived those moments as if I was standing there in my pajamas in the yard all over again. He knew he had used me in his scheme. He knew that I didn't know. He thought nothing of putting his wife at risk! This shouldn't have been a surprise, but seeing my name forged on deeds associated with crimes that landed four people in prison made me both angry and sad at the same time. I still wore a locket of pain like an albatross. Nostalgia for the past contrasted to the defects I recognized in Ted now was cause for conflicting emotions. I remembered the great family times with Kennedy, like Flat Stanley's trip to Florida and the rides at Busch Gardens. I fondly remembered visiting an older woman's home the year Ted and I were married. It was Christmas, and she had a garland that wrapped around the house, constructed from years of Christmas card pictures of her family. I liked it so much I decided to do the same, to start my own tradition. Now I have thirteen Christmas cards corresponding to thirteen years of marriage with Ted. It makes me catch my breath. Maybe not nostalgia so much for the good memories

I carry, but like the garland that never was, nostalgia for what could have been.

Where was all this leading? Was I waxing nostalgic for Ted or life with Ted? I realized how absurd my thinking was and how absurd it was to have given Ted chance after chance. Even when he was released from prison, I wanted to have an understanding, if not a relationship, but each attempt at reaching out was asking to be sucker-punched over and over.

My marriage had been a façade. Behind the light-hearted persona the world saw was a weary, sad and lonely girl trapped by choices made long ago. No amount of Christmas cards on a garland could ever hide that. I was done lying to myself. I hadn't loved myself enough to leave the man who had no respect for me and who'd hoped for my demise. As the saying goes, "Insanity is doing the same thing over and over again, expecting a different result," and now, wiping a tear from my eye as dreams of a happy marriage and all that was promised, faded, I realized it was all over. I never spoke to Ted again. I grieved. I grieved for the irretrievably broken trust that could never be regained. I was facing the world for the first time, my real world.

That night I lay in bed and looked out the smudged window of my tiny apartment. Exhausted, a flood of tears dampening my pillow, I fell asleep. Waking up the next morning, I got heavily caffeinated, reclaiming my sanity. Curious about the properties I allegedly owned, I went back to Jefferson County's online deed records. I scoured the deed site and found a pattern; property after property changing hands, sometimes three times in a week. All the properties ended in foreclosure.

I knew one of the attorneys fairly well and the other was an acquaintance. Deciding I wanted to ask some questions, I grabbed my phone again. My first call was to Bridgett S. Yochum, the notary on many of the deeds. I found her place of business easily on the internet. It had been thirteen years, but I thought, "I have nothing to lose! I already lost it all," including my mind. The receptionist patched me through, and I introduced myself as "Libby Henry," formerly "Libby House," Ted House's ex-wife. Thirteen years may have passed but she knew exactly who Ted was. I wasn't surprised, since Ted's conviction and subsequent incarceration were widely known throughout Louisville's mortgage industry.

Arriving at my point immediately I explained, "On deeds recently located, my name is forged, and you are listed as the notary." I further explained my legal name is "Elizabeth," but my nickname "Libby" was used instead. I didn't expect her to remember, but I did want to know protocol when notarizing legal documents. She claimed there must have been a woman posing as me with identification. I told her that would have been impossible because my name on my ID is "Elizabeth," and anyway, I recognized my ex-husband's handwriting. I felt the tension over the phone.

"Well, someone must have posed as you."

"Again, I clearly recognize the handwriting, there's absolutely no doubt."

"Then someone must have used my seal." I kept inquiring.

"But wouldn't that mean someone would have had to forge your signature?"

"I guess that would be right." Her urgency to terminate the call came across in her voice. I asked if she happened to remember a "Kevin Hickman," since multiple deeds signed by him had her seal and signature. She had no recollection. It had been thirteen years, so that was reasonable. I wrapped up our conversation, but I wasn't satisfied. I went down to the courthouse and checked the deed book (notaries are required to sign when they renew their notary commission). Bridgett S. Yochum's stamp was renewed in July of 2002. I compared her renewal signature to the deeds in question, and it was a spot-on match. A trusted attorney reviewed both signatures and agreed it appeared to be Bridgett S. Yochum's signature, so her seal had not been stolen. I called her back and revealed I checked her signature in the deed book and it matched the signature on the deeds. Of course, something was amiss. Our conversation ended rather quickly. She said, "I can't speak

THE PEOPLE IN MY HOUSE

DB07820PG0766

202978
Kentucky Deed

WARRANTY DEED AND
CONSIDERATION CERTIFICATION

This Deed, made this 4th day of February, 2002, by and between Kevin Hickman, Grantor of

1637 Dumesnil Ave , Louisville, KY 40210 and Libby House, Grantee of 1637 Dumesnil Ave , Louisville, KY 40210

WITNESSETH That, for a valuable consideration in the receipt of which is hereby acknowledged, the

Grantor, hereby conveys unto the Grantee in fee simple, and with convenant of General Warranty, the following

described property located in Jefferson County, Kentucky, to wit

BEGINNING at the Northeast corner of Dumesnil and 17th Streets, running thence East along North side of Dumesnil Street, 57 feet and extending back North of same width, West line binding on East line of 17th Street 117 feet 9 inches to South line of lot conveyed to William J Price and Wife by deed dated May 2, 1955 of record in Deed Book 3298, Page 213, in the Office of the Clerk of the County Court of Jefferson County, Kentucky, and being part of Lot 10 Block 30 in Ormsby Subdivision Bullitt addition

Being the same property conveyed to Willie Mae Hobbs by Deed dated November 24, 1982 and recorded in Deed Book 5322, Page 311 in the Office of the Clerk of Jefferson County, Kentucky

The Grantor and Grantee hereto certify that the fair market value for this conveyance is the sum of

Seventy Thousand Dollars and zero cents ($70,000 00)

The Grantor further covenants lawful seizin of the estate hereby conveyed with full power to convey the

same, and that said estate is free of encumbrances except restrictions and easements of record, situated on said

property, the 2002 State and County, and School taxes and all taxes thereafter, which the Grantee hereby

assumes and agrees to pay

274

CHAPTER 12

DB 07820 PG 0767

Provided, however, there is excepted any restrictions, stipulations and easements of record affecting said property

IN TESTIMONY WHEREOF, WITNESS the signature of the Grantor and Grantee the day and year first mentioned

Kevin Hickman
Kevin Hickman

Libby House
Libby House

STATE OF KENTUCKY)

COUNTY OF Jefferson

The foregoing was acknowledged, subscribed and sworn to, before me this 4th day of Februry, 2002, by Kevin Hickman, Grantor and Libby House, Grantee

Notary Public, Jefferson County, KY

My Commission Expires 7/20/02

Notary Public, State at Large, KY
My commission expires_____

THE PEOPLE IN MY HOUSE

DB 0782 0PG 0768

CONSIDERATION CERTIFICATE

We, the undersigned, hereby certify that the consideration reflected in the forgoing deed is the full
consideration paid for the property herein conveyed

Kevin Hickman
Kevin Hickman

Libby House
Libby House

STATE OF KENTUCKY)

COUNTY OF Jefferson

The foregoing Consideration Certificate was acknowledged, subscribed and sworn to, before me this
4th day of February, 2002, by Kevin Hickman Grantor and Libby House, Grantee

Notary Public, Jefferson County, KY

My Commission Expires 7/20/02

This Instrument Prepared Without Title Examination By

David P Haick
David P Haick
Attorney at Law
1717 Alliant Avenue, Ste 5
Louisville, KY 40229
(502)357-6000

Document No.: DN2002029636
Lodged By: ASK TITLE.10983
Recorded On: 02/13/2002   10:28
Total Fees: 82.00
Transfer Tax: 70.00
County Clerk: Bobbie Holsclaw-JEFF C
Deputy Clerk: TERHIG

Notary Public, State at Large, KY
My commission expires_____

END OF DOCUMENT

276

CHAPTER 12

DB 0 7 8 4 6 PG 0 7 7 2

3⁵

202988
Kentucky Deed

WARRANTY DEED AND
CONSIDERATION CERTIFICATION

This Deed, made this 6th day of February, 2002, by and between Libby House, Grantor of Louisville, *and Ted House*
↳ *1637 Dumesnil Ave*
Louisville, KY 40210

Kentucky and Kamal Stoddard, Grantee of Decatur, Georgia
↳ *1637 Dumesnil Ave*
Louisville, KY 40210

WITNESSETH That, for a valuable consideration in the receipt of which is hereby acknowledged, the

Grantor, hereby conveys unto the Grantee in fee simple, and with convenant of General Warranty, the following

described property located in Jefferson County, Kentucky, to wit

BEGINNING at the Northeast corner of Dumesnil and 17th Streets, running thence East along North side of Dumesnil Street, 57 feet and extending back North of same width, West line binding on East line of 17th Street 117 feet 9 inches to South line of lot conveyed to William J Price and Wife by deed dated May 2, 1955 of record in Deed Book 3298, Page 213, in the Office of the Clerk of the County Court of Jefferson County, Kentucky, and being part of Lot 10 Block 30 in Ormsby Subdivision Bullitt addition

Being the same property conveyed to Libby House by Deed dated February 4, 2002 and recorded in Deed Book 7820, Page *766*, in the Office of the Clerk of Jefferson County, Kentucky

The Grantor and Grantee hereto certify that the fair market value for this conveyance is the sum of

Seventy Thousand Dollars and zero cents ($70,000 00)

The Grantor further covenants lawful seizin of the estate hereby conveyed with full power to convey the

same, and that said estate is free of encumbrances except restrictions and easements of record, situated on said

property, the 2002 State and County, and School taxes and all taxes thereafter, which the Grantee hereby

assumes and agrees to pay

Provided, however, there is excepted any restrictions, stipulations and easements of record affecting said

property

277

THE PEOPLE IN MY HOUSE

DB07846PG0773

IN TESTIMONY WHEREOF, WITNESS the signature of the Grantor and Grantee the day and year first mentioned

Libby House
Libby House

Ted House
TED House

K. Stoddard
Kamal Stoddard

STATE OF KENTUCKY)

COUNTY OF JEFFERSON)

The foregoing was acknowledged, subscribed and sworn to, before me this 6th day of February, 2002, by Libby House, Grantor and Kamal Stoddard, Grantee
↳ and Ted House

Notary Public, Jefferson County, KY

My Commission Expires ___7/20/02___

Notary Public, State at Large KY
My commission expires_____

278

DB07846PG0774

CONSIDERATION CERTIFICATE

We, the undersigned, hereby certify that the consideration reflected in the forgoing deed is the full

consideration paid for the property herein conveyed

Libby House
Libby House

Ted House
TED HOUSE

K. Stoddard
Kamal Stoddard

STATE OF KENTUCKY)

COUNTY OF JEFFERSON)

The foregoing Consideration Certificate was acknowledged, subscribed and sworn to, before me this

6th day of February, 2002, by Libby House, Grantor and Kamal Stoddard, Grantee
↳and Ted House

_____
Notary Public, Jefferson County, KY

My Commission Expires 7/20/02

This Instrument Prepared Without Title Examination By

David P Haick
David P Haick
Attorney at Law
1717 Alliant Avenue, Ste 5
Louisville, KY 40299
(502)357-6000

END OF DOCUMENT

Notary Public, State at Large KY
ID #200205606500000205606500000000566065
Lodged By: ask title
Recorded On: 03/21/2002   12:09:57
Total Fees: 82.00
Transfer Tax: 70.00
County Clerk: Bobbie Holsclaw-JEFF CO KY
Deputy Clerk: YOLLOG2

DB 08086PG0208

∂

GENERAL WARRANTY DEED

THIS DEED dated March 5, 2003 is between Edward N. House and Elizabeth House, husband and wife (herein "Seller") whose mailing address is 1 Indian Hills Trail, Louisville, KY 40207; and Diane Noble and Joseph Noble, wife and husband (herein "Buyer"), whose mailing address is 132 Boston Court, Louisville, KY 40210.

In consideration of Sixty Thousand dollars and Zero cents, which the parties hereto certify is the full consideration paid for the property, the receipt of which is hereby acknowledged, the sellers hereby convey to the Buyers, for their joint lives with the remainder in fee simple to the survivor of them, with Covenant of GENERAL WARRANTY, the following described property located in Jefferson County, Kentucky, to-wit:

Being The Northern half of Lot 24, as shown on the plat of Westholme Annex, an Addition to the City of Louisville, which plat is recorded in Plat and Subdivision Book 2, Page 274, in the Office of the Clerk of Jefferson County, Kentucky.

Tax ID #01-009H-0024-0000

BEING the same property conveyed to Edward N. House, by Deed dated January 31, 2003, of record in Deed Book 8066, Page 430, in the Office of the Clerk of the County Court of Jefferson County, Kentucky.

Said estate is free from all encumbrances except restrictions and easements of record, zoning regulations and real estate taxes not yet due and payable.

The Buyers execute this Deed for the sole purpose of certifying the consideration pursuant to KRS Chapter 382; and IN AFFIRMATION of this conveyance, witness the signatures of the Sellers, on March 5, 2003.

DB 08086PG0209

Diane Noble (BUYER)

Diane Noble (BUYER)

Joseph Noble (BUYER)

Joseph Noble (BUYER)

Edward N. House (SELLER)

Edward N. House (SELLER)

Elizabeth House (SELLER)

Elizabeth House (SELLER)

COMMONWEALTH OF KENTUCKY
COUNTY OF JEFFERSON

The foregoing Deed and Consideration Certificate was acknowledged and sworn to before me on March 5, 2003, by Edward N. House and Elizabeth House, husband and wife, Sellers; and by Diane Noble and Joseph Noble, wife and husband, Buyers.

My Commission Expires: Apr. 15, 2004

NOTARY PUBLIC, State at Large, Kentucky

PREPARED BY: Mooser & Freibert, LLC
161 St. Matthews Ave., Suite 5
Louisville, Kentucky 40207
(502) 893-6688

Exam No. 2302085

END OF DOCUMENT

THE PEOPLE IN MY HOUSE

DB 0 8 1 2 8 PG 0 3 8 4

2

AND WHEN RECORDED RETURN TO
Mooser & Freibert Land Title, LLC
161 St Matthews Avenue #5
Louisville, Kentucky 40207
File# 2564-002

GENERAL WARRANTY DEED

THIS DEED dated April 23, 2003 is between Edward N House and Elizabeth House, husband and wife (herein "Seller") whose mailing address is 1 Indian Hills Trail, Louisville Kentucky 40207, and Diana Noble and Joseph Noble, wife and husband (herein "Buyer"), whose mailing address is 2306 St Louis Avenue, Louisville, KY 40211

In consideration of *Fifty Six Thousand dollars and Zero cents*, which the parties hereto certify is the full consideration paid for the property, the receipt of which is hereby acknowledged, the sellers hereby convey to the Buyers, for their joint lives with the remainder in fee simple to the survivor of them, with Covenant of GENERAL WARRANTY, the following described property located in Jefferson County, Kentucky, to-wit

BEING the West 20 feet of Lot 37 and the Eastern 10 feet of Lot 36, Block 7, Standard Land Company's Subdivision of Newcomb's Addition to Louisville, Kentucky, map or plat of which is of record in Deed Book 343, Page 640, in the Office of the Clerk of Jefferson County, Kentucky, and being 30 by 135 feet on the South side of Stratton Avenue, the East line of which is 78-1/2 feet West of 23rd Street

BEING the same property conveyed to Edward N House, by Deed dated January 31, 2003, of record in Deed Book 8066, Page 433, in the Office of the Clerk of the County Court of Jefferson County, Kentucky

Said estate is free from all encumbrances except restrictions and easements of record, zoning regulations and real estate taxes not yet due and payable

The Buyers execute this Deed for the sole purpose of certifying the consideration pursuant to KRS Chapter 382, and IN AFFIRMATION of this conveyance, witness the signatures of the Sellers, on April 23, 2003

282

08128PG0385

_____   _____
Diana Noble   (BUYER)   Edward N House   (SELLER)

_____   _____
Joseph Noble   (BUYER)   Elizabeth House   (SELLER)

COMMONWEALTH OF KENTUCKY
COUNTY OF JEFFERSON

    The foregoing Deed and Consideration Certificate was acknowledged and sworn to before me on April 23, 2003, by Edward N House and Elizabeth House, husband and wife, Sellers, and by Diana Noble and Joseph Noble, wife and husband, Buyers

My Commission Expires 9-15-03

_____
NOTARY PUBLIC, State at Large, Kentucky

    CAROLYN M HOBACK
    Notary Public, State at Large, KY
    commission expires Sept 15, 2003

PREPARED BY   Mooser & Freibert, LLC
                161 St Matthews Ave., Suite 5
                Louisville, Kentucky 40207
                (502) 893-6688

                Exam No. 2304002

END OF DOCUMENT

DB0860 3PG0205

DEED

THIS DEED, made and entered into this 7th day of April, 2005, by and between **ENH Enterprises, LLC**, Grantor(s), whose address is 136 St. Matthews Ave. Louisville, KY 40207 and **Peacock Anchorage, LLC**, Grantee(s) , whose address is 836 E. 64th Street Indianapolis, IN 46220.

WITNESSETH:

THAT, for and in consideration of the sum of *SIXTY FIVE THOUSAND DOLLARS AND 00/100 ($65,000.00)*, and other good and valuable consideration, the receipt and sufficiency of which is hereby acknowledged by the Grantor(s), the Grantor(s) has this day BARGAINED and SOLD and do hereby GRANT and CONVEY, unto Grantee(s), as joint tenants in common with rights of survivorship, his heirs and assigns forever the following described property located at 4217 Sunset Avenue Louisville, KY 40211, to wit:

BEING Lot No. 10 and the Western 15 feet in width of Lot 11 in Block #1 of Lewis' Subdivision, as shown on plat recorded in Deed Book 531, Page 638, in the office of the Clerk of Jefferson County, Kentucky.

Being the same property conveyed to ENH Enterprises, LLC, a Kentucky Limited Liability Company, by deed dated September 27, 2004 and found of record in Deed Book 8551, Page 740 in the Office of the Jefferson County Recorder.

TO HAVE AND TO HOLD the above-described property together with all appurtenances thereunto belonging unto Grantee, in fee simple, his heirs and assigns forever.

Said Grantor(s) do hereby release and relinquish unto the said Grantee(s), his heirs and assigns, all of their rights, title and interest in and to the above-described property, including homestead and all exemptions allowed by law, and hereby covenants to and with the said Grantee(s), his heirs and assigns, that they are lawfully seized in fee simple to the said property and have good and lawful right to convey the same as herein done, and that said property is free and clear of all encumbrances of whatsoever nature and that they will WARRANT GENERALLY the title to said property.

Provided, however, that there is excepted from the foregoing warranties and covenants, the following:

1. All conditions and/or restrictions, if any, affecting the property herein conveyed and contained on any plat of record in the aforesaid Jefferson County Clerk's Office.

2. Zoning and building restrictions, regulations and ordinances, if any.

3. Easements and rights-of-way of whatsoever nature and kind reserved and recorded in the aforesaid Clerk's Office.

4. Lien for 2004 State, Jefferson County and school ad valorem taxes and subsequent years.

Page 1 of 2

284

DB 08603PG0206

The parties hereto state that the consideration reflected in this Deed is the full consideration paid for the property. The Grantees joins this Deed for the sole purpose of certifying the consideration pursuant to KRS 382.990.

IN WITNESS WHEREOF, the Grantors and Grantees have hereunto set their hand this day and year first above written.

ENH Enterprises, LLC by:

_____
Edward N. House, as member

Peacock Anchorage, LLC by: House Development

_____
Michael P. House, as member

STATE OF ~~KENTUCKY~~ Florida)
)
COUNTY OF Collier)

The foregoing Deed and Consideration Certificate was acknowledged and sworn to before me on this 7th day of April, 2005, by ENH Enterprises, signed by Edward N. House as member of said company, Grantor and the foregoing Consideration Certificate was acknowledged and sworn to before me on the 7th day of April 2005, by Peacock Anchorage, LLC signed by Michael P. House as member of said company, Grantee

My Commission Expires: 8/19/07

_____
Notary Public, State at Large, Kentucky

This instrument prepared by:

MEGAN BERNASCONI
NOTARY PUBLIC - STATE OF FLORIDA
COMMISSION # DD242963
EXPIRES 08/19/2007
BONDED THRU 1-888-NOTARY1

This instrument prepared by:

Jason Kron, Esq.
Heritage Title Services, LLC
159 St. Matthews Ave., Ste 4
Louisville, KY 40207
502.895.5045

Jason A. Kron
159 St. Matthews Ave. Ste. 4
Louisville, KY 40207

Page 2 of 2

4/8/05

Document No.: DN2005056547
Lodged By: HERITAGE TITLE LLC
Recorded On: 04/13/2005   09:50:26
Total Fees: 77.00
Transfer Tax: 65.00
County Clerk: BOBBIE HOLSCLAW-JEFF CO KY
Deputy Clerk: EVEMAY

END OF DOCUMENT

with you again without consulting our legal department. "You do that!" I responded.

My next call was to David Haick, the attorney who prepared the deeds. I didn't have to make much of an introduction, he knew who I was. I explained my purpose and questioned the deeds. Disclosing that I had spoken to the notary and relaying her response, he told me he was doing his job. I asked how a property sold twice in the same day, escalating in value from $35,000 to $70,000, could be an ethical transaction? He became defensive, saying, "I hope you don't think I was involved?"

I didn't know what to think. He went on to say he was "thrown under the bus" by another attorney but didn't elaborate. He asked for Bridgett Yochum's number. I obliged, or so I thought, though after our call, I realized I had accidently given him the number of a podiatrist I had recently seen. Surprisingly, a hearty laugh escaped me. "Good!" I shook my head in some sort of agreement with my involuntary laugh. It had been a heavy week. I needed a laugh.

I didn't call David Haick back. I figured he knew how to find Ms. Yochum. My final calls regarding forged deeds were to Chris Mooser. I knew Chris. We had dined together with his ex-girlfriend and attended his company Christmas parties. Chris was a congenial person with a quick wit, and Chris and Ted had a cozy business relationship. He was easy to like, no effort required. However, he wasn't that person on the phone a decade later. He expeditiously reminded me, "Libby, you said yourself you signed anything Ted put in front of your!" insinuating it was my fault. When I referenced a transaction between Ted, myself and Diane and Joseph Noble on April 23, 2003, I said, "I did sign what I thought were innocent transactions. I trusted my husband and that's *all* I did! I believe I've paid a hefty price for my ignorance." Why was I suddenly trying to justify my innocence to him? Heat was creeping up my neck. I was angry and I was tired of life teaching me lessons.

"Chris, the deed I legitimately signed was on March 5, 2003 and on the other deed, with "The Noble's, dated April 23, 2003, Ted forged my signature! Do you have any idea how that happened?"

"I have no idea, Libby."

"What about the notary on the deed? Carolyn Hoback, does she still work for you?" Chris answered, clearly irritated.

"She's retired and elderly, lives somewhere in the South End."

"How did any of those three statements have anything to do with notarizing a deed?" I thought. I had many more questions, but they weren't going to be answered by Chris Mooser. I thought of the one person I trusted in the banking and mortgage industry, maybe the only person I trusted anymore, Monroe Jett. He was my friend and husband of my dear friend, Christine from college. We had known each other for twenty-six years. I would go to him for answers.

Monroe is one of the very few men in my circle with whom things haven't changed since "The Fall." Monroe worked in the family business, The Bank of The Bluegrass, and in 2005 started his own company, Jett Title. Who better to answer questions and confirm my suspicions regarding the land deeds?

I spread my documents out on the conference table, and within a minute or so, he outlined how the scam worked.

"I don't know how these guys thought this could end well," he said.

With a second look, it's such a transparent and obvious scam, it's incredulous that Ted and Co. thought they could get away with it. Ted's hubris must have been so strong that he convinced himself and the others that nothing would come of it. Monroe's validation sent a warm glow through me. He offered to write up the ins and outs and how the players might be complicit. I'm so grateful (see addendum).

In my digging into the past, I turned up more than just forged deeds and shady deals. I turned up a transaction between ENH (Edward Needham House) Enterprises and Peacock Anchorage LLC. Of the many documents I reviewed, this one caught my eye. "Peacock" in German is "Pfau," Ted's mother's family name, and they lived in Anchorage when Ted was growing up. I immediately suspected it was a family transaction, I just didn't know between whom. One click revealed the sale of a property owned by Ted's LLC to his brother, Michael Pfau House's company, Peacock Anchorage

LLC. The property was sold for $65,000 on April 7, 2005, the very day our divorce petition was filed.

The papers were signed in Collier County, Florida, the same day Ted left to stay with his parents in their winter home for spring break. "The monster in me and my Jewish attorney are going to tear you apart!"

I heard Ted's cold declaration of war again. He spewed the words to me shortly before he flew off to Florida and secretly sold the property to his brother. It stung, not because I had unearthed more evidence of Ted's dishonesty – that had become commonplace – but because I didn't want to think his brother could be party to deceiving me as well. I had liked him so much.

My last conversation with Ted ended with him affirming, "If you would have kept your mouth shut, you would have gotten more child support!" GOODBYE! CLICK. Ted had done many vile things to me, and yet I still hadn't set up appropriate boundaries. I stayed in the ring, hoping not to take a punch. That was my fault. He took a shot at me that day, because I addressed the ripple effect his actions had on my financial, mental and physical health. For over a decade, my credit had been in the gutter. Ted doesn't like the truth, especially from me. He has no empathy. He never did. Ted always must be the center of attention and, even though his aura is the biggest in the room and his personality is magnetic, in the end he only accepts adulation from those around him.

Life has moved him along. He lives in a $400,000 condo overlooking the Ohio River. His parents provide a safety net, so he never worries about the roof over his head. I, on the other hand, remain saddled with the fallout of his crimes and financial instability. Ted once told me I didn't lose anything, because none of it was mine anyway, which speaks to Ted's sense of entitlement and superiority, not just in relation to me but, to the world at large. I know Ted is thinking of only material things. My loss was far greater. I lost the ability to trust. I lost credibility in the eyes of those who presumed I must have been complicit, or at least, knew of Ted's criminal activity. I lost my place in a circle of friends, or those I thought were friends. What hurt more was the realization that I was liked and accepted more for my social standing than for who I was. Most importantly, I lost my way and our daughter suffered. I can't take that back. It's a stain that doesn't wash away.

I don't know why those words on that particular day caused me to stop engaging, to stop pleading, to stop hoping for a different outcome. I just stopped. I wish for our daughter's sake that Ted and I could have been one of those couples who communicated cordially. The logical part of me knows that would have been best, but life is messy. Will Ted ever understand? Can he ever understand? Or, is he so narcissistic, that he can't see the plight of others? I don't know. I know I'm done trying to understand Ted. Now, each day is an opportunity rife with possibility, though sometimes it's a hard row to hoe, but I'm trying.

Epilogue

I drive past the Corinthian-style tower through stately iron gates. Enveloped by the splendor of springtime, Cave Hill Cemetery looks like it's been stroked by an artist's brush. Cherry trees, Dogwoods, and Lilac bushes are in full bloom, the mixture of carefully selected trees never failing to impress. They have proudly unfurled their finery. I weave my way down the path towards Earl's grave, a magical pond in full view. I fondly think of Kennedy holding a plastic bag filled with torn pieces of bread. She's standing close to the bank tossing its contents towards a glass-like fountain hoping a swan will glide by. My attention back on the path, I make a hard right at the rugged cross to where Earl rests. We need to have a conversation.

My face is buried in a bouquet of wildflowers, rose crocus, lilies, violets, iris, and larkspur. Their fragrance is strong, permeating the air around me. Earl would have preferred geraniums, but they aren't in season. He loved them just like his daddy did. I place the bouquet in a recessed vase and wipe fresh blades of grass off his gravestone. Earl likes it tidy. Taking a soft seat on the grass beside him, I listen quietly to the familiar sound of harmonizing birds.

"Dad, I came here today to tell you I've been up to something. I wrote a book about my life and before you make any judgements, let me tell you why? I've been suffering for a long time. Life didn't turn out the way I imagined. Can you understand? I feel like it cruelly robbed me of my "happily ever after," but that's not true, I never had the "happily" in the first place. I'm sorry I revealed our dark family history to the world. I needed to free myself from the grip it has had on me. Writing is my release. I was tired of denying my own feelings, making everyone else comfortable. Expressing myself was necessary for my own self-preservation. I'm trying to find the inner peace you never could. Can you understand that? I know you were in a world of pain all your own. I was, too. If you can't understand, can you forgive me? I forgave you."

Wiping away a salty stream of tears, I softly run my fingers across my father's name etched in stone.

"Earl Hazelrigg Henry." It comforts me to feel the depressions under my fingers. I look up at the pignut hickory standing guard close by and smile. I like to think I have Earl's blessing.

"Dad, I love you. I'll be back next week."

"Libbah, you know I'm not going anywhere!" he replies.

ADDENDUM

Summary of the Ted House Fraud as written by
Monroe Jett of Jett Title Co.

When a person sells a house, all the loans against the house must get paid off, and the seller gets to keep the difference.

Example:

- A married couple has a house worth $100k (something they own), and a loan of $90k (something they owe). They hire a realtor and list the house for sale. and they get a contract for a sale price of $100k.

At closing, here is what happens:

- The seller side of the settlement statement looks like this:
- Take the $100k sales price the seller is getting...and
- Subtract from the $90k payoff of their loan; also subtracted is the $6k realtor commission (6% is typical)
- The difference of what they get and give is what the sellers walk away with. $100k - $96k = $4k. $4k is what the seller receives.
- That amount, the $4k, is called the sales proceeds...or one could call this net amount their equity.
- What if their loan amount was only $40k instead of $90k? The sellers in this case would walk out of the closing with $54k in sales proceeds. So, the higher the sales price, and the lower their loan payoff amount...the more sales proceeds the sellers get at closing.

The Wrongdoer's thought process:

- Sellers who have a surplus of equity in their house walk out of closings with a surplus of cash.

- How can I be a seller of a house that has a lot of equity, so I receive most of the sales proceeds? Maybe it would be easier to find out how to be a seller of a house with a surplus of equity, so I can receive most of sales proceeds – it doesn't have to be a "lot of equity" in each deal, if I repeat the process numerous times.

Solution:

2 Transactions, closed back to back with persons A, B and C:

- A to B (A is a legitimate seller. B is the Wrongdoer)
- B to C (B is the Wrongdoer, C is hired by the Wrongdoer. He's a "fake" buyer, not intending to live in the house or pay back the loan he gets to buy the house. C is called a "straw" or fake buyer.)

B is "flipping" this house. He buys it from A, flips it by selling it immediately to C.

A (Legit Seller) to B (Wrongdoer):

Wrongdoer arranges to buy a cheap house from a legitimate seller. The house is in the "hood" or some emerging neighborhood where sellers are eager to get cash, and maybe even a bonus (a higher than normal sales price), over and above the house's value.

Why in the 'hood? 1) There are more lower value houses, and sellers are more likely to jump at a higher than normal sales price, even if only slightly higher than normal. 2) It is easier to forge smaller-income documents for the fake buyer than it is to fake, say, a doctor's income to buy an expensive house – it's also far less conspicuous and less likely to raise suspicions. 3) These are less risky deals to lenders, so they are more readily approved: the bank stands to lose less than if it were a $1 million house and a high loan amount with stricter loan approval standards.

B (Wrongdoer) to C (Fake Buyer):

Wrongdoer immediately sells to a Fake Buyer for an inflated sales price, often at the same closing table that the first transaction took place, with all three parties present to sign all documents for each. The Fake Buyer does this for an agreed upon fee from the Wrongdoer. The Wrongdoer gets the Loan Officer to use a crooked appraiser to produce an appraisal showing a high, fake value. Appraiser possibly does this for some agreed upon fee, paid by the Wrongdoer, in addition to the appraisal fee he charges. It is NOT likely the appraiser was doing this under a "don't ask, don't tell" understanding with the Wrongdoer in order to get many appraisal fees…because the appraiser KNOWS the true values of these properties, and KNOWS he/she can NOT legitimately justify the inflated values reported on the appraisals.

The Fake Buyer applies for and gets a maximum loan amount in order to buy the house for the fake sales price. The Fake Buyer has NO intention of paying the loan back, make any payments nor live in the house. The Fake Buyer provides fake supporting documentation for his fake income (paystubs, W-2s, tax returns) supplied by the Criminal.

The Loan Officer that the Fake Buyer gets the loan from is either:

- The Wrongdoer himself (easily creating LLC's or other companies, or forging real persons' names [wife], to act as the flipper party "B" in the above two transactions). AND he ALSO gets as large as possible fees/commissions he can charge on all the processed loans.
- OR: In a "don't ask, don't tell" understanding with the Wrongdoer, in order to get the large, inflated commissions charged on a number of loans, the appraiser inflates the home's value and the loan officer approves the loans even though they might be suspect. If the appraiser gets caught, the loan officer pleads that he never suspected anything due to the Fake Buyer providing all necessary documentation, and it's "not his job" to verify any of the documents – which is true. However, it IS the Loan Officers' job to refuse loans if something seems amiss, or if there's suspicion of loan fraud. (At the time of the events the book presents, there was little

verification of the documents submitted by the Fake Buyer.) The Loan Officer is "shady" and the lender who supplies the loan suffers the loss.

The Loan Officer then sends to its underwriters a loan application for the buyer:

- With inflated income docs
- With an inflated appraisal
- For an inflated loan amount

Once the loan is approved, both deals close (all the documents to finalize the deal are signed) at the same time at a Closing Attorney's Office. The Fake Buyer closes the purchase from the Wrongdoer, and the Wrongdoer gets the sale proceeds. The Wrongdoer closes on the purchase from the Legit Seller...using some of the sales proceeds he received to pay the Legit Seller his sales price. The Wrongdoer keeps the rest of the sales proceeds.

Regarding the Closings:

Wrongdoer gets a closing attorney who is willing to close these deals, back to back: a home purchased at a low purchase price, then immediately closed at an inflated price. The closing attorney may not ask questions about any of the many "holes" or questionable parts of these transactions...either because he is in a:

- "Don't ask, don't tell" understanding...in order to get paid fees on all the closings of a number of transactions, including, likely, owners title insurance on every one of these deals, which is usually only sold in about 10% of average deals in KY. Owners' title insurance provides the closing attorney with even more income than normal, in addition to his likely inflated closing fee charges to the Fake Buyer, on all the closings.
- OR: The closing attorney is in on the deal and being paid additional fees or cuts of the Wrongdoer's income in exchange for participating in the scam...some or many of the closing attorney's employees may suspect something

but don't say anything so they can keep their jobs – and/or they may be paid based on the amount of volume processed for the closing attorney. More closings are better for them financially.

- OR: There is a bad employee in the closing attorney's office with an owner that is "out to lunch" and not paying attention to what's going on – like an alcoholic, drug user or absentee owner. Regardless, employees/notaries used in this scam may sign docs at the closings of their own free will to get paid OR as a result of being bullied by the closing attorney. Some employees may participate in illegal doings to keep their jobs.

The result of the Scam:

The result of each scam is that the lender has made a loan to a fake buyer, on a home worth only a small percentage of the actual loan. The lender won't know this, however, until the Wrongdoer stops making the loan's payments. The Wrongdoer may make payments to keep the loan out of foreclosure, while he continues to repeat this scam as many times as possible.

Everybody makes money – stealing it all from the lender (the original Seller, Bad Guy, Fake Buyer, Loan Officer, appraiser and closing attorney…but, especially the Wrongdoer.)

How the deal unravels and the actors get caught:

As soon as any of the parties involved begin to get scared, they bail out and may possibly be replaced. Once there are no more willing parties to recruit as replacements to keep the scam alive, the Wrongdoer has no more (or greatly reduced) ill-gotten income, so he has to stop making some or eventually all loan payments on the fake loans. When this happens, the loans go into default after three payments are missed and the loan goes into foreclosure. This is simply a lawsuit filed by the lender against the fake borrower, the result of which is the lender repossesses the house with the intention of selling it to get the loan paid back. At the beginning of this foreclosure process, the lender gets a legitimate appraisal and this is when they find out they have been duped. The house is not worth anything near the outstanding loan balance, so the house is sold for a loss. The Wrongdoer makes off with most of the loan proceeds that were used to buy the house from him.

Example:

- Wrongdoer gets a legitimate seller to sell his house to him for $30,000, which is higher than the actual $25,000 value.
- Wrongdoer has appraiser do a fake appraisal, for the Fake Buyer, showing a $75,000 value.
- Fake Buyer applies for and gets a maximum loan amount of $73,000 to buy the house from the Wrongdoer, and has come to closing with $2,000 in cash – cash that is provided to him by the Wrongdoer. The loan costs a lot of fees, so about $65,000 goes to the seller…the Wrongdoer.
- Wrongdoer gives Legit Seller his $30,000, Legit Seller leaves and is happy and likely has no knowledge of the scam.

$75,000 price
Less $2,000 down payment
Less $8,000 in closing costs & lender commissions
Less $30,000 purchase price from Legit Seller
Less $5,000 in kickbacks to Fake Buyer, appraiser, Loan Officer and closing attorney
$30,000 net profit to the Wrongdoer.
Wrongdoer may have to pay some monthly payments

Wrongdoer pockets the difference of $30,000

- A complicit loan officer – Ted
- A complicit straw (fake) buyer – a real person with a real SS#, who has real credit…for whom the Loan Officer creates doctored income verification (tax returns, W-2s, paystubs) to qualify him to buy the house.

- A complicit appraiser who artificially inflates the values of properties

What if I could be the seller of a house and have no debt, so I get to keep all/most of the sales proceeds

Loan Officer, the bad guy, makes most of the money in the scheme.

Loan Officer creates a shell company to buy cheap houses for low prices, say $35k.

Turns around and sells them to a fake buyer for $75k.

The fake buyer is able to buy the house, because the Loan Officer gets him a loan of $73k using faked income documents that say he can afford the payments, and a fake appraisal shows the house is worth $75k.

Close the two transactions back to back.

The loan for B is where the money is obtained to pay the seller in Sale A the sale price of $35k.

Seller A is legitimate. He gets his sales price of $35k.

The Loan Officer's shell company is the seller in the B transaction, and he gets the $75k - $35k, nets $40k.

Buyer on B never makes a payment on the loan. He gets $1,000 for going along with the Loan Officer on the deal and signs the loan documents. He may even be using a fake ID with a stolen SS#.

Profile of B, the Wrongdoer:

- **The key: Be a Loan Officer – or bribe a loan officer:** Have to have intimate knowledge of loan approval process in order to make C, the fake buyer, look real enough to get approved by the lender by faking his income documentation (fake pay stubs, fake W-2s, fake jobs for fake companies, etc.).
- Have a close relationship with the **appraiser** so he can be bribed or persuaded to fake appraisals to make them look legitimate. Like a $100k house on the appraisal form, when it is really only a $30k house.
- Have a close relationship with a **real estate attorney** so you can bribe him or persuade him to agree to close all the deals and not ask questions – because when the attorney sees the

deals' numbers, they will NOT make sense. How can a house be bought for $30k and 5 minutes later be sold for $100k?

I am a former banker, trained by the FBI and the local police in identifying fraudulent personnel types, their personal and financial situations, and internal controls for fraud prevention. I am a former bank officer in charge of bank security on all fronts.

Monroe Jett
October 29, 2017

Made in the USA
Monee, IL
16 December 2023

49352926R00180